FABRIC[ated]

T03997769

FABRIC[ated] examines fabric as a catalyst for innovation, reflection, change and transformation in architecture.

This book explores the ways in which research and development of fabric can, and historically has, influenced and revolutionized architecture, teaching and design. Responsive, flexible, impermanent, fluid and adaptive—fabric interacts with, and influences architecture, offering innovative solutions and increased material responsibility. Foundation and theory chapters establish clear precedent and futures for fabric's position in architectural discourse. The case study section examines 14 international projects through three different threads: Veiling, Compression and Tension. Case studies include a diverse range of projects from the HiLo unit at Nest and CAST's fabric formed concrete projects to a discussion of the impact of fabric on SO–IL and Kennedy & Violich Architecture's professional work, demonstrating new and fresh methods for addressing sustainability and social justice through the use of fabric in architecture. Through the work of the many authors of this book, we see fabric as drape, skin, veil, mold, concept and inspiration. Fabric, in its broadest definition, is an important and innovative material in the development of socially conscious architecture.

Offering readers pedagogical and practical models for international projects highlighting fabric's use in architecture, this book will appeal to the novice and the expert, architecture students and practitioners alike.

Tolya Stonorov is Associate Professor of Architecture and Associate Director of Norwich University's School of Architecture + Art. Tolya has practiced design-build since 2006, when she co-founded her design-build collaborative firm, Stonorov Workshop Architects. She has received multiple awards for excellence for her professional and academic work from the American Institute of Architects' New England and Vermont chapters, among others. In addition, she received the Vermont Women in Higher Education Peggy Williams Award for her teaching and scholarship. Tolya gives lectures and participates in symposium panels nationally and internationally. Her latest book, *The Design-Build Studio: Crafting Meaningful Work in Architecture Education*, was published in 2017 by Routledge.

FABRIC[ated]

Fabric Innovation and Material Responsibility in Architecture

Edited by Tolya Stonorov

Routledge
Taylor & Francis Group

NEW YORK AND LONDON

Cover image: Juney Lee, Block Research Group

First published 2024
by Routledge
4 Park Square, Milton Park, Abingdon, Oxon OX14 4RN

and by Routledge
605 Third Avenue, New York, NY 10158

Routledge is an imprint of the Taylor & Francis Group, an informa business

British Library Cataloguing-in-Publication Data
A catalogue record for this book is available from the British Library

Library of Congress Cataloging-in-Publication Data
Names: Stonorov, Tolya, editor.
Title: Fabric[ated]: fabric innovation and material responsibility in architecture / edited by Tolya Stonorov.
Other titles: Fabricated: fabric innovation and material responsibility in architecture
Description: Abingdon, Oxon: Routledge, 2023. | Includes bibliographical references and index.
Identifiers: LCCN 2022049311 | ISBN 9780367686628 (hardback) | ISBN 9780367686635 (paperback) | ISBN 9781003138471 (ebook)
Subjects: LCSH: Textile fabrics. | Building materials. | Architecture—Study and teaching. | Design—Study and teaching.
Classification: LCC TS1767 .F32 2023 | DDC 677—dc23/eng/20230130
LC record available at https://lccn.loc.gov/2022049311

ISBN: 978-0-367-68662-8 (hbk)
ISBN: 978-0-367-68663-5 (pbk)
ISBN: 978-1-003-13847-1 (ebk)

DOI: 10.4324/9781003138471

Typeset in Univers
by Apex CoVantage, LLC

Printed in the UK by Severn, Gloucester on responsibly sourced paper

This book is dedicated to my mother, Elinor Bacon, who embodies strength, inspiration, risk taking, kindness and generosity.

Contents

Contents

Professional Inquiry

Academic Inquiry

Professional Inquiry

Contributors

Emily Baker is an inventor, fabricator, architect, and educator. Her work investigates the adaptation of the choreography of construction to emerging technologies, hand capacities, and joy in creation. Full-scale constructed experimentation informs her creative practice, research, and teaching, centering on self-structuring material systems. She holds degrees from University of Arkansas and Cranbrook Academy of Art. She taught previously at Tulane University and the American University of Sharjah, and now at University of Arkansas's Fay Jones School of Architecture + Design.

Christopher Bardt is a founding principal of 3SIX0 Architecture (with Kyna Leski) and a professor of architecture at the Rhode Island School of Design (RISD). His research, drawings and artifacts based on the geometry of sunlight, materials, materiality and tectonics as critical to architectural making and thinking has been widely published and exhibited worldwide. Bardt is the author of "Material and Mind," MIT Press 2019, a cross-disciplinary investigation of our engagement with materials and physical surroundings as formative of thought and imagination. A forthcoming book, "The Feeling of Space," aims to recover the physicality of space from its default isomorphic and Cartesian conceptualization. Chris has been honored with a lifetime achievement award for his design work and inducted into the Rhode Island Design Hall of Fame.

Johanna Beuscher studied architecture in Frankfurt and at SCI-ARC, Los Angeles. Her studies abroad were generously supported by graduate scholarships from InWent and DAAD. She worked in architecture firms in Frankfurt and the US. Her first steps into textile architecture gained awards and several publications for the project "SpacerFabricPavilion". Since 2017 she has explored the field of "Lightweight Textile Construction" as a research assistant at Frankfurt University and investigates architectural applications of spacer textiles in various research projects.

Philippe Block is Professor at the Institute of Technology in Architecture (ITA), ETH Zurich, where he leads the Block Research Group (BRG) with Dr. Tom Van Mele and is Head of the Institute. Philippe is also Director of the Swiss National Centre of Competence in Research (NCCR)—Digital Fabrication. He studied architecture and structural engineering at the Vrije Universiteit Brussel and at the Massachusetts Institute of Technology, where he earned his PhD in 2009.

Timo Carl is an architect and Professor for Digital Design and Construction at the Frankfurt University of Applied Sciences, where he co-leads the interdisciplinary research group ReSULT (Research into Lightweight and Sustainable Building Technologies). His interests include the integration of progressive technologies and design within the fields of architecture, material science, and engineering. For his work on lightweight solar structures, he received two awards: *beyond bauhaus—prototyping the future* and *Blauer Kompass* from the German Federal Environmental Agency.

Ron Culver, AIA, is the co-founder of Form Found Design, an architecture and design firm that pioneers the use of technology to solve design problems to impact society. Prior to starting Form Found Design with Joseph Sarafian, Ron founded design-build companies in the US and Canada and has wide-ranging experience in the design and construction of buildings spanning multiple scopes and sizes. He explores the innovative use of materials and processes to advance the design of the built environment.

Eleanor D'Aponte, Associate Professor, has taught graduate and undergraduate design studios, seminars, and lecture courses for over 20 years. She has implemented curricular strengths including ethics, cultural diversity, and a first-year design experience that considers urban public space and casting in concrete. She recently led a design-build collaboration resulting in town approval for a Community Kiosk in Northfield, VT. She has been awarded grants to study the aesthetics and techniques for casting building envelopes and wall panels using fabric formed concrete to which she brings her study of biophilia and the natural environment. She contributes to her local, academic, and professional community. In 2021 she received a Vermont Master Naturalist certificate and presently serves as President for the Vermont Chapter of the American Institute of Architects.

Florian Idenburg is an architect and educator based in NYC. Together with Jing Liu, he is cofounder of the globally recognized design practice SO–IL.

Nick Jenisch, AICP, is Project Manager for the Albert & Tina Small Center for Collaborative Design at the Tulane School of Architecture, and has been engaged in public interest design for more than ten years. With experience in teaching, public engagement, architecture, and planning, he brings a deep understanding of urban scale and regional context to Small Center's work. Nick conducts research on affordable housing and the impact of policy on urbanization, and works with small and mid-sized cities to aid municipal leaders in understanding and harnessing the value of quality design.

Irene Keil is Senior Professor of Practice at the Tulane School of Architecture where she teaches design studios at various levels. She is also a practicing architect, working in New Orleans and Berlin. With architectural degrees from Germany and the United States, she initially worked in both countries on a range of civic and commercial projects and urban design competitions; for her work she was awarded the German Rome Prize in 1992. In her partnership with David Gregor in New Orleans she concentrates on the design, fabrication, and installation of small-scale structures and interiors.

Judith Kinnard, FAIA, is the Harvey Wadsworth Professor of Landscape Urbanism at the Tulane School of Architecture. Her teaching and practice engage urban themes on multiple scales. Her current research involves the development of innovative pedagogical approaches to exploring mass timber in the design studio. This work studies both formal themes that are specific to the discipline of architecture and addresses the role of building materials in advancing regional economies and combating climate change.

Juney Lee is Senior Computational Designer at Skidmore, Owings & Merrill (SOM) in New York City. His main areas of research include graphic statics, computational form-finding methods, and sustainable construction. He studied architectural design and structural engineering at the University of California at Berkeley and the Massachusetts Institute of Technology. He received his PhD at ETH Zurich in 2018 with the highest distinction, under the supervision of Prof. Dr. Philippe Block.

Claudia Lüling is an architect and Professor for Design and Spatial Arts. She co-leads the interdisciplinary research group ReSULT (Research into Lightweight and Sustainable Building Technologies) and has recently gotten one of the innovation professorships of Frankfurt UAS. Her research focus is on textile-based, lightweight design in architecture in a holistic way, including material research, production processes, and design. Her team with Johanna Beuscher won several prizes, including finalist of 2021 DGNB Sustainability Challenge. Claudia Lüling is a member of the expert board research "Zukunft Bau" at BMI.

Aura Luz Melis is educated as an architect at the Technical University of Delft and The Faculty of Architecture and Urbanism in Sao Paulo. She is a partner at Inside Outside since 2016 and is connected to the office since 2005, where her interdisciplinary approach was formed through the wide range of projects and scales she has worked on, many of which connect architecture to interior design and landscape. These projects include the Shenzhen Stock Exchange, the Rothschild Bank in London, the interior of the Taipei Performing Arts Centre and the landscape master plan competition for the West Kowloon Cultural District with OMA.

As the leading partner of the interior and textile department, she has recently realized among others: the extensive 3 years lasting exhibition for the Humboldt University in Berlin, art implementations in the New Generation trains of the Dutch Railways, auditorium curtains for the Mingei Museum in San Diego, the travelling Inside Outside Retrospective exhibition and the architectural textiles inside a former locomotive hall transformed into the Lochal Library in Tilburg, The Netherlands.

She currently teaches landscape and textile design at the Academy of Architecture in Amsterdam and Rotterdam, and in the Design Academy in Eindhoven.

Erin Moore, AIA is a professor in the Department of Architecture and in the Environmental Studies Program at the University of Oregon. Moore's recent work explores the architectural space of fossil fuel consumption, multi-species design, climate justice, and ideas of nature. She uses her critical spatial practice FLOAT architectural research and design as a testing ground for designing explicit relationships with the material and biological context of buildings.

Thomas Randall-Page is a multidisciplinary designer based in East London. Gaining his B.Arch from The Mackintosh School of Architecture, he went on to study architectural carpentry at Aalto University Finland, completing his diploma at London

Metropolitan University. Before establishing his own studio in 2014 he worked at 6A architects contributing to their new court at Chruchhill Collage Cambridge, and then spent 3 years at Heatherwick Studio working on a variety of projects and scales both in the UK and in China. Thomas has taught at Oxford Brookes University, the University of East London, Umea University, and lectured, tutored and run workshops globally. He currently teaches at the Architectural Association. In 2022 Thomas was shortlisted for The Architectural Review's Emerging Architect Award, and this year won the Bridge Design Award for the recently completed Cody Dock Rolling Bridge.

Joseph Sarafian, AIA, is co-founder and CEO of Form Found Design, a Los Angeles-based architecture and design studio that operates at the intersection of technology and nature. His work explores advancements in robotics, material science, and form-finding. Along with his partner, Ron Culver, he launched Form Found Design to employ innovative technology to create new opportunities for design to impact society. Joseph is a licensed architect in California and Professor of Architectural Technology at Orange Coast College.

Jane Scott is a Newcastle University Academic Track Fellow in the Hub for Biotechnology in the Built Environment where she leads the Living Textiles Research group. Jane is a knit specialist, and her interdisciplinary research is located at the interface of programmable textiles, architecture, and biology. Her recent work examines the potential to design with biology using textile materials, textiles thinking and advanced textiles technology.

Abeer Seikaly is a Jordanian-Palestinian interdisciplinary artist, architect, designer, and cultural producer. Her practice is rooted in memory, utilizing journaling, archiving, and collecting to create "narrative threads." Seikaly explores ancestral and indigenous practices in her homeland and the evolving global landscape. Her 'creative compass' responds to context, considering the situatedness of the bodied subject in space, time, and culture. Seikaly aims to address complex societal challenges through creative solutions that highlight the intersections of design, architecture, and culture.

Antje Steinmuller is Associate Professor at the California College of the Arts where she co-directs the Urban Works Agency research lab. Her research explores the role of design at the intersection of citizen-led and city-regulated processes—from new typologies of urban commons to new forms of collective living. Her work has been exhibited at Yerba Buena Center for the Arts, the Milwaukee Art Museum, the Seoul Biennale of Architecture and Urbanism, and the Venice Biennale of Architecture.

Tolya Stonorov, AIA, Associate Professor of Architecture and the Associate Director of Norwich University's School of Architecture + Art, received a master's degree in architecture from the University of California, Berkeley, where she was awarded the Chester Miller traveling fellowship, the Howard Friedman Thesis prize and multiple grants. Stonorov has practiced design-build since 2006, when she co-founded her firm, Stonorov Workshop Architects with Otto Stonorov. Her work explores the nature of fabrication, examining the relationship between digital and traditional methods of making, with a focus on materiality, process, and craft. Architects Stonorov Workshop, a design-build collaborative founded on the belief that good design makes life better and that making and designing are intrinsically intertwined, strives to use sustainable materials and methods in honest, simple expressions to create spaces that outlast their original use. Stonorov has received multiple awards for excellence for her professional and academic work from the American Institute of Architects' New England and Vermont chapters among others. In addition, Stonorov received the Vermont Women in Higher Education Peggy Williams Award for her teaching and scholarship. She gives lectures and participates in symposium panels nationally and internationally. Stonorov's last book, *The Design-Build Studio: Crafting Meaningful Work in Architecture Education*, was published in 2017 by Routledge.

Tom Van Mele is Senior Scientist and Co-director of the Block Research Group (BRG), ETH Zurich, and lead developer of COMPAS, an open-source computational framework for research and collaboration in architecture, engineering, and construction. Tom studied architecture and structural engineering at the Vrije Universiteit Brussel, where he received his PhD in 2008. His technical and computational developments form the backbone of multiple flagship projects, including the Armadillo Vault (2016), Striatus Bridge (2021), and the NEST HiLo unit (2021).

Juan Frano Violich is co-founder of Kennedy & Violich Architecture with his partner Sheila Kennedy. KVA is an interdisciplinary design practice engaging material fabrication, digital technology, and natural resources conservation, expanding the public life of buildings and cities. KVA's material research unit MATx works with business leaders, cultural institutions, and public agencies designing resilient soft infrastructure for networked cities and urbanizing global regions. Violich has taught and lectured widely in the US, Europe, and Latin America. He holds degrees from UC Berkeley and Harvard's GSD.

Emily Vogler is a landscape architect whose research, design and teaching investigate social-ecological systems surrounding water infrastructure, sense of place and climate uncertainty. She has ongoing research projects looking at the irrigation ditches in New Mexico, aging dam infrastructure in New England and coastal adaptation strategies in Narragansett Bay. In her research and design practice, she investigates methods to address regional environmental and cultural issues at the site and material scale; novel approaches to engaging the public in the design and decision-making process; and strategies for strengthening the collaboration and communication between designers, artists and scientists. Vogler is an associate professor at the Rhode Island School of Design where she served as department head from 2017–19. Prior to teaching at RISD, she was a senior project manager at Michael Van Valkenburgh Associates and the 2010 National Olmsted Scholar.

Mark West taught students of architecture and civil engineering for over 30 years while working as an artist, inventor, builder, and researcher. He is the inventor of numerous fabric formed concrete techniques and was the Founding Director of C.A.S.T., the Centre for Architectural Structures and Technology at the University of Manitoba. Since his most recent appointments teaching at MIT in the U.S. and MEF University in Istanbul Turkey, he is now retired from teaching and is working independently at his *Atelier Surviving Logic* in Montreal, Canada.

Acknowledgements

This book is the culmination of more than a decade of research and teaching. It would not have been possible without the tremendous effort of the contributing authors. Thank you Aura Luz Melis, Christopher Bardt, Jane Scott, Timo Carl, Eleanor D'Aponte, Emily Baker, Erin Moore, Emily Vogler, Abeer Seikaly, Florian Idenburg, Claudia Lüling, Johanna Beuscher, Tom Van Mele, Juney Lee, Philippe Block, Mark West, Joseph Sarafian, Ron Culver, Antje Steinmuller, Judith Kinnard, Irene Keil, Nick Jenisch, Thomas Randall-Page and Juan Frano Violich. Thanks also to Norwich University School of Architecture + Art and specifically Aron Temkin, Cara Armstrong, Faculty Development and President Anarumo for their continued support of this work. My editors have provided invaluable comments and critiques; thank you Alexei Pfeffer-Gillett, Abeer Hoque, Cara Armstrong, Sian Foulkes, Vicki Kuskowski, Elinor Bacon, Miciah Bay Gault and Otto Stonorov. This research began as part of my thesis work at the University of California, Berkeley, and therefore I would like to thank my thesis advisors. I could never have completed this book without the love and support of my friends and family. Thank you MBG, LA, EH, SF, VK, SH, SJ, YM, BM, AD, AT, DS, PG, EO, NM, ETW, JV, NK, HM, MW, JE, MS, CH, JF, JR, SP, OS, SF, SB, TP, ML, ZS, KB, HB, KB, KS, MB, BB, KB, JS, JB, NB, SB, TB, NB, KF, MS, DS, SP, IF, APG, XL and many more.

Lastly, thank you to Otto and my boys, Niko, Luca and Miro. This book would not be possible without you.

FOREWORD

AURA LUZ MELIS

INSIDE OUTSIDE
PETRA BLAISSE

Foreword

Aura Luz Melis

Architect/Partner Inside Outside

ON TEXTILE INTIMACY

Textiles and fabrics are intricately crafted soft materials that allow for continuous adjustability and limitless manipulations. The diverse spectrum of relatively minuscule base yarns and the multiple techniques that can be used to shape or transform to a textile result in this inherently versatile quality. By blending traditional methods with innovative (digital) technologies the possibilities for creation become even more endless. This versatility explains, along with many other reasons, why textiles are such a rich and playful tactile medium for designers to experiment with.

Physically engaging with textiles is a type of primal, haptic experience; a primeval material that when close to the body, serves as a mediating membrane connecting us with our context. The porous characteristic of textiles makes for malleable interior surfaces, which allows the material to insulate or adapt to the body. According to the French phenomenological philosopher Maurice Marleau-Ponty, sensation is an action that records the meaning of things: "Merely by touching things, we know far more about them from a natural approach than the theoretical approach can tell us – and above all, we know it in a different way."[1] Knowing more about things through touching is knowing in a different way. This perception is of particular interest with regard to textiles, as part of the authentic tactile experience of textiles, is precisely this intimacy and its close connection to our body. This is true regardless of whether a textile manifests itself as functional, everyday object or as a work of art.

I was introduced to the vast world of textiles by Petra Blaisse, founder of the multidisciplinary design studio Inside Outside, and my business partner with whom I have been collaborating for over 15 years, witnessing the emancipation of the curtain within the architecture field. Inside Outside's curtains relate in a dynamic manner to architecture, creating a dialogue, while remaining independent. As Petra Blaisse always lectures, "Look at what architecture can't do! Bulging and ballooning in and out of a window frame, blown by the wind."[2]

Often considered an afterthought in architectural discourse, Inside Outside has redefined the curtain: literally embedded in the scale of the architecture; carried by rails casted into ceilings or by helium filled balloons, framing spaces, flowing away from the window plane and becoming a significant object in itself. These curtains transition beyond their cultural significance and burgeoning connotation, leaning towards performative planes and artistic expression. They are not a mere background, but a physical manifestation with a certain goal and *raison d'etre*.

The presence of a curtain parallels a dancer on stage; concurrently mesmerising while making one forget about their highly technical skills. The fabric of architectural scale, too, must comply with the various technical requirements dictated by its context: think of glare and privacy, translucency, acoustic quality and climate control. Inside Outside simultaneously experiments with curtains and textiles in many ways, unintentionally resulting in an applied artistic expression. Through the curtain, we interact with light and shadows, with different layers, with the path of the track, with weight, movement and its speed, with unexpected or decontextualised materials, and we explore depth and dynamic qualities, printing methods, perforations and cutouts, creating contradictions or superpositions that always seem in motion.

And yet, once an elaborate textile has been installed, it slowly starts a process of decay. This awareness of impermanence and time has brought Inside Outside to our latest experiment in which we are researching and developing a textile as a medium to carry plants that don't need soil to grow, but thrive from solar energy and moisture. This bioreceptive, flexible, light and translucent green curtain will grow in time and is biodegradable. In collaboration with a multidisciplinary team of biologists, microscopists and lab specialists, we are merging our landscape knowledge with the one of fibres and yarn molecular structures. Although the first attempts and petri-dishes are developing successfully, a larger question remains: can we find beauty in these lab-grown products? While we try to push the boundaries, aesthetic expression perseveres as an essential component of both the research process and the research result.

Pushing the boundaries is the common thread of this book. In its pages, we read about the exploration of the possibilities inherent to the cutting-edge techniques and materials available to today's designers. Our relationship with textiles today is not exclusively forward looking, but also serves as a means for looking sideways, to other cultures of the world and to the legacy of the past. Weaving is a metaphor for so many things, and this has again been confirmed in this book. The complexity and historical relationship of this artform to humans makes it a foundational area for research and development, physically, methodogically and philosophically. The projects included in this book are a critical reflection, resulting in innovative artistic research and the production of genuinely new knowledge. They raise new curiosities and call for further elaborations and side developments.

I am almost certain that an edition of FABRIC[ated] 2.0 will need to be published in the very near future!

NOTES

1.   Merleau-Ponty, Maurice: *Phenomenology of Perception*, Routledge, UK, 2013
2.   Petra Blaisse

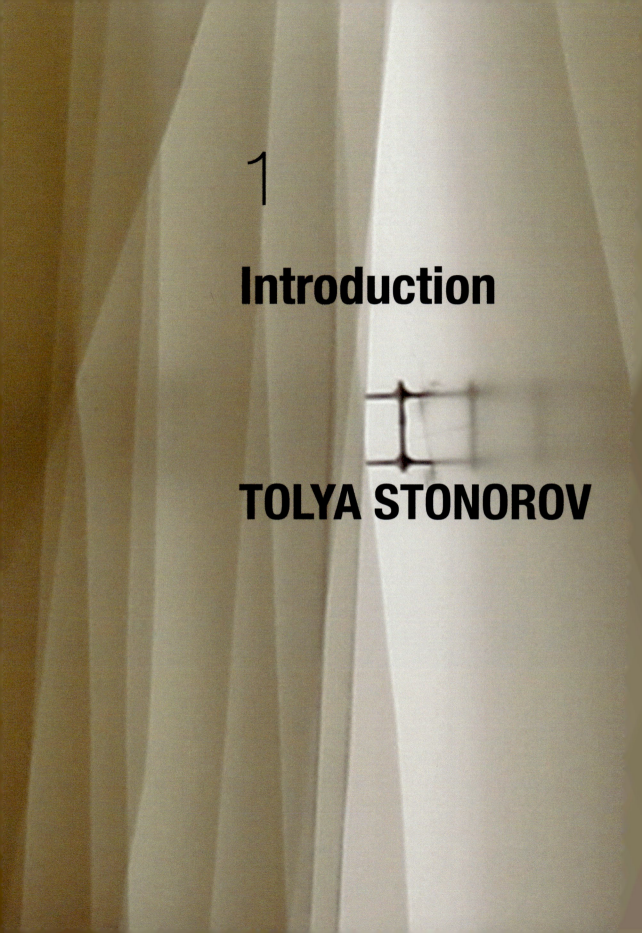

1

Introduction

TOLYA STONOROV

1 Introduction

Tolya Stonorov

FABRIC[ated] examines fabric as a catalyst for innovation, reflection, change and transformation in architecture. This book explores the ways in which research and development of fabric can, and historically has, influenced and revolutionized architecture, teaching and design. From the sustainability of tensile structures,[1] to the relationship of gendered vernacular garments to architectural space, this book uncovers fabric's multidimensional and multifaceted role in architecture and design, as well as its influence on social justice and community inclusion.[2]

Through a multilayered approach, the book studies this topic with sections on fabric used in tensile structures; fabric formed concrete; tent structures; fabric as a gendered translation from the traditional female garment to buildings; smart, responsive fabrics, such as the innovative research conducted by Kennedy & Violich Architecture; and the groundbreaking fabric-focused work of SO–IL and others. Through an examination of community-driven case study projects, the book offers readers pedagogical models for national and international projects that illuminate various aspects of fabric's influence. Woven within this focus is the implicit belief in the importance of full-scale built work. In each of the case study chapters, 1:1 projects are designed and built to fully explore the ideas being researched and tested. The chosen case study projects focus on how these methods are being incorporated into academic architecture and design studios. Specifically, the book documents 14 case study learning environments that explore a myriad of fabric innovations.

FABRIC[ated] brings current research about the relationship between fabric, architecture, design innovation and social justice together under the larger focus of academic and professional learning and exploration. Radical designers like Hella Jongerius have pushed the relationship between fabric, weaving and the body, and revolutionary engineers and architects like Frei Otto, Peter Rice, Herzog and De Meuron and SO–IL have explored how we can re-envision the skin of the built environment—architecture's relationship to structure and material. Leading architects, such as Thom Mayne of Morphosis, have discussed the relationship of skin (it too a tensile fabric) and the body to architecture and thus have established the context for this research:

> The space between the surface of the body and the surface of the skin—the interstitial territory bounding interior and exterior—allows each face of the building to alter as the light conditions change with the movements of the sun across the sky and of pedestrians along the street.[3]

DOI: 10.4324/9781003138471-1

This book takes an inclusive approach to these studies and weaves these inter-related subjects together under the umbrella of the sustainability of social justice, examining each topic holistically in relation to its impact towards human and environmental good.

Figure 1.1
*Transparency
model as concept
development*
Source: Student
work, Translation
Studio, Norwich
University

SITUATING FABRIC[ATED] IN CONTEXT

There is exciting and significant research published about fabric in relation to sustainability, garments and architecture; architecture for the underserved; concrete fabric formwork and tensile structures and innovation. Yet, existing publications tend to be highly focused in their approach or do not take into account new developments in the last few decades. This book updates and integrates existing research and contributes new inquiries in a broad, current and integrated fashion.

Architecture is an art that exists in space. It encompasses the built world and requires experiential understanding. When examining the existing work in the field, precedents may be looked at using two methods. The first involves research and analysis of texts written on the topic. The second, of equal importance, involves an investigation of built work, and how the theories and practices of the relationships between fabric and design are incorporated into the built environment.

Precedent: Textual

In *Architecture in Fashion*, Singley and Fausch examine the relationship between fashion and architecture, drawing conclusions and comparisons between the movements and trends in the two related industries. The editor and chapter authors state, "This . . . cleavage between durable edifice and ephemeral textile motivates not only advertising's use of architecture as a sign for resistance to change, but also fashion's desire to acquire an aura of classic timelessness through a metonymical relationship with the edifice."[4] This text provides important context for the work in FABRIC[ated], in that it deals with the garment/fashion/building relationship and speaks to appropriation and manipulation, both physical and in thoughts.

Another pivotal influence, Ellen Lupton, in *Skin: Surface, Substance, and Design*, writes eloquently about the study of skin in relation to the building envelope: "Skin is a multilayered, multipurpose organ that shifts from thick to thin, tight to loose, lubricated to dry, across the landscape of the body."[5] Lupton thus knits complex responses to the idea of skin through an exploration of precedent projects. She discusses the relationship between interior and exterior space relative to the body: "Skin, a knowledge-gathering device, responds to heat and cold, pleasure and pain. It lacks definitive boundaries, flowing continuously from the exposed surfaces of the body to its internal cavities."[6] This exploration into skin provides a foundation for FABRIC[ated] case study chapters such as SO–IL and Translation.

The study of the relationship between fabric and the built environment demands new approaches to the way we teach. In relation to the pedagogy of teaching methods, Hella Jongerius has been a leader in boundary pushing processes, working with fluid forms and fabric innovation for decades. Her lab, currently located in Berlin, Germany, explores state-of-the-art weaving techniques and other textile innovations. Jongerious writes:

> The unfinished, the provisional, the possible—they hide in the attention for imperfections, traces of the creation process, and the revealed potential of materials and techniques. . . . This working method . . . not only celebrates the value of the process, but also engages the viewer, the user, in her investigation.[7]

Jongerius's highly experimental methods point to potential in the products of studio exploration. As *FABRIC[ated]* explores pedagogy and how these concepts can affect student learning and professional output, work like Jongerius's with Droog Design is essential for pushing the idea of process and product.

Precedent: Built Work

Frei Otto

Frei Otto is one of the leading architects on tensile and lightweight structures. Otto is widely considered to be one of the most important architects of the 21st century, and in 2018, Otto received the Pritzker Prize.[8] In pushing innovative boundaries of materials and engineering, Otto was also deeply concerned with social justice. In an interview with the Pritzker Prize committee, he stated: "I've never done anything to gain this prize. . . . Prizewinning is not the goal of my life. I try to help poor people."[9] Otto's work was rooted in sustainability at its core, though it may not be immediately apparent. The choice to examine how structure might be envisioned as something light and minimalist, as opposed to the heavy, material-abundant traditional forms of wood and steel framing methods, was a political statement as well as a design manifesto. Otto questioned need and excess in his work through rethinking how buildings could be made. "Otto's work was lightweight, democratic, low-cost and sometimes temporary."[10] Similar to Neri Oxman, Frei Otto was inspired and fascinated by examples of lightweight minimalist structures in nature. Otto was fundamentally committed to learning by doing and was known to construct complex physical models to test the tensile structures he envisioned. These examples of societal equity, doing more with less, and physical making, are key themes that point to how fabric innovation has contributed to goals of social justice. "The advantage of cable net structures is that load transfer can be achieved with an enormous saving in material."[11] This material frugality represents a pressing issue in architecture fabrication today:

> The relevance of Frei Otto's empirical model aesthetic lies in identifying the enormous potential of object knowledge and its material-cultural dimension—on the one hand to continue to anchor the perception of the resource between nature and technology, and on the other to allow better investigation of the complex interrelations between digital and analog. So what does it mean for architects and engineers to design in a society that seeks a balance between growing digitalization and increasingly important resource awareness?[12]

In minimizing the sheer amount of material used in construction, the design embraces sustainability at its core, creating a greater focus on resource scarcity.

ORGANIZATION: THE ARCHITECTURE OF FABRIC[ATED]

This book is organized into sections. The first section offers four detailed discussions, providing a foundation from which the case studies springboard: The Philosophy of Fabric Innovation in Architecture, Digital Fabrication and Fabric Innovation, The Sustainability of Lightweight Structures, and The Art and Science of Fabric-Forming. The second section examines 14 international case studies in detail. Case studies are further organized into three different threads: Veiling: Gender, Fabric and Woven Structures, Compression: Fabric Formed Concrete and Dense Applications and Tension: Tensile structures and Inflatables.

SECTION I: FOUNDATION AND THEORY

In The Philosophy of Fabric Innovation, Christopher Bardt examines the relationship of history, cultur, innovation and fabric. "Fabric as both an architectural concept and material has gained importance as the rapid changes in technology and the planet's health have raised questions about the wisdom of an inflexible built environment." Bardt's discussion transmutes beautifully into Jane Scott's Digital Fabrication and Fabric Innovation in which she writes that "digital fabrication has liberated textile making to offer a new vision for architecture where the complex organization of intersecting threads, produces a multisensory experience of tactile surfaces and responsive interfaces." Timo Carl examines the inherent and intrinsic sustainability of fabric in architecture, looking back at Frei Otto's work with a more minimalist, less environmentally cumbersome material palette in The Sustainability of Lightweight Structures. Architecture, fabric and social justice are discussed through a historical and current look at how this method and material has impacted the social thread of architecture in culture. Eleanor D'Aponte's The Art and Science of Fabric-Forming chapter on the history of fabric formed concrete looks at the early relationship of fabric to human experience and comfort in Venice,

Italy, and its relationship to the current use of fabric formwork in concrete. Related to D'Aponte's discussion, Rima Sabina Aouf notes, "according to engineering and architecture firm Atkins, fabric casting could allow architects to create interesting structures with up to 40 per cent less concrete, and may also mean that buildings could be made with less labour."[13] D'Aponte examines fabric formwork as a more socially accessible, sustainable response to the historically carbon heavy use of concrete in buildings.

SECTION II: CASE STUDIES

The case studies section of FABRIC[ated] examines 14 international fabric-focused studios through process, artifact and learning outcomes. Individual chapters are written by the project leads, providing firsthand expertise and knowledge about each distinct process. Questions discussed include: Can working with a light and malleable material effect positive change in housing for the underserved? How is fabric related to the economics of scope and scale? How can fabric contribute to flexibility and adaptability in architecture resilience? How does fabric provide a platform for architectural innovation? How should architecture education engage with community issues? How can fabric help architects reduce our industry's impact on our natural environment? How does hands-on learning affect students' relationship to their work? How does the process of building full-scale architecture impact students' and professionals' learning and process? How does the use of digital design and fabrication methods impact process and final form? Last, and relatedly, how does the use of traditional design and fabrication methods impact process and final form? In each case study chapter, fabric innovation is most successfully explored at full scale in order to fully test and research design and social proposals. The importance of full-scale work and material testing is twofold: students and practitioners gain a more holistic understanding of material realities and are forced to test their design ideas through realized fabrication.

Case Studies: Veiling: Gender, Fabric + Woven Structures

The first section, Gender, Fabric + Woven Structures, focuses on how fabric has played a pivotal role in gendered relationships between architecture, garments and culture.

Seaming: The Fabrication of Keswa

In this chapter, Emily Baker, discusses KESWA: AN UNCOVERING, where she worked with Muslim female students at the American University of Sharjah, to develop a project that examined the veil, *the abaya*, in Arabic culture today. Female students digitally fabricated a steel enclosure that abstracted the abaya and encouraged the community to inhabit this enclosure. "*Keswa* invites the public to enter the space of the *abaya*, simultaneously venerating the garment and subverting its power to subordinate."[14]

This reinterpretation of the traditional female garment starts to dissolve gender-imposed boundaries and barriers and encourages users and viewers to question their own perception and preconceptions. Beatriz Colominia's essay in *Gender Space Architecture*, sheds light on this point when she notes:

> [Silverman] points to the role of the object in forming both its own image and that of the spectator. Moreover, by stressing the notion that seeing and being seen are reciprocal positions in the same operation, she returns us to the dual nature of representation: at once inscribing the image of the thing represented and revealing its own culturally constituted structure.[15]

Translation: Female Garment to Architecture Studio

In my own chapter, Translation: Female Garment to Architecture, based on an upper-level architecture studio taught at Norwich University School of Architecture + Art and my graduate thesis completed at the University of California, Berkeley, I discuss the studio's research on fabric and architecture through the relationship of the garment to the body and the translation of the garment to the building. This analogy can be examined through the relationship of the kimono and the veil to the traditional Japanese and Islamic house. From this study, lessons can be extracted, abstracted and applied to built form.

Pipeline Resistance and Feminist Spatial Practice

In this chapter, which documents the research and fabrication of the Pipeline Resistance project, Erin Moore discusses methods of defining a feminist spatial practice through resistance architecture installation interventions. Moore, along with her students, constructed three nature-based woven pavilions, using local rush plants as the material for construction, on private land that was designated for

future pipeline construction. Together with the landowners, Moore sees the Portal constructions as a protest of the pipeline project. Moore notes:

> The Portals are intended as direct-action pipeline resistance as they visibly place something of value in the path of potential destruction. The Portals are intended to transform perception of these places by demonstrating their value in terms of ecological holism, nutrient cycling, multi-species sheltering, and habitat biodiversity rather than in terms of extraction and profit. In this way, and as they subvert extraction-based power structures, the installations are meant to embody an ecofeminist ethic and to build on dialogues in new materialisms, speculative design, critical spatial practices, and the environmental humanities.[16]

Emily Vogler, GEO | Textiles: Weaving Restoration Ecology and Cultural Narratives

Vogler's studio, GEO | Textiles, marries landscape architecture and fabric. Through a weaving process, Vogler examines cultural narrative through the lens of ecology. "Weaving and other structural textile techniques will be explored as both a metaphor and a physical strategy to weave together the multiple cultural narratives of a river as well as consider how to support the diverse river ecologies and the unique experiential qualities of being at the water's edge."[17]

Weaving a Home

Abeer Seikaly provides a historical and forward-looking analysis of the Bedouin tent and a proposal for structural fabric-based housing for displaced communities, asking: "Is architecture a social technology?"[18] In her ongoing research, Seikaly's constructs offer dwelling solutions that combine high-tech solar fabric, water

Figure 1.4 *Kukje Gallery mesh closeup*
Source: Copyright SO-IL

collection and ventilation with a beauty that is contextually reflective. Inspired by folded paper constructs, these structures propose that housing should "build awareness of how shelter is a social and cultural process that continues to evolve with our collective values."[19]

Kukje Gallery and Breathe—MINI Living
In an interview about world-renowned architects SO–IL's work with various definitions of fabric, Florian Idenburg discusses the incredible processes that defined the outcomes of the Kukje Gallery, Breath MINI Living and other earlier work. Idenburg leads us into the intricacies of the development of the mesh skin of the Kukje, the fabric double envelope of Breath MINI Living, the ethereal and alternatively dense walls of Logan and the communal structure of the PS2 installation.

06 Case Studies: Compression: Fabric Formed Concrete and Dense Applications
The second case study section focuses on Fabric Formed Concrete and other fabrication methods that result in material in compression. Fabric formed concrete consistently reduces waste from traditional formwork methods and produces sometimes unexpected results in product. There is an element of the unknown in fabric formed concrete, a risk taking that is innovative and experimental in its nature.

Spacer Fabric Pavillion—Advanced 3D Textile Applications in Architecture
Claudia Luling and Johanna Beuscher are leading professors conducting research into fabric innovation in relation to the architectural envelope. Luling and Beuscher's architecture studios have researched how fabric can provide skin and structure through methods of folding and layering with a foam-centered structure. Their work is questioning the typical wood or metal framed building system and suggesting that a digitally produced, 3D printed fabric and foam envelope can provide a streamlined product that will produce significantly less waste than traditional

building processes. Luling and Beuscher's work uses an innovative folding technique with

> Three dimensional, double layered textile structures are used as structural ele-
> ments, which once foamed serve as lost formwork for the fabrication of stable and
> insulated lightweight structural elements. Integrated into this system are hingeless
> folding mechanisms that enable fast building and dismantling.[20]

It is precisely this sort of innovation that is specifically allowed by fabric's material
qualities. The lightweight, transportable design provides a bright and dynamic solution to a basic human need that it currently in crisis.

Lightweight Cable-net and Fabric Formwork System for the HiLo Unit at NEST

Tom Van Mele, Junee Lee and Philippe Block, from the Block Research Group at the
Institute of Technology in Architecture at ETH Zürich, discuss their innovative cable
net, fabric formed concrete technology and how it inherently pushes the boundaries
of sustainability in concrete construction methods. A building material traditionally
shackled by a high carbon footprint, the Block Research Group demonstrates how
the use of fabric can help to redefine the sustainable outcome of concrete materiality. The building process and resulting structure are extraordinarily beautiful.

The Flexible Way

Mark West's discussion of CAST, the fabric formed concrete lab that defined and
set the foundation for much of the innovation associated with this building technique, marries the technical and poetic. In exquisite prose, West allows the reader
to glimpse into CAST's highly complex and experimental process. West highlights

the haptic necessity of material response, that through physical experimentation, innovations can be identified and pursued.

Form-Finding the MARS Pavilion

Ron Culver and Joseph Sarafian, of Form Found Design, discuss the experimental technique of robot-built fabric formed concrete for their winning competition entry for the MARS Pavilion. Their fascinating trajectory from academic research to professional projects paints a fluid understanding of a designer's process. The chapter highlights a focus on learning from the discoveries that are revealed through making.

Case Studies: Tension: Tensile Structures and Inflatables

The section on Tensile Structures and Inflatables presents a method of making that is inherently doing more with less. As a result, these projects are a political undertaking—at their core, addressing the overconsumption of materials by the construction industry. Often temporary in nature, tensile structures reduce construction material and related waste, while providing innovative material assemblies that serve cultural needs.

Fabri[ating] Act[ivat]ion

In this chapter, Antje Steinmuller works with a condensed international architecture studio to examine ground-up activism in the form of an appropriation of underutilized public space. With tensile pavilions, Steinmuller demonstrates how spatial constructs can provide cultural space that encourages community, once galvanized. "As *activators*, architects devise strategies in the form of a long-term plan of action, a process towards a collective goal."[21]

Hollygrove Shade-Water Pavilion

The Tulane Small Center for Collaboration and Design + The Carrollton-Hollygrove Community Development Corporation (CHCDC) joined together to produce Hollygrove Greenline Shade-Water Pavilion in New Orleans, Louisiana. The pavilion is an insertion of protest in a blighted area: seeking to transform a derelict area into an educational beacon that provides for the community. Founded on the simple idea of an inverted series of tents, the Shade-Water Pavilion gathers rainwater that would otherwise contribute to the city's stormwater system, collects it and distributes the water to nearby urban farming gardens.

Airdraft

Thomas Randall-Page and Benedetta Rogers' AirDraft[22] pushes the boundaries of definable space. With inspiration from 1960's Antfarm, AirDraft is an inflatable cultural space that inverts the previous life of an industrial barge and transforms it into a mobile performance/gallery space. Airdraft shines light on the shift that the canal system has undergone from that of industry with utilitarian meaning to conduits of leisure and pockets of cultural experimentation. The form itself references counterculture testing of decades earlier radical designers. Yet, the inflatable nature of Airdraft is born out of a necessity to create space with some permanence, while

Figure 1.6 *Airdraft completed*
Source: Photo credit Jim Stephenson

also being able to dissolve that same space based on the physical constraints of the canal system. The inflatable model provided a solution to this need, allowing the space to be constructed and deconstructed as needed. The use of fabric in this experimental form of cultural space provided a flexible and innovative material answer to the issue and opportunity.

Patchworks: A Report from Three Fabricated Futures

Kennedy & Violich Architecture, KVA, has spearheaded research and implementation of innovative fabric and material studies for decades. In this chapter, three projects are examined and contrasted: 34th Street Ferry Terminal, Soft House and Global Flora Conservatory. KVA's work with the Soft House, in Hamburg Germany, explores how soft surfaces throughout the house may be used to absorb and provide solar energy. Exterior "twisters", flexible photovoltaics, are used to capture energy throughout the day. The innovative use of flexible and moving structure results in a higher energy yield. The Soft House further uses high tech fabric curtains embedded with lights to divide spaces within the dwelling. This highly customizable flexible infrastructure provides the user with enhanced agency to define their experience. Coupled with large expanses of glass, the curtains allow the user to meld and screen their public and private inhabitation of the space. The LED-lit fabric divisions both veil the interior from bright sunlight and create a gentle and luminous wall in non-lit times of the day.

Figure 1.7 *Soft House exterior*
Source: Copyright Kennedy & Violich Architecture

Outcomes + Conclusion

From each introductory foundation and case study chapter examined, we see exciting possibilities demonstrated of how the use of fabric in architecture can expand material potential through sustainability and community justice. Through each project, process is revealed and unraveled, exposing how the use of fabric spurs novel techniques for addressing space, culture and need. These innovative methods and resulting concrete projects provide fresh ways of looking at architecture, incorporating design, use, equity and social justice. Realizing the role of fabric in architecture unpacks a world of possibilities for professionals and teachers to explore socially conscious design. This shift in material and intention provides a more socially minded outcome and a goal of architecture for all.

NOTES

1. Tensile Structures: "A tensile structure is a construction of elements carrying only tension and no compression or bending. . . . Tensile structures are the most common type of thin-shell structures." https://en.wikipedia.org/wiki/Tensile_structure
2. Social justice is defined here under a broad definition of architecture and design as a force that aids humanity and the natural world, while creating an inclusive, diverse and altruistic environment.
3. Quote from Thom Mayne; Lupton, Ellen, with essays from Jennifer Tobias, Alicia Imperiale, and Grace Jeffers. *Skin: Surface, Substance, and Design*, New York: Princeton Architectural Press, 2002.
4. Fausch, Deborah, and Paulette Singley. *Architecture in Fashion*, New York: Princeton Architectural Press, 1996, p. 7.
5. Lupton, Ellen, with essays from Jennifer Tobias, Alicia Imperiale, and Grace Jeffers. *Skin: Surface, Substance, and Design*, New York: Princeton Architectural Press, 2002.

6. Lupton, Ellen, with essays from Jennifer Tobias, Alicia Imperiale, and Grace Jeffers. *Skin: Surface, Substance, and Design*, New York: Princeton Architectural Press, 2002.

7. www.jongeriuslab.com/information.

8. "To honor a living architect or architects whose built work demonstrates a combination of those qualities of talent, vision, and commitment, which has produced consistent and significant contributions to humanity and the built environment through the art of architecture. The international prize, which is awarded each year to a living architect/s for significant achievement, was established by the Pritzker family of Chicago through their Hyatt Foundation in 1979. It is granted annually and is often referred to as 'architecture's Nobel' and 'the profession's highest honor.' The award consists of $100,000 (US) and a bronze medallion. The award is conferred on the laureate/s at a ceremony held at an architecturally significant site throughout the world." www.pritzkerprize.com/about; Last seen 7.15.2022.

9. www.nytimes.com/2015/03/11/arts/design/frei-otto-german-architect-wins-pritzker-prize-posthumously.html Last accessed 11.14.19.

10. www.pritzkerprize.com/laureates/frei-otto Last accessed 11.14.19.

11. Meissner, Irene, and Eberhard Moller. *Frei Otto, A Life of Research Construction and Inspiration*, Munich, Germany: Detail, 2017, Second Edition.

12. Meissner, Irene, and Eberhard Moller. *Frei Otto, A Life of Research Construction and Inspiration*, Munich, Germany: Detail, 2017, Second Edition.

13. www.dezeen.com/2016/06/06/six-examples-fabric-cast-concrete-architecture-design/ Last accessed 3.27.20.

14. Emily Baker, http://architecture.tulane.edu/news/2016/03/article-1909.

15. Rendell, Jane, Barbara Penner, and Iain Borden. *Gender Space Architecture*. London: Routledge, 2000. Essay 34, Beatriz Colominia, Excerpts from 'The Split Wall: Domestic Voyeurism', from Beatriz Colomina (ed.) Sexuality and Space (1992).

16. Moore, Erin, www.floatwork.com/portal-project-statement

17. Vogler, Emily; GEO | TEXTILES: Weaving Restoration Ecology and Cultural Narratives Along the Yuba River; Rhode Island School of Design, 2020.

18. Abeer Seikaly; https://abeerseikaly.com/is-architecture-a-social-technology/

19. Abeer Seikaly, https://abeerseikaly.com/is-architecture-a-social-technology/

20. www.frankfurt-university.de/en/about-us/faculty-1-architecture-civil-engineering-geomatics/contact/professors/architecture/prof-dipl-ing-claudia-lueling/tab-designbuild-e/spacerfabric-home/ Last accessed 1.22.2020.

21. Steinmuller, Antje, The Act(ivat)or's Toolbox: Expanded Roles, Actions, and Parameters in the Production of the Urban Commons, Presented at ACSA Conference.

22. http://thomasrandallpage.com/AirDraft

BIBLIOGRAPHY

Accad, Evelyne, *Veil of Shame: The Role of Women in the Contemporary Fiction of North Africa and the Arab World*, Quebec, Canada: Sherbrooke, 1978.

Balmond, Cecil, *Informal*, London: Prestel, 2002.

Black, Alexander, *The Japanese House*, Boston: Tuttle Publishing, 2000.

Crawford, Matthew B., *Shop Class as Soulcraft, an Inquiry into the Value of Work*, London: Penguin Press, 2009.

Darabi, Parvin, *Rage Against the Veil: The Courageous Life and Death of an Islamic Dissident*, Amherst, NY: Prometheous Books, 1999.

Fathy, Hassan, *Natural Energy and Vernacular Architecture, Principles and Examples with Reference to Hot Arid Climates*, Chicago and London: The United Nations University by The University of Chicago Press, 1986.

Fausch, Deborah, *Architecture in Fashion*, New York: Princeton Architectural Press, 1996.

Fletcher, Kate, *Sustainable Fashion and Textiles, Design Journeys. Earthscan, 2008*, Oxon: Routledge, 2014.

Goodwin, Jan, *Price of Honor: Muslim Women Lift the Veil of Silence on the Islamic World*, Boston: Little Brown, 1994.

Hillenbrand, Robert, *Islamic Architecture*, New York: Columbia University Press, 1994.

Hoag, John D., Pier Luigi Nervi, General Editor, and Harry N. Abrams, *Islamic Architecture*, New York: Inc., Publishers, 1977.

Iwamoto, Lisa, *Digital Fabrications, Architectural and Material Techniques*, New York, NY: Princeton Architectural Press, 2009.

Kinney, Leila, *Fashion and Fabrication in Modern Architecture*. Cambridge, MA: MIT Press. *Journal of the Society of Architectural Historians*, Vol. 58, No. 3 (September 1999), pp. 472–481.

Kinoshita, Masao, *Japanese Architecture*, Tokyo, Japan: Shokukusha Publishing Co., 1964.

Lüling, C., and Richter, I., Architecture Fully Fashioned – Exploration of Foamed Spacer Fabrics for Textile Based Building Skins. *Journal of Façade Design and Engineering*, Vol. 5, No. 1 (2017): Special Issue PowerSkin.

Lupton, Ellen, with essays from Jennifer Tobias, Alicia Imperiale, and Grace Jeffers, *Skin: Surface, Substance, and Design*, New York: Princeton Architectural Press, 2002.

Michell, George, *Architecture of the Islamic World*, New York: William Morrow and Company, Inc., 1978.

Miodownik, Mark, *Stuff Matters, Exploring the Marvelous Materials that Shape Our Man-Made World*, UK: Penguin Books Ltd, 2013.

Musterberg, Hugo, *The Japanese Kimono*, New York: Oxford University Press, 1996.

Pfeffer, Richard M., *Working for Capitalism*, New York: Columbia University Press, 1979.

Rice, Peter, *An Engineer Imagines*, England: Batsford, an Imprint of Pavilion Books Co., 2017.

Rudofsky, Bernard, *The Kimono Mind, An Informal Guide to Japan and the Japanese*, New York: Van Nostrand Reinhold Company, 1965.

Schittich, Christian (Ed.), *Building Skins, Concepts, Layers, Materials*, Basel, Germany: Birkhauser Edition Detail, 2001.

Schouwenberg, Louise, *Hella Jongerius*, London: Phaidon Press, 2003.

Tsutoma, Ema, and Meiji-Shobu, *Kimono: One Hundred Masterpieces of Japanese Costumes*, Tokyo, Japan, 1950.

FOUNDATION AND THEORY

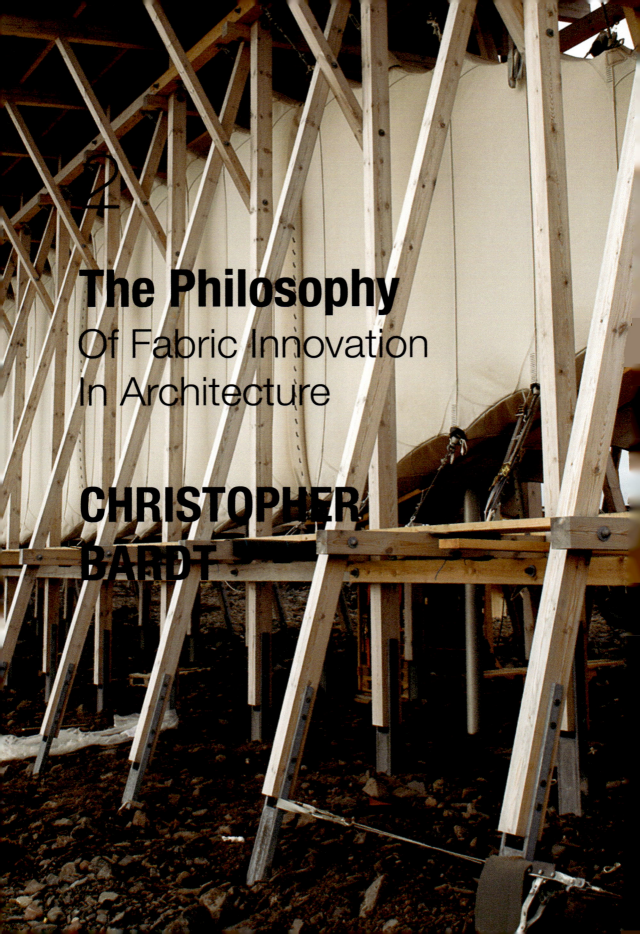

2

The Philosophy
Of Fabric Innovation
In Architecture

CHRISTOPHER
BARDT

2 The Philosophy of Fabric Innovation in Architecture

Christopher Bardt

Missing the architectonic language of stacked solid assembly, massive construction, the immovability of symmetrical vaulted, columnar order, or any other "classical" attributes of the permanence of architecture, fabric architecture is associated with mobility, clothing, impermanence, and regarded as vulnerable, non-resistant, and acquiescent to forces. Through possessing architecture's utility and performative aspects, fabric architecture is not afforded the status of "real architecture." Generally considered to be an ancillary form of building technology and narrowly defined by specific techniques and material, fabric architecture is unable to embody fully the culturally central role of architecture in manifesting the stability and endurance of societal orders and practices—or so it would seem.

FABRIC AS PROGENITOR OF ARCHITECTURE

Architecture's historical and conceptual sources, however, suggest a more nuanced and entangled relationship between fabric and architecture. Indeed, fabric is arguably a progenitor of architecture, and fully present in "real architecture." As Robert Bringhurst has written:

> An ancient metaphor: thought is a thread, and the raconteur is a spinner of yarns— but the true storyteller, the poet, is a weaver. The scribes made this old and audible abstraction into a new and visible fact. After long practice, their work took on such an even, flexible texture that they called the written page a textus, which means cloth.[1]

Language and history implicate textiles and fabric at the heart of architecture's origins and cultural significance. Coinciding with the emergence of textiles, the development of writing and the rise of agriculture and urban settlement in ancient Mesopotamia hint at common origins and conceptual structures. Writing, for example, emerged as a matrix of symbols, eventually organizing itself in horizontal rows similar to a plowed field. The quirk of *boustrophedon* (meaning literally "like the ox turns") writing, seen in later Greek but also in earlier Semitic scripts, is identical to the way that oxen move in a field being plowed, or how the movement of a shuttle carries the weft on a loom. Boustrophedon text is read back and forth, first from left to right; the following line is read from right to left; and so on.

DOI: 10.4324/9781003138471-3

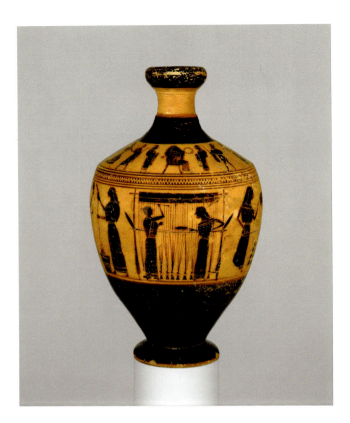

Figure 2.1
*Metropolitan
Museum of Art,
New York*
Source: Public
domain

The etymology of "text" and "textile" share a common root: *teks*, meaning to fabricate, to weave. The words "texture," "tectonic," "architect," "technique," and "context," all have this same etymological origin *teks* and, in an etymological sense, unite "fabric" with text and textile, weaving and making.

In ancient Greece, the loom was not only an engendered technological instrument embodying societal order, but was also connected symbolically and formally to architecture and the city.[2] The Parthenon was dedicated to the goddess Athena, herself associated with handicrafts—weaving in particular. Whether analogous or homologous to the loom, there is strong evidence that temple architecture originated as a reflection and extension of the looms' symbolic role in Greek culture (Figure 2.1).[3] It has been postulated that the frame and warp of the vertical loom were the inspiration for and model from which Greek temple architecture derived its colonnaded architectural form.[4]

For a culture originating in a pre-literate setting, where meaning came from action/making, it would be natural for the meaning and configuration of a temple's columns to be associated symbolically with the vertical threads of a loom, ancient Greece's first pre-eminent technology and concrete symbol of making.[5] The peristasis of the temple and its inter-columnar (warp) space was set aside for priests to circumambulate (weft), and while no explicit references were made between looms and temples, the shared technologies and common terms of both

Figure 2.2 *Egyptian Museum—Georg Steindorff—of the University of Leipzig*

looms and ships is implicit in the symbolic allusions of temples as metaphorical "ships." We can see a small example of a shared symbolism (and technology) in the striking similarities between ship anchors and loom weights (used to tension the warps): the word *histós* in ancient Greek means both "mast" and "loom."[6] As looms predated sailing, it is likely the loom's technology was an important source for both nautical technology and the symbolism associated with ships and temples.

The cultural relationship between fabric and mass construction can be recognized in a small statue from ancient Egypt (Figure 2.2) that echoes contemporary preconceptions: a painted Egyptian stone carving that depicts a husband and wife, Lai-ib and Khuaut, standing side by side. They are both wearing wigs, hers arranged in vertical braids and his in horizontal bands. The form of each wig is contingent on the manner and métier of its making, her braids falling pliantly and his bands, like stacked masonry, assuming a beehive form. The yielding to gravity suggested by her wig, and the resistance against it of his, is gendered and symbolic, each wig constructing meaning from the fluid interdependencies of material, tectonics, and form: an assemblage of stone, hair, artifice (a wig), masonry, weaving, stacking, and braiding.

The architectural wood lattice screen of the Middle East, known as the *mashrabiy'ya*, offers a historic example of gendered social practices manifesting as a phenomenon derived from fabric. It has become widely deployed as an architectural device serving the same purpose as the veil, filtering and regulating the private and public domains of men and women.[7] Performing as a literal veil, the *mashrabiy'ya* is a gendered construction and direct transliteration of a distinct optical trait of fabric: a woven textile held close to one's face is optically asymmetrical, transparent from the close darkened side while remaining opaque on the other, lit side.

This textile-centered phenomenon of transparency is also a general architectural condition. Wooden screens, lattices, perforated surfaces, hollow masonry screen walls, and woven metal screening all exhibit "textile transparency" and, indeed, a strong architectonic affinity with fabric, sharing characteristics of material, optical, and constructed uniformity.

Still, classical architecture's representations of massiveness and stability have persisted and defined architecture in general, even as building techniques have diverged and become fabric-like (such as the curtain wall). Despite the Gothic sensibility of transforming mass-built stone to a weightless, gossamer, transparent, lace-like architecture, and the growing use of architectural screens, the canonical notion of architecture as founded on massive and stacked construction has persisted.

The nineteenth-century fascination with archaeology and anthropology led to a new "scientific" rethinking of architecture's origins, suggesting that architecture was actually Medusa-like, a solidification of an original flexible construction. Based on their catenary geometries, which a rope suspended from two points naturally assumes, Chinese, Japanese, and Southeast Asian roofs were speculated to have had tensile origins.

German architect Gottfried Semper proposed a textile-based beginning for architecture, arguing that the partition wall was originally woven, in part evidenced by the decorative continuity of wall surface patterns, despite their tectonic assembly (such as tiles). German employs two different words for "wall": *Mauer* denotes a mass constructed wall, whereas a partition wall is *Wand* (its complex etymological roots include what was known as a "woven wall"). Semper was making a reasoned argument for a logical and functional correspondence between construction and architecture, wherein the *techne* of building was *the* source material of architecture. This marked an important conceptual shift evident in the anti-gravitational aspirations of twentieth-century modern architecture.

In a sense, Mies Van Der Rohe's radical separation of partition wall from structural column, first manifest in his Barcelona pavilion, conceptually reprised Semper's origin idea of *Wand*—that is, the woven wall. Rem Koolhaas has speculated that creating an earlier full-scale canvas mockup of a house design for Helene Kroller Muller awoke Mies to the new modern sensibility of lightness:

I suddenly saw him inside the colossal volume, a cubic tent vastly lighter and more suggestive than a sombre and classical architecture it attempted to embody. I guessed—almost with envy—that this strange "enactment" of a future house had drastically changed him: were its whiteness and weightlessness an overwhelming revelation of everything he did not yet believe in? An epiphany of anti-matter? Was this canvas cathedral an acute flash-forward to another architecture?[8]

FROM SYMBOLIC ROLE TO DESIGN MEDIUM

I have to this point sketched out the historical roots and background role of woven or textile architecture's shaping of architectural concepts and meaning. Terms such as "urban fabric," "text-tile house," "mat architecture," "cladding," and even "building envelope" and "building fabric" attest to the metaphorical and analogous presence of "fabric" in architecture.

The formal and performative role of fabric as an architecturally generative material constitutes a separate, more familiar lineage apart from the symbolic one discussed earlier. From tents to yurts to the tensile structures of Frei Otto and contemporary large-scale textile roofs, each of these structure's building geometry and form is a direct result of fabric's material traits.

Most fabric architecture forms follow from fabric's tensile properties, but there are exceptions, such as Albert Frei's canvas weekend house on New York's Long Island, in which he used wooden framing as a structure over which to stretch canvas, creating a conventional form with an unconventional material. Ani Albers' bespoke wall textile for the Bundesschule Auditorium in Bernau, Germany, reified the idea of fabric as an integral performative architecture: the weave of chenille, cotton, and cellophane was simultaneously reflective (of light) and absorptive (of sound), in effect, *the* architecture of the auditorium (Figure 2.3).

The work of Antoni Gaudí brought fabric to the center of the design process itself. His funicular models made with suspended cloth, ropes, and weights created tensile structures that when "flipped" over would represent a geometry of pure compression, not unlike the Gateway Arch in St. Louis being a "flipped" weighted catenary (the natural geometry of an evenly weighted rope suspended from two points).

The materials and media of any design process, particularly the *architectural* design process, have long played critical roles in the development of architectural ideas and forms. For instance, a casting plaster will generate thoughts of subtractive space and form, while a chipboard model will reinforce a planar and layered sensibility. Used as a design medium, as Gaudí's funicular models demonstrated, fabric imbues architectural thinking with its materiality (Figure 2.4). The stitches, tears, ripples, draping, creasing, folding, stretching, and wrinkling of fabric all suggest a vast untapped architectural vocabulary and conceptual resource.

Figure 2.3 *Courtesy: Bauhaus-Universität Weimar, Archiv der Moderne* Source: Photographer unknown

Figure 2.4 *Photographer unknown* Source: Public domain

Figure 2.5 *Cover image - Photo by Bjarne Riesto*

The 1993 project "Bad Press" of architects Liz Diller and Rick Scofidio reimagined the simple act of shirt ironing with a series of "dysfunctional" refoldings and shirt manipulations that provoked new associations and architectural potential.

Peter Zumthor's and Louise-Bourgeois' Steilneset Memorial to the victims of seventeenth-century witch trials in Vardø, Norway, is centered around a 400-foot-long structure of fabric and wood (Figure 2.5). Fabric plays an architecturally generative role; it is used to create a metaphorical cocoon, its vulnerability and suspension evocative of a funerary ship or vessel. The folds, ripples, and the manner of the cocoon's hanging from the support structure are rich with symbolism; it is an architecture of fabric no longer confined to tensile structural utility.

In both "Bad Press" and the Steilneset Memorial, fabric is at the center of the design process itself: its material properties, limits, and affordances inform and guide the design. The designers, in other words, would have worked directly with fabric during the design process, in order to gain access to the material-based properties that were incorporated into how they thought through the design.

Figure 2.6 *Photo credit BRG/Mariana Popescu*

THE FUTURE OF FABRIC ARCHITECTURE

Fabric as both an architectural concept and material has gained importance as the rapid changes in technology and the planet's health have raised questions about the wisdom of an inflexible built environment. The broad cultural shift toward a more sustainable, resilient, and flexible relationship with the environment aligns with fabric architecture's attributes, valorizing what had historically been regarded as its limitations. And given fabric's surface complexities and the tendency for digital tools to foreground and easily manipulate surface geometries, fabric has gained a new potential for architectural meaning and form finding—that is, as "real architecture"—well beyond the preconceptions of it as a limited technical form resulting from physical forces (Figure 2.6).

NOTES

1. Bringhurst, Robert, *The Elements of Typographic Style* (Vancouver: Hurtley & Marks, 1992).
2. McEwen, Indra Kagis, *Socrates' Ancestor: An Essay on Architectural Beginnings* (Cambridge, MA: MIT Press, 1997), 89.
3. Ibid., 111.
4. Ibid., 110.
5. Malafouris, Lambros, *How Things Shape the Mind: A Theory of Material Engagement* (Cambridge, MA: MIT Press, 2013), 117.
6. Nosch, Marie-Louise, "The Loom and the Ship in Ancient Greece: Shared Knowledge, Shared Terminology, Cross-Crafts, or Cognitive Maritime-Textile Archaeology?", in *Texts and Textiles in the Ancient World: Materiality—Representation—Episteme—Metapoetics*, ed. Henriette Harich-Schwarzbauer (Oxford: Oxbow Books, 2015).

7. Kenzari, Bechir, and Elsheshtawy, Yasser. "The Ambiguous Veil: On Transparency, the Mashrabiy'ya, and Architecture", *Journal of Architectural Education* 56, no. 4 (2003), 17–25.
8. Koolhaas, Rem, "The House that Made Mies", in *SMLXL*, ed. Rem Koolhaas and Bruce Mau (New York: The Monacelli Press, 1995), 63.

3

Digital Fabrication
and Fabric Innovation

JANE SCOTT

3 Digital Fabrication and Fabric Innovation

Jane Scott

Digital fabrication has liberated textile making to offer a new vision for architecture where the complex organisation of intersecting threads, produces a multisensory experience of tactile surfaces and responsive interfaces. In fact, textiles are a physical manifestation of digital technology; translating code into soft structures that weave together ideas about space and the environment, closely aligned to the concept of *Visionaries* in Radical Architecture: "an interconnective matter that flows between the reality and potential of social spaces, individual lives and materials" (Galilee, 2021:13). This chapter explores the how digital fabrication and fabric innovation is transforming the role of textiles in architecture. Examples illustrate how the relationship between computation and fabrication, seen through the lens of the textile, is leading to fundamental changes in the way that architecture is imagined. This in turn, is resulting in positive changes in how we, both as individuals and communities, experience architecture.

The roots of digital fabrication can be traced through textiles; the Jacquard Loom in 1804 introduced a binary code for weaving, using punchcards to control the lifting of warp threads prior to weft insertion. As well as transforming the complexity of woven fabrics and the speed of production, this innovation was an important conceptual driver for computer programming (Quinn, 2010:22). Fast forward to 1995 and the launch of Shima Seiki's Wholegarment© knitting transformed digital manufacturing of textiles. This technology enabled programmers to design and knit garments in 3D, eliminating waste because garments could be knitted to shape on the machine. It was during the same period that 3D printing was gaining momentum as a medium for prototyping, and this was significant because it directly connected design software with the hardware that produced the physical output.

TEXTILES AS A MATERIAL INTERFACE

The coming together of computation and digital fabrication with textiles and architecture has changed our understanding of materiality. Textile practice is about making materials, even when textiles are digitally fabricated, and this is different to the specification of materials conventionally undertaken by architects. Whilst the ability to programme bespoke textiles optimised to a particular specification has transformed the way that textiles can be used in architecture, it has also changed the way that we understand the potential to design with materials.

DOI: 10.4324/9781003138471-4

Figure 3.1 *Using industrial knitting machine technology a fabric can be detailed to an individual stitch to generate a hyperspecified material*
Source: Jane Scott

For Artist Janet Echelman, billowing canopies such as *Bending Arc* (2020) are a way to reimagine the spaces between buildings. Each sculpture is precisely engineered to move with the wind. They are created from high-performance fibres using brightly coloured, perfectly positioned, interconnecting threads (Echelman, 2020). Architecture relies on performance criteria that can be modelled accurately, but these textiles are soft and malleable as opposed to rigid and stiff, they are not static but responsive and therefore cannot be understood in the same way as conventional building materials. This is where the opportunity that presents computation merging with digital fabrication becomes so exciting. Designers are now able to calculate the performance of materials at miniscule scales, accommodating variation or specifying properties as required (Carpo, 2017:50). Research at The Royal Danish Academy's Centre for Information Technology and Architecture (CITA) aims to move away from standardised information, focusing instead on the complexity of material performance (Ramsgaard Thomsen, 2019). In prototypes such as Hybrid Tower (2015), knitting is understood as a material system that operates across multiple interconnecting scales that determines overall behavior (Ramsgaard Thomsen, 2015). These textiles can be very highly specified: a knitted fabric can be configured to an individual stitch, producing a material with variable properties. This can reduce material usage by placing material only where it is needed to achieve the require performance.

Digital fabrication is already enabling materials that could not conventionally embody the unique characteristics of a fabric to become more textile. Lightweight and efficient composites are emerging that unite the formmaking of 3D knitting with the structural performance of concrete (Popescu et al., 2020). *KnitCandela* (2017) is a highly engineered structural composite, however it retains the imprint

Figure 3.2 *Knit Candela*
Source: Philippe Block

of the textile in its exposed and vibrant formwork, purple and orange knitting juxtaposed against a concrete surface.

Whilst some technologies are familiar, repurposing the traditions of knitting, weaving and non-wovens with new fibres and advanced programming, others take their reference points from alternative experiences of fibre-based materials, such as biomimicry which looks to nature for inspiration.

This is exemplified by robotic coreless filament winding, a bio-inspired additive robotic fabrication process developed by the Institute for Computational Design and Construction (ICD) and the Institute for Building Structures and Structural Design (ITKE) at the University of Stuttgart (Menges and Knippers, 2015). This technique uses industrial robots to precisely wrap high-performance filament yarns around a winding frame to create architectural components. The precision achieved by robotic fabrication enables fibre orientation and density to achieve the structural requirements of the component with high material efficiency alongside a high load bearing capacity (Prado et al., 2017). The implementation of lightweight structures is a critical vision for textile architectures because it shows an alternative way of making buildings with less materials, and less waste in the process of construction offering essential alternatives to current building practices.

TEXTILES AS AN ENVIRONMENTAL INTERFACE

The urgent need to address environmental sustainability in architecture extends beyond construction. Most of the energy used in buildings is required

Figure 3.3 *Robotic Needle Felting* Source: Tsz Yan Ng & Wes McGee

to maintain our comfort through heating, cooling and ventilation (Department of Energy, 2015). Fabric innovation can be used to reduce energy use either through engineering passive, low impact textile materials or by implementing active sensing systems using digital technologies. By embedding sensing systems directly into fabrics smart textiles can act as sensors to monitor the interior environment and produce physical responses. In Soft House (Kennedy and Violich, 2013) flexible textile photovoltaics produce power, whereas fibre optics are woven directly into the structure of *Lit Lace* (Robertson et al., 2019) to generate lighting. These are hi-tech solutions that showcase the latest in digital technologies, but such elaborate engineering requires high-cost materials and electronic control.

Digital manufacture also has the potential to transform low value, locally sourced natural fibres, such as wool, into high-performance textiles. Through novel manufacturing developments these fibres can be used to create engineered nonwoven felt in passive systems such as *Robotic Needle Felting* (McGee et al., 2019) for bespoke thermal and acoustic environments.

Programmable Knitting (Scott, 2017) is motivated by the potential to transform the design potential of programmable and smart materials for the built environment using a textiles interface. The work demonstrates how knitted fabrics can be engineered to act as a sense and response system, directly engaging with an environmental stimulus, and producing real-time, programmed shape change responses. Knitted from wool and linen using 3D knit technologies, these moisture sensitive fabrics change in shape in response to changing humidity levels in a building, providing instant, reversible actuation for example opening up fabrics to enhance airflow. The development of Programmable Knitting demonstrates a critical step towards the implementation of passive responsive material systems to replace energy-intensive mechanised control.

Figure 3.4
*Programmable
Knitting: textiles
provide an
environmental
interface*
Source: Cristina
Schek

Figure 3.5
*Programmable
Knitting: these
fabrics respond
to moisture and
actuate from 2D
to 3D*
Source: Jane Scott

Figure 3.6 *MyThread Pavilion: interior view with photoluminescent yarns activated*
Source: Nike Inc and Jenny Sabin Studio

TEXTILES AS A DATA INTERFACE

Digital fabrication in textiles relies on specialist programming to design not only the colours, structures and shapes of a fabric, but also to communicate how the pattern is developed into a textile structure. Both punchcards and computer programmes present a unique visual language of textiles that we can use as a data interface, to read and comprehend digital information.

Architectural designer Jenny Sabin describes this as the "materialisation of data" (Sabin and Lloyd Jones, 2018:278). In *MyThread Pavilion* (2012), Sabin used biometric data from athletes as a design input, translating it into unique stripe sequences through knit programming. The output, knitted in photoluminescent threads, added both materiality (through changes to fabric handle and tactility) and interactivity (through the use of colour changing yarns) suggesting an intimate connection to architectural spaces by encoding personal data into the very fabric of a building. This allows textile to produce a "tangible code" (Engenhoefer, 2010:141), a trace of the human between a programme and its data. An earlier work by Sabin, *BodyBlanket* (2005), interpreted patient data recorded in a clinical setting into a digitally woven jacquard. Here a textile interface provides alternative ways to make the data visible and use data as a new tool for patternmaking at an architectural scale. In doing so, these projects engage with larger questions around the ethics of data generated by sensing systems within the built environment. There is resonance here with contemporary thinking where the language of textiles provides a powerful visual metaphor for change:

> In the end, if inequity and injustice are woven into the very fabric of society, then each twist, coil, and code offers a chance for us to weave new patterns, practices,

and politics . . . new blueprints. The vastness of the problems we face will be their undoing when we accept that we are patternmakers.

Benjamin (2022:283)

If data harvested in our buildings is materialised through textiles, could this encourage transparency and promote ethical data use?

TEXTILES AS A MULTISENSORY INTERFACE

Textile architecture promotes a haptic experience and digital fabrication reveals the possibilities for new encounters thanks to the scale and the complexity that can be programmed into fabric structures using a digital interface. Architect Sean Ahlquist works with the tactility and responsiveness of knitted fabric to produce extraordinary immersive environments that provide a multisensory experience for children with Autism Spectrum Disorder (Ahlquist, 2018). His Sensory Architectures (Ahlquist, 2015) use bespoke highly elastic knitted forms to create bending active structures that find their form in tension. The fabric can be pressed, pulled, climbed into and over, enabling each child to create their own physical experience of the architecture whilst improving motor skills. The fabric itself is also a touch responsive sensing system connected to a digital interface that projects images on the surface of the fabric. By pushing the fabric, fish appear on the surface; by changing pressure, the fish will swim. For *How Will We Play Together* at the 2021 Venice Biennale Ahlquist presented Social Equilibria (Ahlquist, 2021), an exterior playscape that celebrates the scope for social interaction facilitated by the textile:

> Sensorial abilities—to perceive, motivate and act upon a malleable architecture— become inherently social as they resonate from the textile landscape, moment by moment. Architecture becomes a live canvas for communication, rather than the consequence of a doctrine of preconceived expectations.
>
> Ahlquist (2021)

The textile interface provides a very different kind of learning environment, where the knitted fabric creates a multisensory interface that produces haptic encounters resulting in an inclusive space to encourage learning and play. An alternative play space, the Shadow Gradient *3D Knit Pavilion* (Scott and Chaltiel, 2019) again captures the softness and responsiveness of knitted fabric, but here uses inflatable beams integrated into the knitted panels to provide a pop-up temporary space. This pavilion can be flat packed, transported in a bag and inflated in only a few minutes.

CONCLUSIONS: TEXTILES AS A TEMPORAL INTERFACE

The ephemeral and temporary nature of a fabric is, thanks to digital fabrication, gaining durability and new life spans. After completing the largest ever knitted

Figure 3.7 *Shadow Gradient 3D Knit Pavilion*: the use of multiple yarns enabled by digital fabrication particularly appealed to children who were attracted by the bright coloured yarns and glow in the dark interior
Source: NAARO

installation, *Lumen*, for MoMA's 2017 Young Architects Program, Jenny Sabin Studio is now developing solutions using weather resistant materials to increase longevity for future projects (Sabin, 2019). In the design of Social Equilibria, the material system is transformed for outside use. The technology behind KnitCandela has been developed for the design of a pedestrian bridge (Bouten et al., 2021). This permanent structure using knitted formwork will be located Rotterdam in the Netherlands.

Programmable Knitting has also advanced into new timescales through the establishment of the Living Textiles Research Group. Here new hybrid technologies envision a biological architecture where growth replaces construction, and living organisms such as mycelium and bacteria cellulose are structured using textile principles of knitting and weaving. For *BioKnit Pavilion* time was compressed and

Figure 3.8 *The BioKnit Pavilion incorporates digital fabrication and biotechnology to envision a future living architecture*
Source: Hub for Biotechnology in the Built Environment

expanded by controlling heat and moisture levels to guide the growth of mycelium through a knitted preform (Scott et al., 2022). Here knitting becomes a scaffold and scaling agent in a biocomposite system that lies dormant but has the potential for new life encoded into the material itself.

Digital fabrication has opened up new ways to imagine architecture and to explore the material world of textiles. Each example cited presents a vision for collaboration across multiple domains of knowledge. Digital fabrication has transformed the scale, materiality and performance of a textile architecture but, more fundamentally, introduced new ways of thinking that operate between the digital and physical contexts so that through textiles, architecture can become an interface to engage with people, adapt to change and contribute to a positive society.

REFERENCES

Ahlquist, S. (2015). Social Sensory Architectures: Articulating Textile Hybrid Structures for Multi-sensory Responsiveness and Collaborative Play. In Combs, L. and Perry, C. (eds.), *ACADIA 2015: Computational Ecologies [Proceedings of the 35th Annual Conference of the Association for Computer Aided Design in Architecture]*, Cincinnati, October, pp. 262–273.

Ahlquist, S. (2018). Sensorial Playscape. In Yuan, P., Leach, N. and Menges, A. (eds.), *Digital Fabrication*, Tongi: Tongji University Press, pp. 197–210.

Ahlquist, S. (2021). *Social Equilibria*. Available From: www.labiennale.org/en/architecture/2021/how-will-we-play-together/sean-ahlquist-lab-sociomaterial-architectures-university-michigan. Accessed 20/02/2022.

Benjamin, R. (2022). *Viral Justice: How We Grow the World We Want,* Princeton, NJ: Princeton University Press, p. 283.

Bouten, S., Popescu, M., Ranaudo, F., Van Mle, T., Block, P., Mengeot, P., and Wyns, K. (2021). Design of a Funicular Concrete Bridge with Knitted Formwork. In *IABSE Congress: Structural Engineering for Future Societal Needs*, Ghent, Belgium, 22–24 September 2021, pp. 690–699. http://doi.org/10.2749/ghent.2021.0690.

Carpo, M. (2017). *The Second Digital Turn: Design Beyond Intelligence*, Cambridge, MA: MIT Press.

Department of Energy. (2015). *Quadrennial Technology Review: An Assessment of Energy Technology and Research Opportunities*. Chapter 5: Increasing Efficiency of Building Systems and Technologies, September 2015. Available From: www.energy.gov/sites/prod/files/2017/03/f34/qtr-2015-chapter5.pdf. Accessed 28/02/2022.

Echelman, J. (2020). *Bending Arc*. St Petersburg, FL. Available From: www.echelman.com/st-petersburg-fl. Accessed 20/02/2022.

Engenhoefer, R. B. (2010). Tracking Knitting and Translating Code. In Hemmings, J. (ed.), *In the Loop, Knitting Now*, London: Black Dog Publishing, pp. 140–149.

Galilee, B. (2021). *Radical Architecture of the Future*, London: Phaidon.

Kennedy and Violich. (2013). *Soft House*. Available From: www.kvarch.net/projects/iba-soft-house. Accessed 28/03/22.

McGee, W., Ng, T. Y., and Peller, A. (2019). Hard + Soft: Robotic Needle Felting for Nonwoven Textiles. In Willmann, J., Block, P., Hutter, M., Byrne, K., and Schork, T. (eds.), *Robotic Fabrication in Architecture, Art and Design 2018. ROBARCH 2018*. Cham: Springer.

Menges, A., and Knippers, J. (2015). Fibrous Tectonics. *Architectural Design*, 85(5), London: Wiley, pp. 40–47.

Popescu, M., Rippmann, M., Van Mele, T., and Block, P. (2020). KnitCandela—Challenging the Construction Logistics, Waste and Economy of Concrete-Shell Formworks. In Burry, J., Sabin, J., Sheil, B., and Skavara, M. (eds.), *FABRICATE 2020*, London: UCL, pp. 194–201.

Prado, M., Dorstelmann, M., Menges, A., Solly, J., and Knippers, J. (2017). Elytra Filament Pavilion: Robotic Filament Wingding for Structural Composite Building Systems. In Menges, A., Sheil, B., Glynn, R., and Skavara, M. (eds.), *FABRICATE 2017*, London: UCL, pp. 224–231.

Quinn, B. (2010). *Textile Futures*, Oxford: Berg.

Ramsgaard Thomsen, M. (2019). Complex Modelling, Questioning the Infrasturctures of Information Modelling. In Beesley, P., Hasting, S., and Bonnemaison, S. (eds.), *White Papers 2019*, Kitchener, Ontario: Riverside Architectural Press, pp. 265–281.

Ramsgaard Thomsen, M., Tamke, M., Holden Deleuran, A., Friis Tinning, I., Leander Evers, H., Gengnagel, C., and Schmeck, M. (2015). Hybrid Tower, Designing Soft Structures. In *Design Modelling Symposium: Modelling Behaviour*, Berlin and Heidelberg: Springer.

Robertson, S., Taylor, S., and Bletcher, J. (2019). Collaborative Innovation: Reflections on Research for Smart Textiles in a Theatre and Performance Context. In *Textile Intersections*, London, 12–14 Sep 2019.

Sabin, J. (2019). Lumen. In Beesley, P., Hasting, S., and Bonnemaison, S. (eds.), *White Papers 2019*, Kitchener, Ontario: Riverside Architectural Press, pp. 291–319.

Sabin, J., and Lloyd Jones, P. (2018). *Lab Studio*, New York: Routledge.

Scott, J. (2017). Programmable Knitting. In Tibbits, S. (ed.), *Active Matter*. Cambridge, MA: MIT Press, pp. 213–216.

Scott, J., and Chaltiel, S. (2019). *Shadow Gradient 3D Knit Pavilion, IASS 2019 Barcelona*. Available From: https://www.jjo33.com/iass-barcelona-2019. Accessed 29/11/2022.

Scott, J., Kaiser, R., Ozkan, D., Hoenerloh, A., Agraviador, A., Elsacker, E., and Bridgens, B. (2022). Knitted Cultivation: Textiling A Multi-Kingdom Bio Architecture. In *Proceedings 5th International Conference on Structures and Architecture*, 6–8 July 2022. CRC Press.

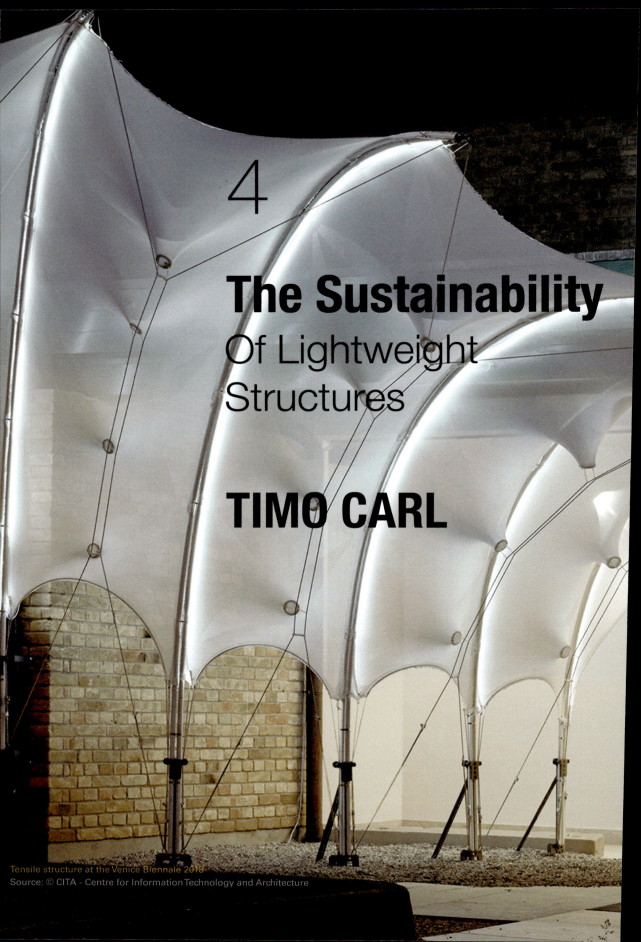

4

The Sustainability
Of Lightweight Structures

TIMO CARL

4 The Sustainability of Lightweight Structures

Timo Carl

INTRODUCTION TO TENSILE STRUCTURES

Textile tensile structures and architecture share an extensive history from the earliest nomads' tent to contemporary, large-span lightweight structures. Tensile constructions, such as tent membranes and tension (cable) net structures, are especially fascinating because of their lightweight nature, light transmission, and space-creating effects that contrast in outcome with more common building methods. The interwoven interplay of physical forces, geometry, material, and aesthetics have inspired a rich history of architectural precedents such as Shukov's Rotunda in 1895, Frei Otto's Olympia Park Roof in 1972, and Fentress Architect's Denver Airport Roof in 1995, to name just a few examples. Lightweight tension structures have an inherently nearer relationship to nature than more traditional structures based on wood, concrete, or steel. Combining the physical realms of material premise and the natural flow of forces situates tensile structures closer to a material-efficient "form follows force" concept in comparison to more traditional architectural notions such as Sullivan's "form follows function." Moreover, they produce a density of sensual experiences through their softness and fluidity, and transgress pure material and technical constraints in their space-creating effects.

In the following, I will outline the main parameters of tensile structures to provide the foundations for the subsequent evaluation of their sustainability. In addition to the aspect of minimal material use, I will expand the scope of the discussion to include alternative material research, contemporary design and fabrication, and the extended functionalities of novel tensile typologies exemplified by three case studies of different scales.

KEY PARAMETERS OF TENSILE STRUCTURES

Tension nets and membrane structures belong to the category of form-active structures. Both carry external loads by a single stress condition of pure tension. For simplicity, we assume the load-bearing principles for tension net and textile membrane structures as identical—imagining the latter as an isotropic, biaxial plain weaved element at a denser scale. As no shear forces or bending moments are absorbed, a membrane stress condition always prevails and form-active tension structures belong to the most efficient load-bearing systems, because failure through buckling is impossible (Knippers et al. 2012, p. 134) (Krauss et al. 2021,

DOI: 10.4324/9781003138471-5

Figure 4.1 *Aerial and detail image of Munich Olympia*
Source: Timo Carl

p. 92). If a series of constraints is considered, non-rigid, flexible matter, shaped in the right way and secured by fixed end supports, spans even very wide spaces.

Similar to a catenary line, tensile structures transfer loads laterally by pure tensile stresses. Additionally, tension nets and membrane structures transfer those loads in more than one axis. Transverse cables and double curved textile geometries increase the overall stability and strengthen resistance against point loads (Engel 1985, p. 79). Therefore, a double curved geometry is favorable to an effective design. More precisely, pure tension nets and textile structures require ideally a combination of anti-clastic and syn-clastic curvatures, that is, saddle shaped geometries, that have a negative Gaussian curvature at any point on their surface. Last, tent membranes often require extra cables at their edges for local differentiation and control of the textile geometry.

This illustrates that architectural form and space are inseparably linked to material behavior and load conditions. Form-active tension structures "show the connection between form, force and mass" (Otto 1998, p. 151). Manuel de Landa describes analog form-finding procedures therefore also as "material computation" (DeLanda 2015, p. 16). Meanwhile, form-finding strategies, pioneered by Antonio Gaudi, Frei Otto, and Heinz Isler, are well established, and computational off-the-shelf tools are nowadays widely available.

Since tensile structures are much lighter than conventional structures, they carry different external loads from wind and snow by deformation (Knippers et al. 2012, p. 139). This requires a pre-stressing of the construction that must be at least half as large as the prime expected load (Krauss et al. 2021, p. 344). The absorption of these, often considerable, horizontal forces at the anchor points is a major drawback of tensile systems that often involves massive foundations (e.g., the single-family-sized foundations of the Munich Olympia Stadium). The floating lightness of the Munich Olympia Roofs required enormous planning and construction efforts in 1972.

One common solution is hybrid systems combining truss rings or girders with membranes or tension nets, so that the respective properties of different load-bearing systems complement each other (e.g., the Rosa Parks Transit Center in Denver by the FTL Design Engineering Studio). Current research taps into bending-active hybrid structures (BAHS) that combine the flexibility of bending elements with tensioning membranes. Examples include the sensory PLAYSCAPE Prototype (Ahlquist 2015, pp. 262–271) and the vaulted gradient textiles of the Danish Pavilion for the 16th Architectural Biennale in Venice (Ramsgard et al. 2018). Besides structural considerations, increased accessibility to computational tools for the simulation of flexible systems supports a growing body of research on the topic.

SUSTAINABILITY OF TENSION STRUCTURES

Lightweight tension structures are sustainable, because they utilize light high per-formance materials within form-active geometries to decrease the required amount of construction material. This leads to energy savings and, in turn, to a reduction in emissions. Using less or lighter material is important, because "Building and con-struction activities together account for 36% of global final energy use and 39% of energy-related carbon dioxide (CO_2) emissions when upstream power generation is included."[1] Beyond material savings, the complexity of the subject matter touches on a comprehensive number of additional quantitative and qualitative aspects.

Textile tension structures are especially captivating due to the use of a mem-brane with minimal thickness and expressive potential which creates architectural space by separating inside from outside. This situates the concept of tensile archi-tectures close to Gottfried Semper's Bekleidungstheorie ("theory of clothing/cladding") where he distinguishes between the primary function of defining space through woven fabrics and the secondary function of structure, holding those tex-tiles in place (Carl, 2019, p. 21). Semper's interest is rooted in the traditions of arts and crafts with their focus on material properties and building processes—position-ing the architect as a weaver who tries to take advantage of technological advances (Feldtkeller 1989, p,. 38). The accessibility of computational form-findings and inter-face design for digital fabrication should therefore be included in the discussion, as it touches on the sustainability of planning efforts.

What about energy? Reynar Banham's attributes deflection, exclusion of rain, maintenance of privacy, and other unwanted physical forces to the environmental behavior of a tent. However, he forgot to include the reflection of radiation, the retention of internal heat, and the exclusion of solar heat to the latter (Banham 1988, p. 20). Any minimal membrane has limitations in terms of building phys-ics, and Reynar Banham is at least wrong in his assumptions concerning thermal performance—anyone who has ever slept in a tent knows this. Lacking mass, mem-brane textiles are inherently ill suited for insulation and soundproofing and present challenges for the introduction of enclosures beyond a single surface (Vandenberg 1998, p. 34). For example, the tension net roof of the Olympic Swimming Pool in Munich has an extra insulation membrane layer, suspended beneath the primary cable net. Because membrane and foil materials are not vapor-tight, condensation and saturation of the insulation must be considered, alongside thermal bridges and intersections with other components (Knippers et al. 2012, p. 217).

Nevertheless, the low weight and transparency of membranes make them well suited for upgrading existing structures (e.g., Leipzig Central Station, Germany) and the layered envelope design provides buffer zones with intermediate temperatures (Knippers et al. 2012, p. 221). This allows for the design of differentiated transitions between exterior and interior spaces. Various layered membranes with diverse specific functions allow for the adjustment of views and privacy, and the control of light, temperature, and spatial atmosphere. Textile membranes are excellent shading devices (e.g., the King Fahid National Library in Riyadh) and are well suited for the design of secondary skins (e.g., Unilever Building, Hamburg, Germany).

MATERIAL RESEARCH

The materials used for textile membranes must meet many different requirements. Whereas the 23,000 m² of tension sails used at the Colosseum in Rome were made of pure woven cotton, nowadays large-span membrane materials consist of composites made from technical fabrics with several layers of plastic coating. Weather resistance (e.g., UV radiation), fire protection, and self-cleaning are all important factors for achieving the longest possible life cycle (Knippers et al. 2012, p. 115).

Additionally, materials with greater tear strength, combined with a low density (i.e., weight) and high elasticity (i.e., flexibility), facilitate minimal membrane constructions that span large spaces without additional cable nets. For this, only polymer-coated synthetic or glass-fiber fabrics currently have the required strength and durability. For load-bearing textile membranes, these include PTFE-coated glass-fiber cloth, or Polyvinyl chloride (PVC). For tension net roofings, PMMA (polymethyl methacrylate—also known as acrylic glass) and PC (polycarbonate) are suitable. Lastly, ETFE (ethylene tetrafluorethylene) is often found in single layer facades (Knippers et al. 2012, p. 100).

In terms of sustainability, oil-based polymers consume a high amount of primary energy.[2] In addition, the emissions from some of these materials (e.g., PVC) pose a risk to the environment, and recycling them is a challenge. On the other hand, these high-tech textiles offer substantial material savings within tension structures. The average weight of textile membrane is only around 1.2 kg/m². Joost Hartwig emphasizes that lightness comes at a cost of other disadvantages, yet in the balance of things is still more resource-efficient than many other forms of construction (Hartwig and Zeumer 2012, p. 124).

Investigations into alternative textile materials (i.e., biopolymers) promise more sustainable alternatives in the future. The Research Lab for Sustainable Lightweight Building Technologies (ReSULT) at the Frankfurt University of Applied Sciences explores, for example, sandwich-like 3D textiles with extended functionalities (Lüling et al. 2021 p. 37). Combining textile fabrication techniques and foam materials allows thickness, density, and porosity to be controlled. This process is discussed in detail in the Spacer Fabric Pavilion chapter in the Case Studies section of this book. The novel use of basalt fibers and foamed concrete, as well as recycled PET fibers and PET foams, permits the production of single origin building elements with good insulation capacity, or in the first instance with excellent fire ratings. Such novel lightweight and self-supporting materials offer fresh applications for more ecological tension net structures. Their low weight and extended functions (i.e., insulation and non-combustibility) provide an excellent ecological alternative for roofing cable net envelopes.

COMPUTATIONAL PROCESS AND DIGITAL FABRICATION

Frei Otto predicted that computational procedures would play a major role in the design of less energy-hungry, multi-functional structures that successfully combine ecological and aesthetic concerns (Otto 1998, p. 13).

Computationally speaking, the analysis of pure tension net structures is well established and a modest number of variables is sufficient to generate meaningful results (Piker 2013). Parametric form-finding tools such as Daniel Piker's Kangaroo, a dynamic relaxation-based solver, is popular within academia and practice—based on Hooke's Law and the Barnes/Adriaenssens (Adriaenssens and Barnes 2001, p. 31) model respectively. The tool is integrated within the Rhino©/Grasshopper© (Rutten 2018) parametric modeling platform, which is available for little cost, and can be easily combined with more sophisticated structural analysis programs (e.g., Karamba3D, Kiwi3D or STiKbug/Sofistik©). With the help of the Kangaroo plug-in, designers can explore a great variety of tensile topologies, because the tool is easy to use and fast.

In the introduction to this book Tolya Stonov points out that "the idea of doing more with less is a key theme that points to the role of fabric innovation in social justice."[3] This notion of efficiency also includes the accessibility of non-expensive and free planning tools that relate the nature of those computational methods to the social relationships they serve. Increasing the amount of sustainable tensile lightweight projects requires a transformative effect on the accessibility of computational tools for both the design and construction process. Ideally, those tools are open-source software that interface well with industrial fabrication processes—developed by a community with a strong regard for knowledge-sharing.

A good example of open-source software is the plug-in Cockatoo (Eschenbach 2022), developed as part of ongoing research by Max Eschenbach and Franz Dietrich. It integrates the design of knitted membranes with the generation of data that functions as a generic exchange format for the control of industrial CNC knitting machines. The plug-in uses graph theory (Narayanan et al. 2018) for a mathematical representation of the textile knits that includes information about the individual stitches and the relationship to their respective neighbors. Mapping the basic measurements of a single stitch and the three basic shaping operations of knitting within a graph allows the knit patterns to be computed directly on the 3D surface or mesh geometry. Last, topological sorting creates a two-dimensional Bitmap image for the import into machine-specific software.

Developing computational CNC knitting workflows opens up extended design possibilities that are at the core of the ongoing research effort at CITA in Copenhagen. Controlling the machining of textiles allows the design of individual and specific gradients within a knitted membrane. This is especially relevant for the design of bending-active hybrid structures (BAHS) that combine membranes with compression rods to create an equilibrium between tension and compression forces (Ramsgard et al. 2018). The lightweight Isoropia canopy embracing the Danish Pavilion integrates channels for tension cables and reinforcement patches for the bent GFRP rods directly into the knit membrane without any additional need for post-fabrication detailing.

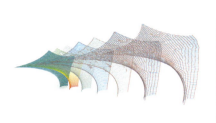
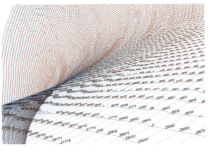
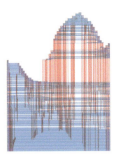

Figure 4.2 *Cockatoo plug-in, workflow images*
Source: © Max Benjamin Eschenbach

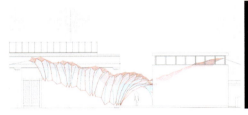

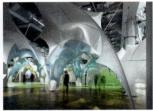

Figure 4.3 *Tensile Structure at Venice Biennale and Installation at ZKM in Karlsruhe*
Source: © CITA - Centre for Information Technology and Architecture

The Zoirotia installation[4] by CITA at the ZKM in Karlsruhe grades the knit properties with regards to stretch and color, allowing for quite dramatic membrane shapes that move without creasing and avoiding extra waste from the cutting and seaming operations (Sinke et al. 2022). The project covers an impressive 500 m^2 and is proof of concept for the scalability of the approach. Design conception to realization only took five months, thanks to the integration of computational membrane design and CNC knit fabrication.[5]

EXPLORING NOVEL TENSION STRUCTURE TYPOLOGIES

Related to the previous case studies, at (Research Lab for Sustainable Lightweight Structures) we are also exploring novel forms of tension typologies, which combine solar energy production and climate regulation for the urban realm. This ongoing research originates in an interest in tensile shading structures, such as the vernacular Spanish toldo ("awning"), which cover public spaces to protect from excessive sun exposure. Our approach is based on exploring flexible lightweight structures that provide habitable shade and combine their capacity for energy reflection (passive shading) with active energy generation. Considering this context, Frank Stepper, Markus Schein, and I have created a contemporary sun-shading typology capable of harvesting energy together with our students. The technological foundations for the project are lightweight organic photovoltaic foils (OPVs).

In order to achieve lightness, both in the aesthetic sense and as an actual reduction of material mass, we decided not to attach the photovoltaic elements as a separate material layer to a tensile membrane. Instead of using organic photovoltaic foils (OPV) as an additional material layer, they are used as space-defining elements

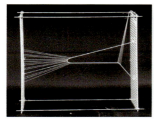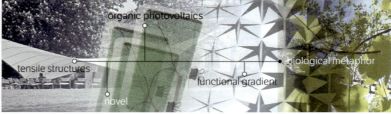

Figure 4.4 *Diagram of tensile structures relationship to nature*
Source: ©Timo Carl and Markus Schein

that create a three-dimensional shading structure (Otto 1984, p. 94). Designing a solar cloud from a series of OPV modules that integrate within a cable net structure circumvents the complexities of double curved surface geometries. Moreover, the concept allows for moving from a single surface layer (i.e., membranes) to an architectural volume with extended design opportunities.

This approach exemplifies the idea of exploiting material properties (in our case the "lightness" of organic photovoltaic cells) to a structural and an architectural advantage (Carl et al. 2018). The 30 m² canopy of this "solar cloud" consists of 300 OPV cells, embedded in three-dimensional thermoformed lightweight carrier tiles. A series of tension rope carriers integrates the shading and energy harvesting modules at the top of their thin metal compression struts. These cable girders are supported by two discrete, pre-stressed tension ropes of roughly 70 m length (diameter = 20 mm) that are anchored by a series of thin supporting cables between a group of trees and the ground. The overall weight, including the tensile supporting structures, is less than 120 kg. The use of computational form-finding tools within a parametric set-up was essential to conduct this research together with a group of students within an educational context in just four months.

In contrast to tensile membranes requiring high pre-tension forces, we chose to allow for a generous amount of flexibility and movement. The solar cloud compensates the wind loads through movement. Observing the modulation of this lightweight structure by environmental forces (i.e., light and wind), it reminds us of our and architecture's connection to nature.

CONCLUSIONS

The presented case studies challenge the notion that the sustainability of tensile typologies is solely defined through the reduction of mass. Instead, a meaningful assessment of the sustainability of tensile structures is multivalent. Nature, as both the problem and the solution, is the point of convergence for the design of green tensile architectures. Expanding the baseline of material efficiency through material research, computational methods, social and sensorial considerations is key. A clever combination of binary conditions such as software and hardware, material and behavior, design and fabrication is required. Nevertheless, exploring the fertile ground of tensile structures in a patient dialogue with nature also promises in the future to produce results that are both sustainable and beautiful.

NOTES

1. Global Status Report 2017; Published by the UN Environment and the International Energy Agency; www.worldgbc.org/news-media/global-status-report-2017, last seen 9.05.2022.

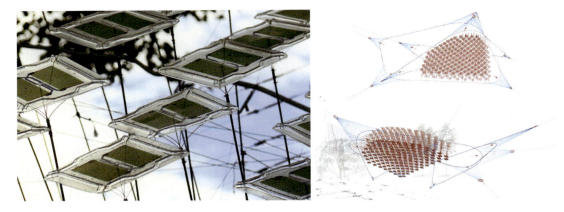

Figure 4.5 *Detail photo of opv panels, form-finding simulations of Solar Spline*
Source: © Timo Carl and Markus Schein

Figure 4.6 *Aerial image of Solar Spline*
Source: © Timo Carl and Markus Schein and Flying Impressions

2. Primary Energy (PE) is an energy form found in nature that has not been subjected to any human-engineered conversion process. It is energy contained in raw fuels, and other forms of energy, including waste, received as input to a system. Primary energy can be non-renewable or renewable. Wikipedia, last seen 9.04.2022.
3. Tolya Stonorov, Introduction, FABRIC[ated].
4. Many thanks to Martin Tamke from CITA for providing material and information on the Zoirotia project.
5. Thanks to Martin Tamke from CITA for sharing his insights on this project.

REFERENCES

Adriaenssens, S. and Barnes, M. R. (2001), Tensegrity spline beam and grid shell structures, *Engineering Structures*, 231, pp. 29–36.

Ahlquist, S. (2015), Social sensory architectures: Articulating textile hybrid structures for multi-sensory responsiveness and collaborative play, *ACADIA 2015: Computational Ecologies: Design in the Anthropocene: Proceedings of the 35th Annual Conference of the Association for Computer Aided Design in Architecture*, pp. 263–273. https://www.researchgate.net/profile/Sean-Ahlquist/publication/290195497_Social_Sensory_Architectures_Articulating_Textile_Hybrid_Structures_for_Multi-sensory_Responsiveness_and_Collaborative_Play/links/56957fe108ae3ad8e33d71f0/Social-Sensory-Architectures-Articulating-Textile-Hybrid-Structures-for-Multi-sensory-Responsiveness-and-Collaborative-Play.pdf, accessed 20.09.2022

Banham, R. (1988), *The Architecture of the Well-tempered Environment*, 2nd ed., 3. [Dr.], Chicago: University of Chicago Press.

Carl, T. (2019), *Deep Skin Architecture—Design Potential of Multi-layered Boundaries*, Wiesbaden: Springer.

Carl, T., Stepper, F. and Schein, M. (2018), Solar Spline—Expanding on traditional sun-sail typologies and Frei Otto's lightweight approach with the help of computational design procedures, *Proceedings of the 36th eCAADe Conference*, Lodz, https://doi.org/10.52842/conf.ecaade.2018.1.149.

DeLanda, M. (2015), The New Materiality. *Archit. Design,* 85: 16-21. https://doi.org/10.1002/ad.1948

Engel, H. (1985), *Structural Systems*, Ostfildern: Verlag Gerd Hatje.

Eschenbach, M. B. (2022), *Cockatoo.* https://github.com/fstwn/cockatoo

Feldtkeller, C. (1989) Der architektonische Raum: eine Fiktion, Vieweg, Braunschweig [u.a.]

Hartwig, J. and Zeumer, M. (2012), Environmental Impact of Polymers. In Knippers et al. (eds.), *Construction Manual for Polymers + Membranes*, Basel: Birkhauser.

Knippers, J., Cremers, J., Gabler, M. and Lienhard, J. (2012), *Construction Manual for Polymers + Membranes*, Basel: Birkhauser.

Krauss, F., Führer, W., Willems, C. and Techen, H. (2021), *Grundlagen der Tragwerklehre*, Band 2 — Gebäude und Tragwerke entwerfen und optimieren, R. Müller Verlag.

Lüling, C., Rucker-Gramm, P., Weilandt, A., Beuscher, J., Nagel, D., Schneider, J., Maier, A., Bauder, H.-J. and Weimer, T. (2021), Ge3TEX-Multifunctional Monomaterials Made from Foamed Glass-, Basalt- or PET-based 3D Textiles, *Powerskin Conference Proceedings*, pp. 37–51.

Narayanan, V., Albaugh, L., Hodgins, J., Coros, S. and McCann, J. (2018, June), Automatic machine knitting of 3D meshes, *ACM Transactions on Graphics*, 37(3), Article No.: 35, pp. 1–15, https://doi.org/10.1145/3186265.

Otto, F. (1984), *Vela, toldos: Sonnenzelte = sun & shade, IL*, Vol. 30, Stuttgart, Germany: University Stuttgart.

Otto, F. (1998), *Lightweight Principles, Institute für Leichte Flächentragwerke*, Stuttgart, Germany.

Piker, D. (2013), Kangaroo: Form-finding with computational physics, *Architectural Design*, 83(2), pp. 136–137, https://doi.org/10.1002/ad.1569.

Proceedings of the 9th PowerSKIN Conference. TU Delft Open. https://doi.org/10.47982/BookRxiv.27

Ramsgard Thomsen, M., Tamke, M., La Magna, R., Noel, R., Lienhard, J., Baranovskaya, Y., Fragkia, V. and Längst, P. (2018), *Isoropia: An Encompassing Approach for the Design, Analysis and Form-Finding of Bending-Active Textile Hybrids*, IASS Symposium: Creativity in Structural Design.

Rutten, D. (2018), *Grasshopper 3d. V. 1.0.0. Robert McNeel & Associates*, www.rhino3d.com/

Sinke, Y., Ramsgaard, M., Thomsen, D. S., Albrechtsen, S. and Tamke, M. (2022), Design-to-production workflows for CNC-knitted membranes, In: *Proceedings of the ACADIA Conference "Hybrids & Haecceities"*, Philadelphia, USA.

Vandenberg, M. (1998), *Cable Nets: Detail in Building*, London: Academy Editions.

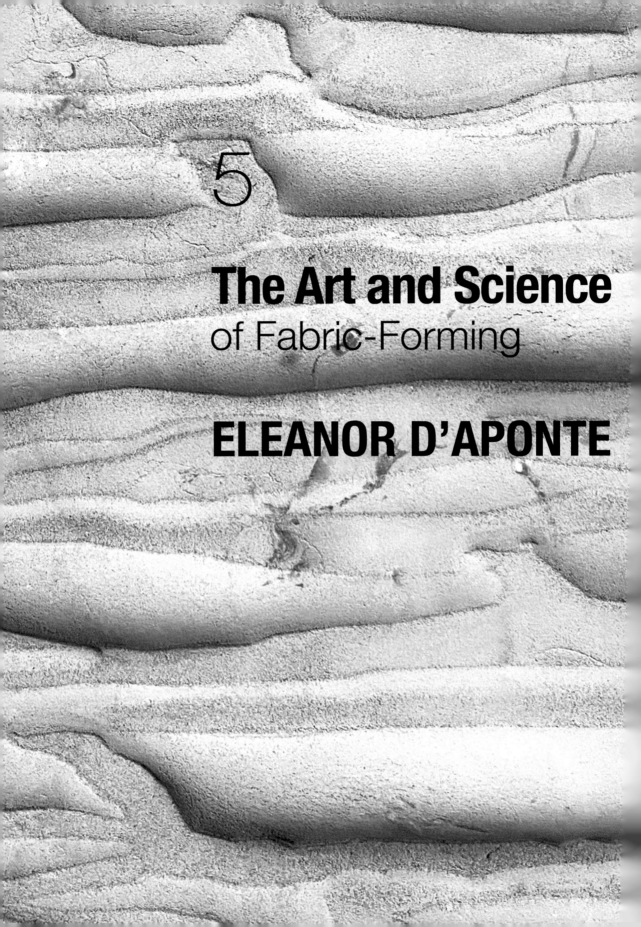

5

The Art and Science
of Fabric-Forming

ELEANOR D'APONTE

5 The Art and Science of Fabric-Forming

Eleanor D'Aponte

> *The beginning of building coincides with the beginning of textiles.*
> *Gottfried Semper*, Style in the Technical and
> Tectonic Arts, or Practical Aesthetics

INTRODUCTION

A human instinct to imitate nature and create ritual has shaped an intertwined story between architecture and fabric. The eighteenth-century architect and art critic Gottfried Semper traced the impact of weaving techniques on the design of the earliest architectural enclosures, or "space-dividers."[1] These dividers or walls were first woven from plant fiber and later from fiber. Stone walls for defense eventually replaced these woven dividers.[2] A woven tapestry often covered the unrefined stone wall as a "dressing" for warmth or decor. German archaeologist Karl Böttiger suggested that the dressing cultivated mediation with the human inhabitant by dematerializing the wall and enhancing its form.[3] As architectural enclosures evolved, patterns from early weavings and tapestries influenced the shape, cut, and assembly of stonework as ornament.[4] Semper analyzed the formal design characteristics (orientation, direction, and placement) of decorative elements such as the band, the seam, and the hem, and traced their cultural and functional origins to clothing, drapery, and tapestry. The resulting visual language in the stone facades of Renaissance buildings, for instance, can poetically express resistance or delight.[5]

A perceptible expression of this intertwinement can be seen on the facades of many buildings in Venice, Italy, where early weaving techniques such as twisting, and braiding are imitated and expressed in stone (Figure 5.1).

Venetian architecture, a city shaped by a dynamic exchange of culture and commodities via the Silk Route, was adorned with tapestries from Egypt, Asia, and East Asia for both simple functions and elaborate ceremonies. *Serenissime Trame*, an exhibition held at the Ca' d'Oro museum in 2017, evidenced the integration of tapestries in everyday life during the Venetian Renaissance.[6] They were used to soften stone seats, windowsills, and balcony railings; a woven carpet placed on the ground could frame a display of merchandise or delineate personal space for prayer in the public sphere. Complicated weaves with precious threads could symbolize social status or sacredness. Paintings by Canaletto illustrate eighteenth-century Venetian and life depict building facades adorned with fabrics to provide shade

DOI: 10.4324/9781003138471-6

Figure 5.1
© Redmond135,
Facade of Ca' d'Oro
or Palazzo Santa
Sofia in Venice, Italy
Source:
Dreamstime.com.
Web August 10,
2022

or serving as flags and banners during religious festivals and rituals. The decorative stone dressings and pigmented stucco layers covering the brick Venetian building facades recall the colorful and lively decor of the city's earlier ornamentation with fabrics.

"Fabric-forming" refers to the use of fabrics to cast architectural elements such as columns, beams, and wall panels. The techniques and effects of this innovative construction method explore and make use of the properties of fabric. Viewed through an evolutionary lens of enclosure that began with woven plant fibers and tapestry design, fabric-formed elements can be seen as expressions of enclosure that dematerialize, soften, personalize, and enhance habitable spaces.

The practice of fabric forming employs the material properties of fabric—weave thickness, elasticity, and permeability—to design and build formwork and drive the resulting shape and surface of the cast. Typically, architectural elements such as walls, columns, and beams are cast by pouring concrete into molds or formwork built of plywood or other rigid, bulky materials. Unlike rigid molds, fabric molds can be stretched, fastened, pierced, sewn, draped, folded, pinched, and combined with rigid materials to produce a variety of effects and forms. As with rigid materials, the precision and craft of the form or "rig," as well as the ingredients of the concrete mixture used, are revealed in surface, shape, texture, and strength of the final cast.[7] In a comprehensive history of fabric forming published in 2011, fabric formed concrete is shown to have three essential and often overlapping roles: as a hydraulic and geotechnical agent, as a shell construction and engineering agent, and as an agent for architectural and cultural expression.[8]

Fabric formwork's potential for architectural and cultural expression has been sustained by the proliferation of high-strength, low-cost geotextile fabrics—woven polyolefin fabrics that allow for the release of excessive bleed water, the filtering

Figure 5.2 *Mark West, Figure 6.53* Source: Eleanor D'Aponte. Photograph, 2009, in Mark West, *The Fabric Formwork Book* (New York: Routledge, 2017), 99

of air bubbles, and a reduction of air pockets, producing a more durable surface (Figure 5.2).[9] In the 1960s geotextiles were used for pouring groundwork such as backfill, earth stabilization, and footings.[10] The Centre for Architectural Structures and Technology (CAST), founded by Mark West in Manitoba, Canada, in 2002, developed techniques using these fabrics for casting wall panels and structural members. The plastic weave of geotextiles is malleable enough to manipulate, yet resistant to ripping and tearing. West explains that the balance between where and how the fabric is constrained and where it is allowed to relax dictates the final form.[11] The weave of the fabric responds to the weight of the concrete pour, and the resulting forms are often sensuous and curvaceous, quite different from typically rectilinear concrete structures.[12] The astounding sculptural potential of the technique can be employed to convey metaphor through ornamentation and, in some contexts, such as North America, the resulting softer and more fluid forms challenge a popular bias against concrete spurred on in the 1950s by the Brutalism movement. An unexpected

Figure 5.3 *Fabric being pulled away from concrete cast to reveal impression*
Source: D'Aponte

masonry surface can "draw [observers] into a dialogue" about concrete and its possibilities.[13]

ARCHITECTURAL EXPRESSION

As an ancient, economical, and ubiquitous building material used across the globe, concrete has been accessible to a wide array of makers and laborers since Roman times. It can be mixed and poured in small batches on remote rural sites or applied on a monumental scale for transportation, infrastructure, and groundwork. Notable architects such as Frank Lloyd Wright recognized the expressive potential of the surface of the concrete cast and employed the imprints of formwork joints, plywood patterns, and form liners to affect the appearance of a pour.[14] Wright was influenced by Semper and in the early 1920s explored the aesthetic expression of concrete, which he described as "masonry fabric." In his textile block houses, he

conceived a broadly accessible American vernacular for a building material that was otherwise considered "ugly" and "cheap." [15] In the 1950s, northern Italian influential architects Luigi Figini and Gino Pollini used an interplay of concrete and stone in works such as the church of the Madonna dei Poveri (1952–54), exploiting associations of concrete with poverty to call out the growing expense and luxury of church buildings. [16]

The immediate relationship between the properties of the fabric and the cast invites the designer to explore its expressive potential, see figure 5.3. In the 1970s architect Miquel Fisac began to experiment with thin plastic sheets as formwork to create billowing concrete wall panels that capture light and shadow for building facades. [17] In the 1990s, in response to the Kobe earthquake, Japanese architect Kenzo Unno developed a zero-waste formwork method for people to economically and simply upgrade interior walls. Unno developed the "quilt-point" system using form ties to restrain and attach construction netting fabric to an existing stud wall frame. [18]

Figure 5.5 *House One. View of fabric formwork in place after pour, removed formwork seen on the right*

Concrete poured into the cavity from above presses against the fabric producing a gridded surface of softly bulging forms.

More recently, ArroDesign, a construction company in Waitsfield, Vermont, has used fabric forming in both single-pour and hybrid framing methodologies for energy- and labor-efficient residential building envelopes. A freestanding prototype inspired by Unno's quilt-point method, designed to eliminate as many skeletal form members as possible, was constructed as an elongated column from a single sheet of fabric (Figure 5.4). In ArroDesign's House One, the Schulz Residence (2009), the thermal envelope of the entire building was cast in a single pour. The structure's 14-foot-high concrete walls comprise a sandwich system of interior and exterior wythes that envelope a layer of insulation. During construction, the fabric was supported on both sides by a wooden frame and horizontal wood whalers held together with form ties woven through the geotextile fabric. The horizontal fabric restraining method imprinted a pillow pattern on the faces of both the interior and exterior surfaces (Figure 5.5). House Two, Climate Resilient House (2019), improved energy and labor performance through the development of a hybrid wall that merged aspects of traditional steel post-and-beam construction and fabric-forming. This technique allowed for more flexibility in the construction sequence and the ability for trades to collaborate; for instance, the chases for plumbing and wiring could be placed independently from the pouring of the exterior walls.[19] When compared with traditional, rigid wood- or steel-panel form-work, less material by weight was required on-site for casting, and there was less ensuing waste.

Concrete is an equal-opportunity resource, and fabric forming techniques can be simple and accessible as well as high-tech and luxurious. In the Dominican Republic, fabric forming was employed in a project for the entry to the site of the Pomier caves, a proposed UNESCO World Heritage site. Hand-mixed and -placed batches of concrete were used along with other simple, readily available materials. The reinforcement was driven into the bedrock ground, and picket forms were installed to hold the locally obtained plastic fabric, which was not a geotextile.[20] Fabric for formwork is lightweight and can be transported to remote sites, thus reducing associated transportation costs and environmental impact. Sometimes geotextile fabric can be reused for multiple casts and then returned to its original use as a groundwork material.[21]

CLIMATE ETHICS

In addition to the sculptural and ornamental possibilities of fabric-forming the techniques for energy savings and structural efficiency are compelling. Concrete is responsible for 8 percent of global carbon emissions. Fabric forming techniques can be leveraged to reduce the amount of concrete necessary to achieve various shapes. Since the fabric stretches in response to the weight of the concrete in tension, naturally occurring geometries can be cast that also yield efficiencies in material. Mark West has explored these geometries in structural elements like beams, where the deflected or relaxed geometries, when inverted, resist compressive forces.[22] These efficient structural shapes are made with less concrete mix than conventional casts. The production of Portland cement, a key component in concrete, contributes the most to carbon emissions; next-generation concrete mixes include geopolymer concrete, which replaces 80 to 90 percent of Portland cement with industrial waste additives such as fly ash (light coal ash) and ground granulated blast furnace slag (GGBS).[23] Glass fiber reinforced concrete (GFRC) is a mix that allows for thinner, lighter, and stronger panels and reduces the amount of concrete used. A thin face coat is sprayed or poured onto a piece of fabric, and a glass fiber-filled back coat is applied to build up the desired thickness of the piece. GFRC mix is practical for making repetitive ornamental wall panels to enclose an interior or exterior space, or to enhance a special moment or ritual a special moment or ritual. Curved elements can also be cast using this technique, and fabrics can be layered and combined with other materials for desired effect, see figures 5.6 and 5.7. Finishing techniques like acid staining, lime wash, beeswax, and concrete paint can further enhance the texture, color, and feeling of a surface as well as improving its resistance to environmental conditions such as insects and moisture, see figure 5.8. The overall economy of fabric formwork material and construction operations is consistent with the sustainable practices of using less material and energy in construction.

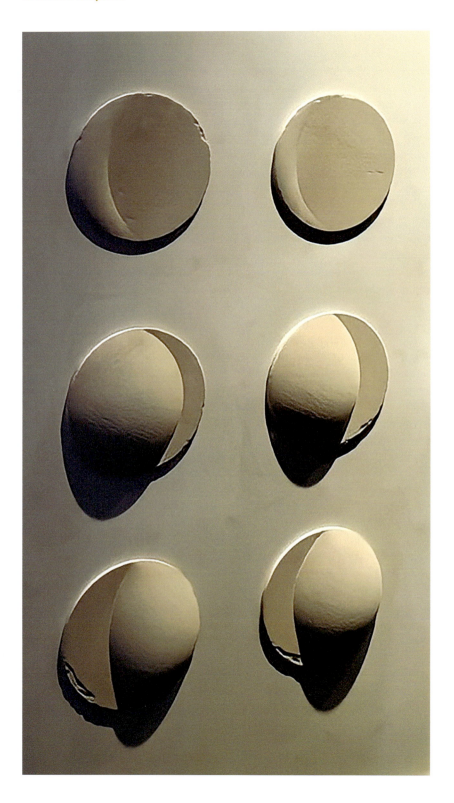

Figure 5.6 *GFRC panel cast with elastic spandex fabric and plexiglass*
Source: D'Aponte 2018

Figure 5.7 *GFRC panel cast with fabric and plexiglass*
Source: D'Aponte 2019

Figure 5.8 *Cast surface finished with acid etch stain*
Source: D'Aponte 2015

DIGITAL ADVANCES

Digital fabrication technologies, including CAD, CNC sewing machines, and robotics, have also amplified the potential to envision and construct new architectural forms and increase material efficiencies. Furniture, wall panels, columns, beams, and other elements can be cast in suspended fabric molds which have been laser cut and sewn either by hand or by an automatic industrial embroidery machine.

As digital technologies develop, the methods for generating geometrically complex, large-scale forms increase. An innovative research project by Zaha Hadid Architects combines fabric formwork methods with a cable-net technology. Collaborating with Block Research Group (BRG) of ETH Zurich, developers of KnitCrete formwork technology, the firm designed and cast a thin, double-curved concrete shell in the form of a pavilion at the University Museum of Contemporary Art (MUAC), in Mexico City, where it was installed from November 2018 to March of the following year. The form is in the spirit of hyperbolic paraboloid geometries that the pioneering architect and structural engineer Felix Candela (1910–1997) combined to reuse formwork and reduce waste. The fabric knit pattern and form design were digitally generated and fabricated. The lightweight textile was transported from Switzerland in a suitcase, sewn, and reinforced on-site, where it was suspended from an engineered scaffolding and stiffened to create the formwork for an applied layer of concrete. In fabric forming, the fabric is generally used as formwork and removed; here the colorful striped textile is integrated and exposed and, along with the structure's undulating shape, recalls the pattern and billowing skirt of a traditional Mexican dress.[24] Efforts aimed at reducing concrete usage, increasing the durability and life cycle of the material, and sequestering carbon during the manufacturing process are developing swiftly.

CONCLUSION

Human connection to patterns, textures, and interactive surfaces that imitate nature (biophilia) have been found to improve well-being.[25] Early on, "space-dividers" and, later, colorful tapestries brought elements of the natural world into human habitations. Images of plants, animals, human rituals, and interactions with nature created a connection to place and a significance for ornament in daily life. Fabrics for formwork can be chosen for their weave patterns and textures, which leave impressions on the surfaces of casts, offering the potential for dialogue between inhabitant and enclosure. Textiles have been employed in architectural expression from the brilliant facades of Venice to fabric-formed climate-controlled houses and environmentally sound innovations. The human instinct to connect with nature, engage the senses, and meaningfully celebrate surface and form endures.

NOTES

1. Wolfgang Herrmann, *Gottfried Semper: The Four Elements of Architecture and Other Writings*, trans. Harry Francis Mallgrave (Cambridge: Cambridge University Press, 1989), 104.

2. Gottfried Semper, *Style: Style in the Technical and Tectonic Arts; or Practical Aesthetics* (Los Angeles: Getty Research Institute, 2004), 248.

3. Herrmann, *Gottfried Semper*, 39.

4. Semper, *Style*, 729.

5. Ibid., 734.

6. Accessed April 14, 2017, www.serenissimetrame.it/en/the-exhibition/.

7. Anne-Mette Manelius, "Fabric Formwork: Prototyping Concrete as Material, Process, and Context," in *Prototyping Architecture: The Conference Papers*, ed. Michael Stacey (Toronto and London: Riverside Architectural Press and London Building Centre, 2013), 14.

8. Diederik Veenendaal, Mark West, and Philippe Block, "History and Overview of Fabric Formwork: Using Fabrics for Concrete Casting," *Structural Concrete* 12, no. 3 (September 2011): 137–220. https://doi.org/10.1002/suco.201100014.

9. Mark West, "Fabric-Formed Concrete Members," *Concrete International* 25 (October 2003): 55–60.

10. John J. Orr et al., "Concrete Structures Using Fabric Formwork," *Atkins Technical Journal* 7, no. 1 (2011): 101, accessed July 30, 2022, www.snclavalin.com/~/media/Files/S/SNC-Lavalin/download-centre/en/technical-journals/technical-journal-07.pdf.

11. Mark West, *The Fabric Formwork Book: Methods for Building New Architectural and Structural Forms in Concrete* (1st edition, Routledge, 2016). West has been pivotal in advancing and disseminating the technical language of fabric forming. His 2017 book, *The Fabric Formwork Book,* delves into the material culture and imaginative context of methods for fabrication.

12. Manelius, "Fabric Formwork," 14.

13. Anne-Mette Manelius, "Fabric Formwork for Concrete—Investigations into Formwork Tectonics and Stereogeneity in Architectural Constructions," (PhD dissertation © 2012 Royal Danish Academy of Fine Arts School of Architecture, Institute of Architectural Technology), 193.

14. Tod Williams and Billie Tsien, "Surface as Substance," in *Liquid Stone: New Architecture in Concrete*, ed. Jean-Louis Cohen and G. Martin Moeller Jr., (New York: Princeton Architectural Press, 2006), 106.

15. Karen Cilento, "Frank Lloyd Wright's Textile Houses," *ArchDaily*, September 14, 2010, accessed July 30, 2022, www.archdaily.com/77922/frank-lloyd-wrights-textile-houses.

16. Adrian Forty. *Concrete and Culture: A Material History.* London: Reaktion Books, 2016, 183.

17. Mark West and Ronnie Araya, "Fabric Formwork for Concrete Structures and Architecture" (lecture, International Conference on Textile Composites and Inflatable Structures, Barcelona, Spain, 2009), accessed March 30, 2022, https://fdocuments.in/document/fabric-formwork-for-concrete-structures-m-west-r-araya-2-has-invented.html?page=1.

18. Kenzo Unno, "Fabric Formed Walls," accessed June 15, 2022, http://fabwiki.fabric-formed-concrete.com/lib/exe/fetch.php?media=unno:kenzo_unno_article.pdf.

19. Eleanor D'Aponte, Sandy Lawton, and Ronnie Araya, "Bringing Fabric Forming to the Market with Composite Structures in North America," (IASS 2015 International Association for Shell and Spatial Structures, Future Visions Conference, August 17–20, 2015), Amsterdam, The Netherlands.

20. Eleanor D'Aponte, A. Lawton, and Russell Johnson, "Fabric Formwork for Architectural Concrete Structures," (iCERI 2009 International Conference of Education, Research and Innovation, November 16–18, 2009).

21. Mark West, "High Tech/Low Touch," (lecture, School of Architecture + Art Symposium, Norwich University, Northfield, VT, April 1, 2022).

22. West and Araya, "Fabric Formwork," 2.

23. T. Ch. Madhavi and P. M. Rameshwaran, "Geopolymer Concrete—The Eco-Friendly Alternate to Concrete," *NBM&CW Infra Construction and Equipment Magazine*,

May, 2020, accessed July 30, 2022, www.nbmcw.com/product-technology/construction-chemicals-waterproofing/concrete-admixtures/geopolymer-concrete-the-eco-friendly-alternate-to-concrete.html.

24. Preema Anand, "Zaha Hadid Architects Uses KnitCrete Technology for Experimental Structure," *Sawdust*, November 26, 2018, www.sawdust.online/news/zaha-hadid-architects-uses-knitcrete-technology-for-experimental-structure/.

25. Xiaomin Yue, Edward A. Vessel, and Irving Biederman, "The Neural Basis of Preference for Natural Scenes," *Journal of Vision* 6 (June 2010): 474. https://doi.org/10.1167/6.6.474.

CASE STUDIES

6
VEILING
Gender, Fabric and Woven Structures

ACADEMIC INQUIRY

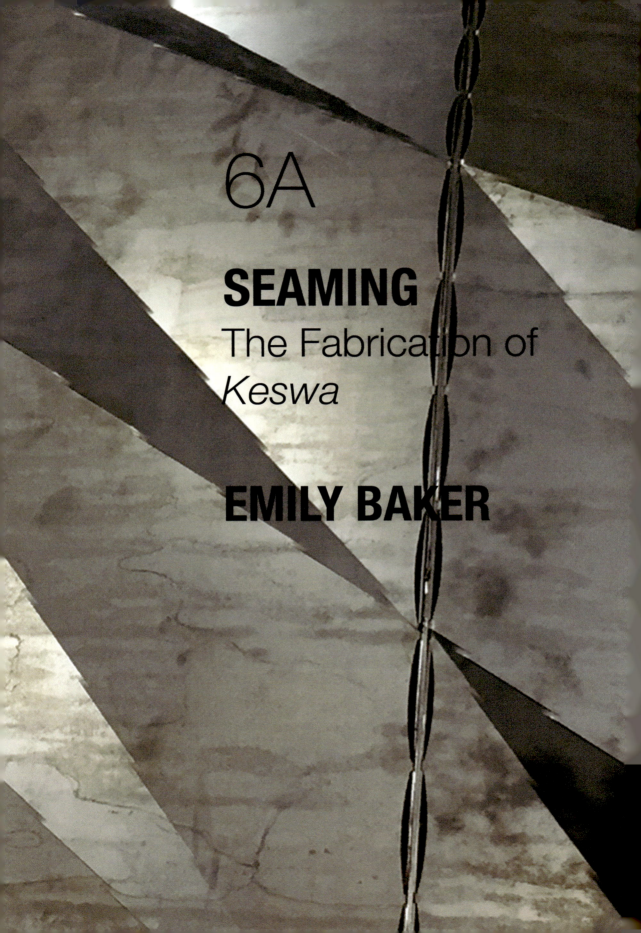

6A

SEAMING

The Fabrication of *Keswa*

EMILY BAKER

6A Seaming

The Fabrication of *Keswa*[1]

Emily Baker

In the fall of 2014, two architecture students approached me to act, with sup-port from instructor Daniel Chavez, as the faculty mentor for their Christo and Jeanne-Claude Award submission. The award program, administered by the Abu Dhabi Music and Arts Foundation (ADMAF) and NYU Abu Dhabi, elicits submis-sions for works of public art from emerging artists studying in the United Arab Emirates (UAE). Nada Al Mulla and Salwa Al Khudairi, then students at the American University of Sharjah, originally from Saudi Arabia, developed a design that evokes the form of Arab Gulf women in public space, and won the competition. The result-ing public installation, *Keswa*, was prototyped and produced in the following three months and toured public spaces around the UAE in the spring of 2015. The team was given $5,000 to produce the work and a $10,000 prize to encourage future creative endeavors. The piece represents the confluence of a culturally significant (or loaded) formal language, a design process based on iterative prototyping, digital fabrication techniques for forming and structuring steel, and detailing that blends technical necessity with allusive pattern language.

DOI: 10.4324/9781003138471-10

Figure 6A.2 *Initial conceptual rendering of the competition entry. Several stretched curving figures punctuate a park-like landscape*
Source: Image by Nada al Mulla and Salwa al Khudairi

CONTEXT AND ALLUSION

Keswa is a high Arabic word for vesture or clothing, but the more essential meaning is covering. In naming their piece *Keswa*, the students evoke the *abaya*, or long black robe, worn by many Muslim women in the Arab Gulf states to cover their clothing in public spaces. The effect of the ubiquitous use of the *abaya* in the region, both as modesty device and emblem of cultural and religious identity, is, from a distance, an abstract uniformity of black silhouettes, distinctly female, moving through public space—women's forms seem to glide, hovering slightly above the ground as they move. *Keswa* (sometimes *kiswah*) is also the term used to indicate the black silk covering on the Ka'aba at the Muslim holy site in Mecca. Both instances describe a distinct, revered, and conspicuously concealed black form that is set apart from its surroundings.

Initial renderings (Figure 6A.2) show a design that conjures the image of the *abaya*, exploring the abstracting effect of the wrapping or covering of women's forms in public space and paying homage to the fabric works of Christo and Jeanne-Claude, which reveal and celebrate architectural or landscape forms by abstracting them. The stretch and flow of fabric-like forms wrought in folded steel, rather than cloth, emerged in the design as a powerful inversion of the traditional association of women with textiles, softness, and pliability. Formally, the piece seems to lift at the corners of a curving plane, thus inviting the public to peer into and enter the space of the *abaya*, either passing through its central arch or stopping to sit in the shade of its wings.

Keswa was commissioned as a piece of public art intended to travel the Emirates, temporarily inserted in various sites—university campuses, commercial centers, desert landscapes and governmental properties (Figure 6A.3). Thus, the piece addresses a public that is not only Emirati, not only Arab or Muslim, but the multiethnic and multicultural public typical of the UAE. The site could also be said to be more generally, simply "the public" because of its transitory nature. The *abaya* is

a garment made for public space. Elizabeth Diller's essay "Bad Press" begins with a description of the "body as a legal site," comparing property lines on land that defend private space from public transgression to ways of bounding the body: "property lines that define the socially 'decent' body defend public space from transgressions of the private(s)." She goes on to reference Michel Foucault's discussion of institutionalized bodies in uniform and "the fashionable body produced by popular media."[2] *Keswa* could be said to be site-specific in that it addresses the site of women's bodies in public space in the Arab Gulf region as delineated by the cultural uniformity of the *abaya*.

In *One Place After Another*, Miwon Kwon discusses the various uses of the term "site-specific" to describe public art and defines three initial categories of site-specificity—phenomenological/experiential, social/institutional, and discursive—maintaining that all compete and overlap in their current and historical use.[3] All three can also be discussed in relation to *Keswa*. The piece calls attention to strong desert sunlight as it passes through seams in the steel, and it provides a moment of shaded relief to the intensity of heat and light. Set within a more populated area, such as a university campus, it becomes a momentary experience as one passes through while walking between buildings. In the desert setting, it is first viewed from afar, and if approached, is likely experienced as a point of stasis and temporary shelter within the extreme environment. However, Keswa's site-specificity is not only linked to its locale, but rather addresses specific local identity and the particulars of a regional culture in which it is common for some women to cover themselves in public. *Keswa* appropriates the *abaya*, a garment commonly used by Arab Gulf states as a means to retain a uniqueness of place in the face of massive influx of globalized culture,[4] and renders the normally pliable and flowing fabric in steel. While embodying a cultural emblem, *Keswa* provides a platform for discourses around gender, public space, and labor.

As in Jane Rendell's "An Embellishment: Purdah," *Keswa* deals with gendered space as defined by veiling or covering of women's bodies. Similarly, "the work changes according to the position occupied."[5] When viewed at a distance (the desert

Figure 6A.4 *Editing notes in chalk on a full-scale steel prototype aid the team in refining the cut files that will produce steal parts for the final fabricated piece* Source: Emily Baker

siting lends itself to this perspective), the piece recalls women moving through the world, conspicuously covered. When encountered at close range, the work asks viewers to consider and question notions of within/without, protection, and enclosure.

PROCESS AND DETAILING

The development of *Keswa* after initial design sketches proceeded largely within the fabrication lab. My experience through personal research and teaching with iterative design processes and techniques in digital steel fabrication[6] allowed me to impart proven strategies, giving the students a base of knowledge to begin iterating. This teaching method involves familiarizing students with processes of manipulating full-scale materials as early as possible. Students test details in real material while simultaneously envisioning the whole through paper models. Early prototypes not only tested cut patterns that produce a specific effect in the steel, but also allowed the students to develop a haptic awareness of the material and understand its relationship to their digital processes (Figure 6A.4). In all acts of constructing, but particularly within digital fabrication processes, not only the properties of the material, but also the properties that emerge in the pairing of a material with a specific tool or process become the milieu for the designer.[7] The students became comfortable in the milieu of digitally-cut steel, and they quickly took ownership of fabrication techniques, discovering the parameters within each technique that might be explored and exploited in their design (Figure 6A.5).

Developing the design within the context of what would become the final construction process allowed the layering of conceptual significance onto fabrication techniques. A detailing language emerged and evolved through our conceptual dialog and iterative design process that resulted in two distinct perforation patterns for folding and attachment. This language was tuned to meet requirements for strength, constructability,

Figure 6A.5
Designers Nada al Mulla and Salwa al Khudairi assemble the structural ribs for Keswa in the fabrication labs at the American University of Sharjah

and ease of assembly, while simultaneously mined for aesthetic potential, light effect, and specific reading (Figures 6A.6 and 6A.7). Perforations that allow folding and attachment of structural ribs rise off of the triangulated surface at each steel seam. These create curved gaps, allowing light to pass through the steel skin and form shadows on the exterior surface. This manipulation of the steel produces an effect much like the embellished stitching that commonly adorns the *abaya*. Fold lines on each triangulated panel use a second seam-like perforation pattern that works to minimize stress, thus protecting the steel seam from breaking due to excessive bending during assembly.

Keswa transforms sewing techniques for both functional seams and ornamental embroidery into techniques for digital steel fabrication. The fabrication method necessarily leaves some aesthetic trace on the finished piece, and in this case varying levels of ornamentation were cultivated out of functionally tuned seaming methods. Decoration, traditionally assumed to be a feminine aspect of architecture,[8] is here embedded in joints and cut-lines that enable the structuring and constructing of steel through digital manipulation. Collapsing the binary of masculine/structure, feminine/decoration,[9] *Keswa* is at once structure and decorated fabric.

CRITICAL REFLECTION

Keswa's reading spans between a piece of public art that can elicit changed viewpoints or altered awareness and the typology of the pavilion—a favored vehicle for architectural experimentation. As a pavilion, it postulates a way of embedding structural capacity in form through the digital manipulation of steel—a monocoque; form and structure in one. It points toward potential ways of building and aesthetics that arise with and through those means. But *Keswa* moves beyond a mere fabrication study

Figure 6A.6
Cover Image. Variations on perforation patterns cut in sheet steel are tailored for precise assembly, create patterns of light and shadow, and embellish the surface of the piece much like the ornamental stitching in abayas
Source: Emily Baker

and takes on cultural content. The enmeshing of symbolic allusion with fabrication techniques gives birth to a distinct design language that plays out on multiple levels.

In the conclusion to *One Place After Another*, Kwon discusses efforts to retain specificity of place in the face of the homogenizing forces of mass globalization, suggesting that certain works are "efforts to retrieve lost differences, or to curtail their waning." She asks: "What would it mean now to sustain the cultural and historical specificity of a place (and self) that is neither a simulacral pacifier nor a willful invention?"[10] Arguably, the UAE has employed both, with its quixotic skylines and nostalgic use of faux wind towers. However, *Keswa*'s allusion to the *abaya* is not simply a regurgitation of a symbol. It refers to, but also recasts the *abaya*, altering the boundaries of its space.

This piece represents work that was done by female students under the primary direction of a female mentor. The debate lingers as to the existence or import of an architecture that is distinctly feminine, but in a country whose name almost universally conjures the image of the skyscraper, it is not insignificant to find young female architects evoking their own image through built work, *because* and *despite the fact that* that image is a covered body. The practice of architecture in Arab Gulf countries is often divorced from materiality and construction processes, with architects expected to create the image of a building that engineers will then detail.[11] Architecture is seen as a profession appropriate for women precisely because its practice does not include physical labor. An article by Noor Al Qasimi suggests that women in Arab Gulf states make use of the *abaya* as a means of maintaining association with their culture and religion while at the same time moving away from traditional gender roles.[12]

Keswa references the form of Muslim women in public space, and in so doing it lifts the corners of its covering and allows people of all genders, ages, and backgrounds to enter the space of the *abaya*. The two women who created the piece undertook the labor of steel fabrication and assembly, and they were adamant that viewers know that they did this work personally. This is significant because, while the

Figure 6A.7 ►
Drawings show perforation pattern tests along with the constituent ribs that assemble to create the overall form of Keswa
Source: Drawing by Nada al Mulla

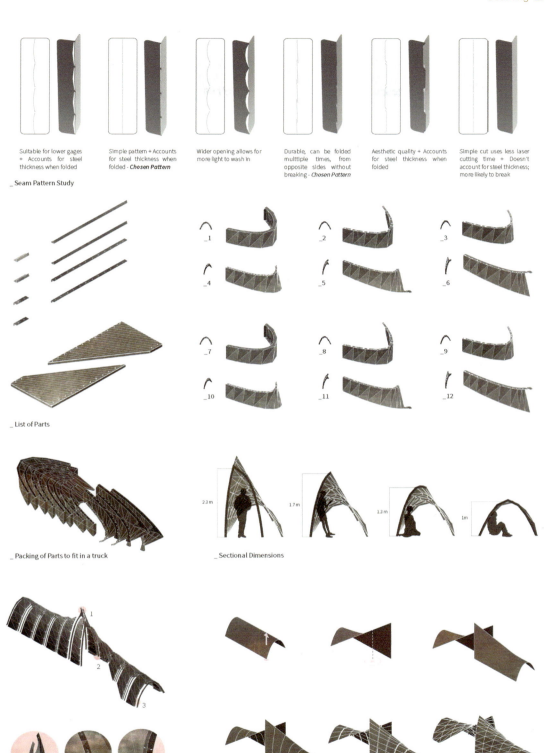

Suitable for lower gages + Accounts for steel thickness when folded

Simple pattern + Accounts for steel thickness when folded - *Chosen Pattern*

Wider opening allows for more light to wash in

Durable, can be folded multiple times, from opposite sides without breaking - *Chosen Pattern*

Aesthetic quality + Accounts for steel thickness when folded

Simple cut uses less laser cutting time + Doesn't account for steel thickness; more likely to break

_ Seam Pattern Study

_ List of Parts

_ Packing of Parts to fit in a truck

_ Sectional Dimensions

2.3 m   1.7 m   1.3 m   1m

Figure 6A.8
*Students direct the
initial installation
of* Keswa *on the
campus of NYU
Abu Dhabi*
Source: Emily Baker

piece venerates the *abaya*, the work of fabrication subverts any attempt of the garment to be used or viewed as a limiting or subordinating device. Labor of construction in the Arab Gulf states is not seen as merely a male pursuit, but notably one relegated to men of a certain socio-economic class. Because the designers of *Keswa* broke with this cultural norm and took on the labor of its construction, they opened technical detailing to their symbolic and aesthetic use, and their labor brought nuance and complexity to the reading of the piece as an *abaya*. The use of digital fabrication processes further complicates the role that labor plays in the reading of this piece. Though the piece could be endlessly re-produced without the direct involvement of the designers, their hand labor was essential to a design process reliant on close interrogation of prototypes as well as to a nuanced reading of *Keswa* within its cultural context.

Kwon proposes "relational specificity" as a way of moving beyond the potential limitations of site-specificity in public art.[13] Within the context of the Emirates, *Keswa* is received as a veneration of an important cultural nexus, recognized as a sign that this symbol is moving forward with the advance of technology, while (perhaps covertly) forcing its admirers to accept the agency in the physical labor of women and the redefining of the space of the *abaya*.

ACKNOWLEDGEMENTS

Thanks to Nada and Salwa for adding dedication and enthusiasm to their talent and for trusting me to be a part of their work. Thanks to NYU Abu Dhabi, ADMAF and the Christo and Jeanne-Claude Award administrators. Thanks to the American University of Sharjah (AUS) College of Architecture, Art and Design (CAAD) Labs for facilitating the production process and to the AUS community for supporting the team. Thanks to my co-mentor, Daniel Chavez. Special thanks to and in fond memory of the incomparable Christo for his enthusiastic and encouraging words to young designers as they embark on their careers.

Project Information:

Chapter: Seaming: The Fabrication of *Keswa*

Professor/Faculty Mentor: Emily Baker, Assistant Professor of Architecture; Daniel Chavez, Visiting Instructor

University/Organization: American University of Sharjah

Students: Nada al Mulla and Salwa al Khudairi

Project Location: traveling piece, initial installation at NYU Abu Dhabi, United Arab Emirates

Client: Abu Dhabi Music and Art Foundation

Donations/Financial Support: $5000 from Abu Dhabi Music and Art Foundation through the Christo and Jeanne-Claude Award; American University of Sharjah provided space/equipment

Awards: Christo and Jeanne-Claude Award for Public Art

Project Timeline:

Development of Competition Submission:	2 Weeks
Selection as one of four finalists	
Material Prototyping and Design Development:	4 Weeks
Selection as competition winner	
Full Scale Detail Refinement:	4 Weeks
Fabrication:	2 Weeks
Total:	12 Weeks

NOTES

1. (First published in the Journal of Architectural Education 70.1(2016) as "*Keswa*: An Uncovering." Used with permission from Taylor and Francis.)
2. Elizabeth Diller, "Bad Press," in *Gender Space Architecture*, eds. Jane Rendell, Barbara Penner, and Iain Borden (New York: Routledge, 2000), 385–386.
3. Miwon Kwon, *One Place After Another: Site Specific Art and Locational Identity* (Cambridge, MA: MIT Press, 2002), 2–4.
4. Elizabeth D. Shimek, "The Abaya: Fashion, Religion, and Identity in a Globalized World" (Lawrence University Honors Project, 2012): 10.
5. Jane Rendell, "An Embellishment: Purdah," *Architectural Design* Vol. 76 Issue 6 (2006): 97.
6. Emily Baker, "Search for a Rooted Aesthetic: Study in Spin-Valence," in *Fabricate: Negotiating Design & Making*, eds. Fabio Gramazio, Matthias Kohler, and Silke Langenberg (Zurich: GTA Verlag, 2014), 128–135.
7. Gail Peter Borden and Michael Meredith, "Introduction: Foreign Matter," in *Matter: Material Processes in Architectural Production*, eds. Gail Peter Borden and Michael Meredith (New York: Routledge, 2012), 1–3.
8. Jane Rendell, "Gender Space Architecture: An Introduction," in *Gender Space Architecture*, eds. Jane Rendell, Barbara Penner, and Iain Borden (New York: Routledge, 2000), 228–229.
9. Rendell, "Gender Space Architecture: An Introduction," 233.
10. Kwon, *One Place After Another*, 164–166.
11. William Sarnecky, "Building a Material Culture in Dubai," *Journal of Architectural Education* Vol. 65 Issue 2 (2012): 80–88.
12. Noor Al Qasimi, "Immodest Modesty: Accommodating Dissent and the 'Abaya-as-Fashion in the Arab Gulf States," *Journal of Middle Eastern Women's Studies* Vol. 6 Issue 1 (2010): 46–74.
13. Kwon, *One Place After Another*, 166.

6B

TRANSLATION
Female Garment to Architecture

TOLYA STONOROV

6B Translation

Female Garment to Architecture

Tolya Stonorov

The Translation: Female Garment to Architecture Studio examines fabric through the relationship of the garment to the body and the translation of the garment to the building. This undergraduate studio taught at Norwich University's School of Architecture + Art, was born out of my own master's thesis research at the University of California, Berkeley[1], where I examined how the physical ritual of dressing, the layered relationship between public and private space, can be seen as "housing." This idea can inform how we look at the correlation between the garment and architecture, where architecture may be envisioned as our third skin and the garment as our most immediate second skin.

Like the garment, our dwellings at once shield and expose. Building and garment share a parallel language, both affording refuge to the body. The focus of each is concurrently external and internal and what is divulged is selected by choices of spatial immediacy, permeability, and layering. The passage towards private space in built form is analogous to the movement towards the body through the layers of a garment. This analogy began with a historical analysis of the relationship of the kimono and the veil to the traditional Japanese and Islamic house. From this study, lessons were extracted, abstracted, and applied to the garment and built form.

Figure 6B.1 *Garment/Architecture*
Source: Tolya Stonorov Graduate Thesis, University of California, Berkeley

DOI: 10.4324/9781003138471-11

THE KIMONO AND THE TRADITIONAL JAPANESE HOUSE

The construction of the kimono shares with its architectural counterpart, the traditional Japanese house, a true economy of means. Both space and fabric are intricately thought out, rejecting wastefulness. The kimono is based on a bolt of cloth that is typically 14 inches by 12.5 yards. Its construction follows this standard fabric size and uses a minimal amount of cutting to achieve the final garment. The main body of the garment is two lengths of the bolt sewn together in the back and left open in the front. An additional length is divided in two and sewn to each open length in the front, providing overlap. The entire pattern for the kimono is laid out on a single bolt, perfectly divided to ensure no wastage of material. The obi, a belt-like attachment that keeps the kimono closed, is the single part of the kimono that is separate from this concise pattern; it is also the component of the kimono that most transformed over the centuries.[2]

The garment is modified from person to person, but instead of excess material being cut and discarded, it is folded into the seams, allowing for change. The kimono is the antithesis of a pair of stereotypical American jeans that are discarded yearly or with a change in weight; it is a garment for the life of the person and accordingly transforms to fit the current form of that person, similarly to how buildings change over time to accommodate new uses and new owners. This described flexibility perhaps implies a certain generosity and lack of rigidity that may be misleading. Different styles of the kimono throughout history have inhibited women's movement. In the Edo period during the late 18th century, the length of the kimono was several inches longer than the height of the woman and the obi was widened to 12 inches; both of which made walking difficult. It transformed from a simple and functional rope meant to fasten the garment, to an elaborate and wide mechanism that could not be tied by the person wearing the garment. To get in or out of this kimono, a woman had to be assisted, which points to a built-in dependence that the garment itself imparted on women. In *The Kimono Mind*, Rudofsky notes that

> as far back as 1887 the empress condemned the wide obi as 'unsuited to the human body,' and it would indeed seem a senselessly vicious constriction....[3]

The vernacular Japanese house translates many of the characteristics of the kimono. The house, as with the garment, has an economy of space and materiality. Corresponding to the kimono standard bolt of the fabric that is derived from the basic width of the human form, the Japanese house is based around the tatami mat whose dimensions stem from the shape of the human form, 90 centimeters wide and 180 centimeters long. The tatami was originally conceived of as a floor covering that could be used to sleep on, but was also used to cover the entire floor.

> When the designer of a traditional Japanese house first begins drawing up plans for the building, she first determines how many tatami mats will be needed to cover the floor. By designing different layouts, the final configuration of the mats will determine the shape and size of the house. In this way the architecture employs a unit of measurement that is standardized and originates from the proportion of a person.[4]

The idea of the human scaled module translated to how spaces within the house are used. Instead of delineating exact placement of walls and doors, the house is constructed around sliding screens that move in response to season or mood. The use of the shoji screen further emphasizes the subtle expressiveness of the space. Light is softened as is enters through the paper screens, creating complex shadows that bring a specific emotion to the room. The house responds to changing conditions of nature and use, as the kimono responds to the changes of its wearer. The subtle complexity of the kimono and Japanese house creates a sensuous interaction between body and form. Shelter, in both garment and built form, is seen as something that can be opened or closed revealed or hidden, depending on the degree of privacy and warmth desired to respond to the exact needs and desires of the user.

THE VEIL AND THE TRADITIONAL ISLAMIC HOUSE

The relationship between the veil and the traditional Islamic house is highly complex. The veil by nature establishes duality. It determines two things as separate. A is made aware of B to the extent permitted by X, the veil. X becomes the interface between A and B, the public and private spaces of house, and body. The degree of privacy required determines the nature of the veil. In 1999, I spent several months in Northern India, where, during my time in Pushkar, Rajasthan, I saw that women donned the veil only in certain occasions. I spent a day with a local family, where I noticed a young woman putting on and removing her veil (a thin piece of colorful cloth), depending on who was in the room. I was told that she only wore her veil around her husband's older brothers and father. Around his younger brothers, she did not wear the veil, shedding light on the relationship of the veil in this instance to the hierarchy within a family and society.

The traditional Islamic house has an inward facing design. Like the screening of the veil, the intricately carved facades of the Islamic house create a veil through which the public street or courtyard is viewed.

> The veil performs many of the functions of seclusion and introversion as expressed in Islamic domestic architecture. . . . In house architecture, the screened balcony allows the female occupants to view the outside world without being seen.[5]

The house, then, subtly mirrors the garment, articulating the edge between public and private. Furthermore, it delineates the importance of this interface and highlights the desire to control visibility. The veil is a highly complex topic and this investigation inevitably provides only a small glimpse into the political and social issues that it represents. The study highlights the relationship between and the translation from the traditional female garment to the vernacular house.

This research into the relationship between female garments and architecture provides an entry point from which a design prompt was proposed, a test case on which we can examine the ideas embedded within the investigation. Bringing this research into the studio setting spured complex conversations around the ideas of layering, permeability, voyeurism, feminism, chauvinism and public and private space.

CONTEXT THROUGH TRANSLATION

We typically consider context as related to our immediate surroundings, yet context has deeper meaning and influence within our subconscious realms. Context informs our decisions in nuanced, complex ways: the path towards home, the structure of a bird's wings, the patterned light through a deep wall. We may begin to explore the concept of context by examining our own skin, the fabric that becomes a vessel for our most personal interior. Our organic skin, our most immediate context, may be reinterpreted to the framework of the garment, the skin that covers our bodies, and finally to structures, the skin of our built environment. How we contain our bodies in the second skin of a garment relates to the way we surround ourselves with our built environment as seen in the examples of the kimono and veil.

TRANSLATION: FEMALE GARMENT TO ARCHITECTURE STUDIO: OUR BODIES HOUSED

This chapter details a body of research undertaken as part of the undergraduate architecture studio, Translation: Female Garment to Architecture, taught at the School of Architecture + Art, Norwich University in 2014 and 2021 with David Woolf.[6]

Figure 6B.2 *Veiling, Transparency Conceptual Model* Source: Stonorov, Student work, Norwich University

The Translation studio investigated fabric in relation to skin, garment, and the built environment. This chapter documents the findings of the studio and specifically explores the concept of the body's skin as a fabric envelope, architecture as a vessel, and how architecture relates to its inner workings. As the final exploration of the building to garment relationship, the studio developed the program of a garment factory to explore the relationship between design and manual work in America. The Translation Studio employed a three-part process: research, 1:1 making, and finally, interpretation through translating and applying knowledge. The *research* phase of the studio began with a study of an organic skin, the 1:1 *making* phase involved fabrication of a full scale garment in relation to the skin and the interpretation took this preceding work and viewed it through the lens of a building, the *translation* phase.

BODY

As our bodies are made up of more than 60 percent water, we may think of our skin as a housing, a container, for water, malleable and fragile like fabric—ductile like a tensile structure. To ease into the study of the body as context, students began by physically mapping their own bodies. Based on a tutorial by Handimania,[7] the first assignment looked to the body as the initial map for the semester's work. Students were tasked to make the form of *their own* body by fabricating a physical likeness. These custom duct tape mannequins populated our studio and provided a first analysis of the body, the initial landscape, the initial context. To provide uniformity, each form was made out of silver duct tape. These forms provided the foundation upon which students could react/mold/enclose/hide/reveal/protect/expose.

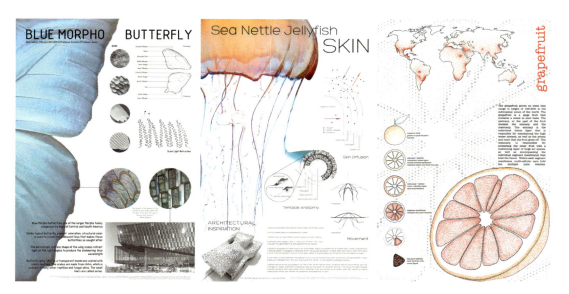

Figure 6B.3 *Skin research posters, Translation Studio, Norwich University*
Source: Glen Lambert, Caleb Menard, Shannon Haggerty, Translation Studio, Norwich University

SKIN

From this initial haptic self-exploration, students selected, researched, and analyzed an organic skin that would provide the foundational context for their future work. These included the skins of the snake, grapefruit, mantis shrimp, jellyfish, trout, and bark, lichen, butterfly, chameleon, stingray and others. Our skin, like the skin of reptiles, organic materials and fruits, is a complex system that both contains and protects. "Skin is a multilayered, multipurpose organ that shifts from thick to thin, tight to loose, lubricated to dry, across the landscape of the body."[8] Students diagramed and analyzed their chosen skin over a two week process that culminated with a poster and critique.

Special attention was given to the different ways that the skin interacts with exterior and interior conditions of the organic body, whether the protective thick and spongy skin of a grapefruit or the directional and complex scales of a fish. Students investigated how the skin protects the body from the environment; how it translates information to the body's internal processes, what drives skin's thickness and texture, and how it moves and transitions from an exterior surface to an internal one. "Skin, a knowledge-gathering device, responds to heat and cold, pleasure and pain. It lacks definitive boundaries, flowing continuously from the exposed surfaces of the body to its internal cavities."[9]

A rich body of knowledge was developed from these studies. This knowledge helped to inform students' understanding of the complex and multidimensional nature of our own skin and that of those in nature.

GARMENT

Next, the class examined the concept of architecture as our second skin, and its relationship to the garment, our most immediate second skin. Based on the initial Skin research, students fabricated a garment that required an exploration of how their research on skin could be translated into a piece of clothing. They examined how this translation might result from (emerge from) form, pattern, 2-Dimensional and 3-Dimensional layering, use, and so on. Most of the students had never operated a sewing machine or worked on full-scale body architecture and thus did not understand the complexity of constructing a housing for a moveable and malleable form such as the body.

Each student undertook intricate, iterative studies to gain the knowledge and understanding needed to finalize the ultimate form of the garment. Students took cues from their skin research and used digital fabrication tools to create mass customized prototypes. Though the garments were informed by the skin project, they were documented and developed as an architect would design a building. Several projects were notable for their creative interpretation of skin to garment including the jellyfish skin, which a student used as a foundation to fabricate a water catchment jacket that could be worn in the wilderness to gather water for drinking or bathing.

Students spent five weeks of the semester considering SKIN and the GARMENT. Concepts of layering, blending, camouflage, transparency, need, armor, and comfort shaped the conversation. As the students moved into the final project that explored a textile/garment factory, they called on their learning from the skin project, and translated the conceptual ideas of the relationship between skin and what it encompasses into built form.

Figure 6B.4 *Garment explorations at 1:1 scale, Translation Studio, Norwich University*
Source: Sam Libby, Translation Studio, Norwich University

The unfinished, the provisional, the possible—they hide in the attention for imperfections, traces of the creation process, and the revealed potential of materials and techniques. . . . This working method . . . not only celebrates the value of the process, but also engages the viewer, the user, in her investigation.[10]

The studio began by conceptually considering the third SKIN, building, as constructed of layers of transparency, which when built up, can provide privacy and comfort to differing degrees, much like a garment. Students were tasked to design an abstract built form that used only mylar or vellum as its construction material with the addition of one material to provide structure: metal wire, concrete, chip board, or wood. The structural material could act only as an armature for the translucent/transparent material and was not permitted to be used to form edge conditions between inside and outside. The form of the transparency model echoed the proportions of the final building (3 inches by 15 inches by 4 inches).

The studio discussed how their garment/structure responded to its own site: the interior body and the outside environment. Students attempted to identify and embody the strengths of their garment proposal: Where were the moments of reveal? Where did the garment retreat? Where were the moments of visual entry? Was it welcoming or protective? Was its exterior envelope dictated by the internal workings occurring within the structure? The transparency model project provided a conceptual entry to the final building project. It allowed the physical, although often metaphorical, garments to find a more traditional built form, while maintaining abstraction. This allowed a slower, more nuanced transition from concept to the concrete.

BUILDING: GARMENT FACTORY

The studio considered built space as our alternative skin, a third iteration based on the foundation research the organic skin and garment. As a studio, we looked at how the conceptual, sensual, and scientific learning from the Skin and Garment projects could translate into space and built structure. Relating back to the garment

Figure 6B.5 *Water Gathering Garment, Translation Studio, Norwich University*
Source: Caleb Menard, Translation Studio, Norwich University

study, the program built on prior studies of skin and garment, as students developed the design for a Textile/Garment Factory.

The studio researched American made textiles, and the process for creating/manufacturing those textiles. We questioned context, the nature of work in this industry, and queried how to infuse the program of work with richness. We asked: how can architecture better fuel a progressive and constructive work environment; how can architecture realize the complexity of its context and provide a nuanced response—one that considers the people, (a fundamental part of the inner workings of the structure), who are producing the textiles and not simply the product itself?

Changing gears from the abstract, we began to investigate the nature of manual work in America. Reading from the text *Working for Capitalism*,[11] the studio became acquainted with one person's experience performing manual factory labor. Though a singular account, the insight of one worker provided an often ignored window into how the products we use every day are produced and how individuals are affected by production. The physical energy and monotony of manufacturing was discussed in relation to making and customization.

> The quality of work . . . is determined by and in turn determines the nature of society. Thus, for any society, if we understand the essential quality of its work, we will better understand the essential nature and purposes of its social organization; and if we understand the essential nature and purposes of its social organization, we will better understand the essential quality of its work.[12]

Though written in the 1970s, the book's account of working in a factory is still largely relevant today. The quality of the work day has not dramatically changed.

The studio embarked on the final building project through the lens of trying to negotiate the nature of work with a heightened sensitivity to the quality of life of those employed within the factory, the skin, and how they could be supported to thrive. The skin covers the inner workings of the body, the organs, guts, and complex systems, like the building covers the inner workings of the factory—the people, the production line, and so on. The project challenged the essence of the workplace spatially, materially, and programmatically, using the garment/architecture relationship as the framework for its alteration. The program housed a new factory making space for two small American fabric-based companies. This project asked students to insert a programmatic element that could enhance the life of the worker holistically. The students were left to decide individually if this part of the program augmentation was to be public or private (Read: bathhouse, pool, theater, gym, sauna, etc.). Hella Jongerius & Louise Schouwenberg note in their manifesto: Beyond the New:

> Count the blessings of industry. Industrial processes have greater potential than low-volume productions of exclusive designs, which reach such a limited market

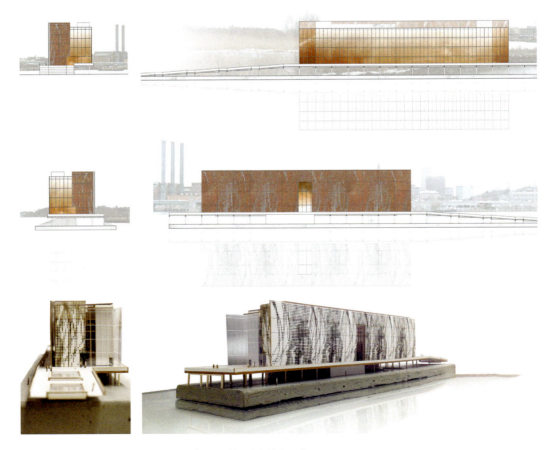

Figure 6B.7 *Garment Factory, Translation Studio, Norwich University*
Source: Caleb Menard, Translation Studio, Norwich University

that talk of "users" can hardly be taken seriously. Industries can make high-quality products available to many people. We should breathe new life into that ideal.[13]

One of the simplest, yet perhaps most astute programatic elements added was a childcare center. With this choice, the student acknowledged one of the great shortcomings in working conditions in our country. She recognized how the inclusion of childcare would relieve workers of a significant expense and result in dramatic improvement in the workers' quality of life knowing their children were well cared for. Other students focused on the body of the workers and how they could be supported by the program of the building, such as a bathhouse or sauna. This type of addition recognized the need for attention to the soul and the physical needs of workers, those who are integral to the functioning of the of the building—if the body and mind are cared for, the worker and management will benefit because of an increased harmony and ease. Caring for the worker performing the work will benefit the work itself.

SITE LOCATION

With a rich industrial history that includes textile manufacturing, the site for the final garment factory was Providence, Rhode Island. The site is a thin land mass that extends out to the bay of the Providence River. Returning to water as context and content, we researched the intersection of water and building.

THEORETICAL STUDIO PROMPT

In an effort to redefine Providence as a "Center for Creativity," the city has decided to focus their economic efforts on revitalizing areas of the city. Wilkesbarre Pier has been identified as a key site in this effort. The city agreed to do site remediation and provide a clean landscape as long as the new building focuses on arts and crafts, employs a local workforce and provides the dual use of a community gathering space that connects to the water. The city has approved the new Garment Factory, provided that the products be made in the USA and that at least 60% of the site be used for an outdoor community park.

As an introduction to the site and the city in which it was located, the 2014 studio traveled to Providence and spent several hours conducting on-site analyses through gesture drawings, photographs, and diagrams. (In 2021, the studio was taught virtually in the height of COVID and all research was conducted online.) Students produced a site model as a group that diagrammed the depth of the brackish river.

Next, program was introduced and developed, and students began the design phase by producing two divergent concept models with maximum dimensions and proportions, but loose expectations for the incorporation of a specific code or program at this point. In this exercise students considered structure in relation to skin, investigating whether the structure was an internal skeleton hidden by a multidimensional layered "skin" like the feathers of an owl, or brought to the edges and expressed like a lobster? Is it intermeshed and integral to the outer skin like a jellyfish? "What are they if not powerful diagrams of structural forces, and organic metaphors turned into emphatic form."[14]

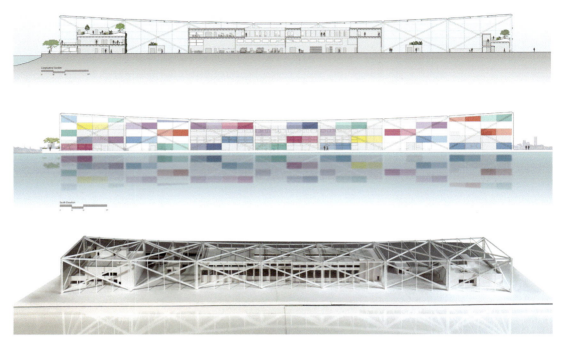

Figure 6B.8 *Garment Factory*
Source: Sam Libby, Translation Studio, Norwich University

Because of the preceding studies of skin and garment, the design development of the building had a robust foundation. Envelopes were complex and multidimensional. The relationship between skin, interior, and exterior showed movement and enriched understanding of a highly nuanced sense of place. Context was explored from the most intimate understanding our own immediate context, outward to how we first house ourselves through our garments, towards an exploration of how we interact with work and finally to the surroundings that influence our physical movement. The ultimate resulting garment factory was an expression of a skin that best houses the internal workings while at the same time presents to the outside world a form that honors the functions of the structure itself.

In sum, after an initial examination of an organic skin, students extracted the lessons they had learned and fabricated a garment related to that skin. These garments were constructed at full scale and represented the first housing of the body. Second, the studio moved into an exploration by conceptually examining the third skin, the building. Third, the students constructed a "building" out of layers of mylar films, that when built up, provides privacy and comfort to differing degrees, much like a garment. This study allowed the physical, although often metaphorical, garments to find a more traditional built form, while maintaining abstraction. By approaching the design of a building through an alternate lens of creativity through the skin/garment/body/building research, the final building allowed for a more nuanced and complex development. It further afforded students an examination of their own cultural constructs to question how they clothe themselves may be related to a building's envelope. Finally, it highlighted how the garment can be influenced by and influence in return, the built environment.

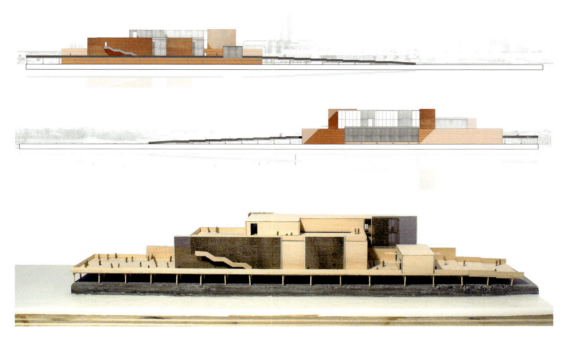

Figure 6B.9 *Garment Factory, Translation Studio, Norwich University*
Source: Adam Wiles-Rosell, Translation Studio, Norwich University

Project Information:

Chapter: Translation: Female Garment to Architecture Professor: Tolya Stonorov, Associate Professor 2014, Co taught with David Woolf 2021

University/Organization: University of California, Berkeley and School of Architecture + Art, Norwich University

Students: 2014: David Burke, Adam Wiles-Rosell, Sarah Bedard, Jess Dahline, Sheridan Steiner, Shannon Haggerty, Jennifer Bauser, Dan Wheeler, Caleb Menard, Jade Burkart 2021: Sam Libby, Michaila Furchak, Glen Lambert, Ethan Miller, Victoria Geraw, Alex Bourbeau, John Delisle, Ben Carlson, Allie Austin, Bekah Chabot, Kyle Pevonis, John Lawson, Vova Quigley, Nichole Thibeault, Sheldon Rogers, Brendon Maxson, Sierra Kornetti, Hayden Carleton, Joseph Cavataio, Keaton Hankus

Project Location: Initial research: University of California, Berkeley, California; Norwich University, Vermont Theoretical Site: Providence, Rhode Island

Project Timeline:

Make Yourself:	1 Week
Skin Research:	2 Weeks
Garment Research, Prototype and Fabrication:	3 Weeks
Garment Factory:	9 Weeks
Total:	15 Weeks

NOTES

1   Portions of this chapter originally published in Pfeffer-Bacon, Tolya. "Office Redressed.'" Master's thesis, University of California, Berkeley, 2003.
2. Tsutoma, Ema, *Kimono: One Hundred Masterpieces of Japanese Costumes*, Tokyo, Japan: Meiji-Shobu, 1950.
3. Rudofsky, Bernard, *The Kimono Mind, An Informal Guide to Japan and the Japanese*, New York: Van Nostrand Reinhold Company, 1965, p. 44.
4. www.swifty.com/apase/ charlotte/@A4.html
5. Edwards, Brian, Sibley, Magda, Land, Peter, Hakmi, Mohamad, *Courtyard Housing: Past, Present and Future*, Oxon: Taylor and Francis, 2006.
6. A portion of this chapter was published in the conference proceedings for the National Conference on the Beginning Design Student, 2019.
7. www.handimania.com/diy/your-own-shape-sewing-mannequin.html
8. Lupton, Ellen, with essays from Jennifer Tobias, Alicia Imperiale, Grace Jeffers, *Skin: Surface, Substance, and Design*, New York: Princeton Architectural Press, 2002.
9. Lupton, Ellen, with essays from Jennifer Tobias, Alicia Imperiale, Grace Jeffers, *Skin: Surface, Substance, and Design*, New York: Princeton Architectural Press, 2002.
10. http://www.jongeriuslab.com/news, Last seen: 3.27.2023, BEYOND THE NEW A SEARCH FOR IDEALS IN DESIGN Hella Jongerius & Louise Schouwenberg
11. Pfeffer, Richard M., *Working for Capitalism*, New York: Columbia University Press, 1979.
12. Pfeffer, Richard M., *Working for Capitalism*, New York: Columbia University Press, 1979, p. 2.
13. www.jongeriuslab.com/news
14. Balmond, Cecil, *Preface by Rem Koolhaas*, Informal, Prestel, 2002.

BIBLIOGRAPHY

Accad, Evelyne, *Veil of Shame: The Role of Women in the Contemporary Fiction of North Africa and the Arab World*, Quebec, Canada: Sherbrooke, 1978.

Al-Nafeez, Ibraheem A., *Privacy and Thermal Comfort in the Saudi's House*, Howard University Thesis in Science of Architecture, Washington, DC, 1985.

Black, Alexander, *The Japanese House*, Boston: Tuttle Publishing, 2000.

Crawford, Matthew B., *Shop Class as Soulcraft, An Inquiry into the Value of Work*, London: Penguin Press, 2009.

Darabi, Parvin, *Rage Against the Veil: The Courageous Life and Death of an Islamic Dissident*, Amherst, NY: Prometheous Books, 1999.

Edwards, Brian, Sibley, Magda, Land, Peter, Hakmi, Mohamad, *Courtyard Housing: Past, Present and Future*, Oxon: Taylor and Francis, 2006.

Fathy, Hassan, *Natural Energy and Vernacular Architecture, Principles and Examples with Reference to Hot Arid Climates*, Chicago and London: The United Nations University by The University of Chicago Press, 1986.

Fausch, Deborah, *Architecture in Fashion*, New York, NY: Princeton Architectural Press, 1996.

Fletcher, Kate, *Sustainable Fashion and Textiles, Design Journeys*, Earthscan, 2008, London and New York: Routledge, 2014.

Goodwin, Jan, *Price of Honor: Muslim Women Lift the Veil of Silence on the Islamic World*, Boston: Little, Brown, 1994.

Hillenbrand, Robert, *Islamic Architecture*, New York: Columbia University Press, 1994.

Hoag, John D., Pier Luigi Nervi, General Editor, *Islamic Architecture*, New York: Harry N. Abrams Inc., Publishers, 1977.

Itoh, Teiji, *Traditional Japanese Houses*, Tokyo, Japan: A.D.A. EDITA, 1980. Edited by H. Kitao; Chanoyu-House; Shokuku-sha, 1961.

Iwamoto, Lisa, Digital Fabrications, *Architectural and Material Techniques*, New York: Princeton Architectural Press, 2009.

Kinney, Leila, Fashion and Fabrication in Modern Architecture, MIT Press, *Journal of the Society of Architectural Historians*, Vol. 58 No. 3 (September 1999), pp. 472–481.

Kinoshita, Masao, *Japanese Architecture*, Tokyo, Japan: Shokukusha Publishing Co., 1964.

Lüling, C., Richter, I., Architecture Fully Fashioned—Exploration of Foamed Spacer Fabrics for Textile Based Building Skins, *Journal of Façade Design and Engineering*, Vol. 5 No. 1 (2017): Special Issue PowerSkin.

Lupton, Ellen, with essays from Jennifer Tobias, Alicia Imperiale, Grace Jeffers, *Skin: Surface, Substance, and Design*, New York: Princeton Architectural Press, 2002.

Lupton, Ellen, Tobias, Jennifer, Skin, Surface, *Substance and Design*, New York: Princeton Architectural Press, 2002.

Michell, George (ed.), *Architecture of the Islamic World*, New York: William Morrow and Company, Inc., 1978.

Miodownik, Mark, *Stuff Matters, Exploring the Marvelous Materials that Shape Our Man-Made World*, London: Penguin Books Ltd, 2013.

Musterberg, Hugo, *The Japanese Kimono*, New York: Oxford University Press, 1996.

Rice, Peter, *An Engineer Imagines*, Batsford: An Imprint of Pavilion Books Co., 2017.

Rudofsky, Bernard, *The Kimono Mind, An Informal Guide to Japan and the Japanese*, New York, NY: Van Nostrand Reinhold Company, 1965.

Schittich, Christian (Ed.), *Building Skins, Concepts, Layers, Materials*, Birkhauser, Basel, Switzerland: Edition Detail, 2001.

Schouwenberg, Louise, *Hella Jongerius*, London, England: Phaidon Press, 2003.

Tsutoma, Ema, *Kimono: One Hundred Masterpieces of Japanese Costumes*, Tokyo, Japan: Meiji-Shobu, 1950.

Zuhur, Sherifa, *Revealing Reveiling: Islamist Gender Ideology in Contemporary Egypt*, New York: State University of New York Press, 1992.

6C

PIPELINE
Resistance and Feminist Spatial Practice

ERIN MOORE

6C Pipeline Resistance and Feminist Spatial Practice

Erin Moore

The Pipeline Portals, completed in 2019, are three pavilions on three different sites along the surveyed route of a proposed natural gas pipeline that was planned for the export of fracked gas from the North American interior to markets in Asia. The Portals are a protest against the construction—and the ecocultural impacts—of the proposed pipeline. Each of the design sites is ecologically complex: One is estuarian, one is wetland, one is riparian. As the Portals shape habitat for both human and non-human visitors and as they shape human views of the sites, the Portals are intended to enrich perception of these places by demonstrating their value in terms of biodiversity, ecological holism, nutrient cycling, and multi-species sheltering. This is to offer an alternative vision for the future of these lands in the face of fossil fuel extraction and climate change.

MULTI-SPECIES SHELTERING

> Our existence depends from one moment to the next on myriad micro-organisms and diverse higher species, on our own hazily understood bodily and cellular reactions and on pitiless cosmic motions, on the material artifacts and natural stuff that populate our environment.
>
> Diana Coole and Samantha Frost, *New Materialism: Ontology, Agency, and Politics*, 2010: 1

Each pavilion is a light, wood-framed cylinder made up of circular trusses on a pair of grade beams that are connected to the ground with reversible helical piers. The cylinders are each clad around their circumferences with a spiral of loose thatch. The thatch that spirals around each of the Portals sheds rainwater down one side of the pavilion and provides some shelter for humans. On the other side, the thatch collects water and nutrients and so provides terrible shelter for humans but achieves a very active habitat for other species of all sizes. This is an intentional subversion of human supremacy in architectural space and a purposeful inclusion of habitat for other species of various scales. While there are surely many, many essential organisms that are imperceptible, the growing list of species that have been observed in these pavilions is long: birds, fishes, frogs, and insects of many niches, and many mammals including a bear and some otters. Notably, bats appear to be roosting in the Haynes Inlet Portal and a mink has been sheltering in the Salmon Portal.

DOI: 10.4324/9781003138471-12

Figure 6C.1 *Just after construction on the Haynes Inlet* Source: Image: David Paul Bayles

As places for human observation of ecological complexity, the Portals—along with their documentation in time-lapse video—are intended to choreograph human experience of time as cyclical. This is in weather, tides, water levels, and planetary movement, and as material decays and accumulates. At the Haynes Inlet Portal, twice daily high tides wash close to the Portal edges and, seasonally, very high tides come up into the Portal. At the Coquille Portal, the surrounding pasture is dry in summer. In the wetter seasons, the pasture is inundated and the same water floats frog eggs up under the floorboards. At the Salmon Portal, varying water levels in the creek under the lip of the Portal change the sound of water on rocks that also host spawning salmon and lamprey. The Portals are also places for observation, either in person or by time-lapse video, of seasonal change in sun path, moon path, and of weather and atmosphere. In this way, the pavilions draw attention to the simultaneous ecological past and future of these lands.

The Portals shape visitor experiences with seating, shelter, and views. Each pavilion includes a built-in bench that is supported by additional members pinned into each hoop truss and includes a narrow floor. Each pavilion is sited to be entered by humans on just one end. At the entry end, the floor is built right up to the entry edge but ends before the overlook edge of the cylinder. The bench is built right up to the overlook edge but starts only a pace into the cylinder. In this way, visitors may sit on the bench on the overlook end while looking down into the everchanging ground. While sitting on the bench, visitors are sheltered from the elements by the layers of tule or soft rush overhead that shed most of the rain. On the facing surface of the interior, the tule and soft rush are layered upside down and leave openings for filtered views directly across and through the walls of the pavilions.

The circular thatch design comes from a sketch about nutrient cycling in architecture that I did many years ago. I developed that sketch into a spiral-thatched

Figure 6C.2 *Haynes Inlet Portal at low tide.*
Source: Image: David Paul Bayles

Figure 6C.3 *The portals are designed to position humans in a more-than human world*
Source: Image: David Paul Bayles

Figure 6C.4 *The FLOAT team enclosesd the portal with thatch made of soft rush*
Source: Image: David Paul Bayles ▼

model at the University of Tokyo while working with a team for a competition in the Kengo Kuma lab in 2013. The truss design itself started out with a full-scale sketch of double hexagon trusses that I made in the sand on the beach in Oregon while on a hike. Back on campus, I worked with graduate student Mike Kwilos to scale and prototype the truss designs from this sketch. Once we refined the details, we built several iterations of full-scale mockups of the trusses and the purloin and grade beam connections. Kwilos and several colleagues pre-cut and partially assembled

the pavilions in the on-campus shops. Installation on each site took one to two days for the primary structure and one day for the thatch. Students who helped with the construction were all hired and compensated through the university.

BORROWED MATERIAL

> *[Architecture] is made possible by the confrontation of a precise form with time and the elements, a confrontation which lasted until the form is destroyed in the process of this combat.*
>
> Aldo Rossi, A Scientific Autobiography, 1981: 2

The Portals are very simple, lightweight installations that resemble woven or thatched baskets. They were partially prefabricated for straightforward installation on site. They are cylindrical structures, each made up of ten prefabricated circular truss hoops set into slits along pairs of grade beams. The truss hoops are stitched together on site by longitudinal purloins. The purloins are woven into recessed cuts in the truss members, junctions that provide lateral strength in the longitudinal axis. Each hoop truss is made up of 12 individual members composing two offset hexagons with pinned connections. The hoop trusses have a very high strength-to-weight ratio in the rotational axis. The result is a cylindrical structure that looks like a loosely woven, twined basket where the purloins are the basket staves, the trusses members are the weavers, and the pinned connections between the truss members mark the lapping of the twining inside and outside of the weavers.

The Portals are designed for reversible construction in consideration of their intended short lifespan and for their end of life. Each is anchored temporarily into the ground with helical piers that, for the moment, hold tight to the tideland, riverbank, and floodplain beneath each of the Portals. The wood in the pavilion is young Douglas Fir (*Pseudotsuga menziesii* or mankw in Hanis Coos) from stewarded forests. This is a lower-grade biproduct of the milling of higher-quality structural lumber. The pavilions have a lifespan for human use of about two to three years before moisture and nutrient cycling begin to erode the lightweight fir construction. With time, the Portals will become even richer habitats for moss, algae, mycelium, and the many other organisms for which these dynamic environments are also habitat. As the plant material of the pavilions becomes part of the nutrient cycle in these places, only several pounds of coated steel hardware will remain to be collected for re-smelting. While the lifespan of the Portals is short, the materials that make up the construction are part of perpetual cycles of biological succession in plant and forest materials.

Each Portal is wrapped with loose thatch that spirals around the entire structure. The thatch is locally-harvested soft rush (*Juncus effuses*) and tule (*Schoenoplectus acutus*) (Phillips 2016). Both plants are indigenous to the Pacific Northwest and have an extremely long, rich history of cultural use for weaving baskets and for making mats, boats, and other household items. The thatch for the Haynes Inlet Portal and the Coquille Portal was harvested in large quantities from the restored tideland area very close to the Haynes Inlet Portal dried off-site, and then tied in interconnected bundles with hemp cord. The tule for the Salmon Portal was harvested from a deep irrigation pond also nearby the pavilion.

Figure 6C.5
Tule bundles, just harvested
Source: Image:
E. Moore

The tule, with a much higher initial moisture content, was dried off-site in a custom structure and then also bundled and fastened to stretchers for transport and installation.

In each case, I worked with local land stewards, student research assistants, and my own family members to harvest the plant material and to dry it. I recruited neighbors and others with experience in knotting and weaving to bundle and tie the dried tule and rush and to fasten the bundles to long stretchers for transport to the installation sites. In consultation with natural scientists and in keeping with local ecological knowledge, we harvested both the tule and the soft rush at their

Figure 6C.6 *Weaving detail*
Source: Image: E. Moore

Figure 6C.7 *Installing on site*
Source: Image: E. Moore

Figure 6C.8 *Tule bundles, just harvested View of the watershed* Source: Image: David Paul Bayles

growth peak and, as expected, both harvest sites grew back with the next season and continue to be rich habitats for turtles, birds, and many other species.

SPACE AND RESISTANCE

> *[Feminist spatial practice] can be understood within a critical feminist tradition examining how power, in the form of political hegemonies and social injustice has been resisted and reconstructed through spatial practice.*
> Schalk et al. 2017, *Feminist Futures of Spatial Practice*

Each of these three pavilions is constructed to challenge the expropriation of land for pipeline construction. As they draw attention to the ecological richness, the Portals are intended as direct-action pipeline resistance as they publicly draw attention to the value of the places that are in the path of potential destruction, to evoke public dismay.

This pipeline was just one of many proposed or under construction for transport of fossil fuels from the interior of North America to the West Coast during the same period. The fuels that these pipelines will carry are material threats to the future of the global climate, to regional ecosystems from leaks and explosions, to indigenous sovereignty, to indigenous sovereignty, and to rural communities. Studies demonstrate correlations between gender-based violence and drug use around extraction industry construction camps and show disproportionate harm to indigenous women. In this context, potential harm to land and potential harm to women is inseparable, especially where livelihoods and wellbeing are connected to whole ecosystems and where the extraction industry is implicated in the epidemic of missing and murdered indigenous women (Morin 2020).

Where the Pacific Northwest has faced pressure from expanded pipeline construction and, where climate change threatens global ecosystems, the Portals are just one of many acts of local resistance to the global threats of pipeline construction. As such, the Portals are meant to protest impacts of construction—from local to global—that are extensions of the extreme environmental and cultural threats to indigenous sovereignty and survivance that are well-rooted in the colonial settlement of North America and that continue in the powerful socioeconomic forces of industrial extraction and climate change (Bosworth 2020).

Pipeline construction and pipeline resistance are both necessarily spatial practices. Energy companies and climate change activists vie for spatial control of the linear—often very remote—spaces of pipeline routes, associated pumping stations, and construction camps along with associated watersheds, territories, and ports. In many cases, resistance has been particularly effective as it engages the unique spatiality of pipeline construction where geography and the linear morphology offer "pinch points" for resistance (Moore 2021).

The Portals are located on land that is within the traditional homelands of the Coos, Coquille, and Upper Umpqua peoples who were forcibly removed from these lands by the United States government. Today, descendants are citizens of the Confederated Tribes of the Coos, Lower Umpqua & Siuslaw Indians, the Coquille Indian Tribe, and the Cow Creek Band of Umpqua Tribe. The Portals are a response to the inseparability of colonial settlement, extraction industries, and the future of the climate and are built on private land in consultation with current landholders who were just three of many who volunteered to host the pavilions on their land as part of their own work to stand against pipeline construction.

Project Information:

Case Study: Pipeline Portals Project, 2019
Project Lead: Erin Moore, Professor, University of Oregon Department of Architecture and Environmental Studies Program
Students: Research assistants Mike Kwilos (lead), Zach Bradby, and Molly Winter.
Project Location: Oregon, USA

Project Timeline:

Design:	6 Weeks
Fabrication:	12 Weeks
Total:	18 Weeks

REFERENCES

Bosworth, Kai. 2020. "They're Treating Us Like Indians!': Political Ecologies of Property and Race in North American Pipeline Populism." *Antipode: A Journal of Radical Geography* 53: 667. http://doi.org/10.1111/anti.12426.
Coole, Diana H., and Samantha Frost. 2010. *New Materialisms: Ontology, Agency, and Politics*. Durham: Duke University Press.
Demos, T. J. 2020. "Extinction Rebellions." *Afterimage* 47(2): 14–20.

Moore, Erin E. 2021, June. "Four Lessons on Land, Space, and Resistance." *e—flux Architecture*. Solomon R. Guggenheim Museum and e-flux Architecture. www.google.com/search?client=firefox-b-1-d&q=erin%2Bmoore%2Bsurvivance.

Morin, Brandi. 2020. "Is Resource Extraction Killing Indigenous Women?" *Indigenous Rights | Al Jazeera*. Al Jazeera, May 5, 2020. www.aljazeera.com/features/2020/5/5/pipelines-man-camps-and-murdered-indigenous-women-in-canada.

Phillips, Patricia Whereat. 2016. *Ethnobotany of the Coos, Lower Umpqua, and Siuslaw Indians*. Corvallis, OR: Oregon State University Press.

Rossi, Aldo. 1981. *A Scientific Autobiography*. Cambridge, MA: MIT Press.

Schalk, Meike, Thérèse Kristiansson, and Ramia Mazé. 2017. *Feminist Futures of Spatial Practice: Materialism, Activism, Dialogues, Pedagogies, Projections*. Baunach, Germany: Art Architecture Design Research (AADR).

6D

GEO | TEXTILES

Weaving Restoration Ecology And Cultural Naratives

EMILY VOGLER

6D GEO|TEXTILES

Weaving Restoration Ecology and
Cultural Narratives

Emily Vogler

INTRODUCTION

Critical making combines the analytical, evaluative, and reflective aspects of critical thinking with the material, iterative, and embodied aspects of making.[1] At Rhode Island School of Design (RISD), the core principles of critical making, embodied knowledge, material explorations, and the iterative creative process, guide studio work and emphasize the importance of the development of ideas through hands-on practices. However, unlike the fine arts disciplines that work directly with the final objects of their practices, landscape architects and architects work with large complex sites and systems and rarely have the opportunity to construct their final designs. As Associate Professor of Landscape architecture at RISD, I have sought to integrate the core principles of critical making into my teaching and find meaningful opportunities where students can build knowledge through hands-on experiences.[2] My goal is to provide students with the design and critical thinking skills that will help position them to address large-scale regional environmental and social issues with concrete, action-based, creative solutions at the site and material scales.

One way I have done this is to offer interdisciplinary classes that allow students and faculty to explore the relationship between landscape architectural practices and the fine arts disciplines. In 2017 and 2018, I co-taught an interdisciplinary studio between landscape architecture and ceramics, looking at modular ceramic and concrete forms to reduce erosion along the water's edge. In 2019, in response to the work from the ceramic/landscape studio and fieldwork that introduced me to the use of geotextiles, I reached out to Mary Anne Friel, an Associate Professor in Textiles, about the possibility of co-teaching an interdisciplinary studio between the landscape architecture and textiles departments. We applied for and received an "Academic Enrichment Grant"—an internal RISD grant that aims to foster interdisciplinary collaboration. The grant covered materials, travel, and extra teaching funds so we could both teach the studio. We had to postpone the studio and shift sites due to COVID, but were able to offer the studio in the fall of 2021.

SITE CONTEXT

The Blackstone River provided the geographical, cultural, and ecological lens for the studio. The Blackstone River runs 48 miles from its urban headwaters in Worcester, MA to Pawtucket Falls where it flows into the tidal Seekonk River. The river passes

DOI: 10.4324/9781003138471-13

through channelized granite walls in downtown Worcester, alongside rural agricul-
tural farms in Massachusetts, over dams in old mill villages, and through the cities
of Woonsocket and Pawtucket.

The Blackstone River watershed is the homeland of the Nipmuc, Pokanoket,
Wampanoag, and Narragansett Nations with the majority of the watershed falling within the Nipmuc territory. Starting in the 1600s, European colonists spread
throughout New England, expropriating the land from the indigenous communities
and settling along the abundant rivers and streams of the region. These rivers facilitated transportation, provided water for agriculture, and were dammed to supply
the power for the early colonial settlements. The early dams within the region were
primarily used to power grist mills and sawmills. However, in 1792 in Pawtucket,
Samuel Slater dammed the Blackstone River and built the first successful textile manufacturing facility in the United States. This development transformed the
economy and spurred the start of the Industrial Revolution within the United States.
In 1809, there were 40 textile mills within 30 miles of Providence (or two-thirds
of total production in NE), and after a period of explosive growth, by 1832 there
were 119 in Rhode Island.[3] At some point there were 34 dams along the 46 miles
of the Blackstone River and hundreds more along the tributaries. This led to the
Blackstone River getting the reputation as "America's Hardest Working River" in
1909.[4]

The Blackstone River was once the backbone of settlement in the region, and
the mills were dependent on the river—it was the lifeblood of the community.
However, with the advent of steam power in the mid- to late 1800s, mills were
no longer dependent on rivers for water power. Beginning as early as the end of
the 19th century, the textile industry began to shift out of New England, first to
the South, and ultimately offshore. During the 20th-century period of deindustri-
alization, the communities both physically and figuratively shifted their orientation
away from the river, and reoriented towards highways, strip malls, and new economic opportunities. Although the mills have mostly closed, the industrial legacy
remains in the dams that continue to block fish passage and the toxic heavy metals
that remain in the sediments behind the dams. In 1990, the U.S. Environmental
Protection Agency (EPA) declared the Blackstone River "the most polluted river in
the country with respect to toxic sediments."[5] Significant efforts have been made
to clean up the river over the past 50 years, but it still is not safe to swim or fish
in the river.

STUDIO APPROACH

In the studio, students were asked to consider the relationship between textiles
and landscape architecture practices to address, reconcile, and interpret the complex ecological and cultural histories of the Blackstone River. Weaving and other
structural textile techniques were explored as both a metaphor and a physical strategy to weave together the multiple cultural narratives of a river as well as consider
how to support the diverse river ecologies and the unique experiential qualities of
being at the water's edge. There are many ways that weaving and landscape intersect along the Blackstone River from basket-weaving traditions of the indigenous

Figure 6D.1 *Map of the Blackstone River Watershed*

communities, to the textile mills, to the contemporary geotextiles that are used to restore the banks of the river.

Some of the overarching material, formal, and performative questions we hoped to explore in the studio were: How can textiles be used to interpret or reveal the multiple stories, histories, and layers of the landscape? Can fibers be used to stabilize the water's edge, direct flows, improve water quality, and provide habitat for riparian plant and animal species? Can the woven materials become "unglued" from the ground plane to shape the human aesthetic experience of the water's edge? How can basket-weaving traditions inform the way we manage the landscape? How can woven materials be integrated with living plant material, mycelium, and soil? How can the density of a textile aggregate and disperse to respond to different site conditions or to shape the pattern of plant growth? How long should the materials persist? Could they be designed to degrade overtime? What is the relationship between traditional craft practices and digital fabrication or scripting? Can community groups be involved in the construction and installation of the textiles as a way of rebuilding a connection between people and place?

STUDIO STRUCTURE

In the fall of 2021, 15 students enrolled in the geotextiles studio. Six students came from landscape architecture, four from textiles, one from architecture, one from furniture design, one from printmaking, and one from Brown University's literary arts program. The studio was divided into two main phases—the first phase included research and material studies which led into the second phase where each student developed a textile/textile inspired response to the river.

Phase 1—Grounding and Exploring

The first phase of the studio was intended to ground students in an understanding of the Blackstone River and material and fabrication techniques in textiles. Three skills-based workshops were offered at the start of the semester. On the first day of class, each student was given a frame loom and we offered a workshop on the basics of structural textile techniques (weaving, netting, braiding). After the workshop, each student was expected to apply what they learned and develop seven woven and netted material samples using techniques learned in the workshop. In the material studies, the students were asked to consider materials, textures, scale, permeability, density, and gradients. The second skills workshop we offered was an introduction to textiles dying in the textiles dye labs. The third skills workshop took place over a weekend at a site along the river and was run by Howard Peller, a willow farmer and basket weaver.[6] During the workshop, students learned basic techniques of working with willow basket weaving. Over the course of the weekend, the students constructed a 4 foot by 6 foot oracle (basket boat) and a 10 foot willow spilled edge along the river. Willow spilling is a practice of weaving willow stakes together vertically to reduce stream bank erosion.

Alongside the skills workshops and material-based explorations of Phase 1, students began to build their knowledge of the river and current geotextiles techniques through research and field trips. The students were able to select from three possible research topic groups: (1) Geotextiles—History + Patents + Case Studies; (2) Blackstone Ecology—Flora + Fauna; (3) Blackstone River—History + Geography. Each group was expected to research their topic and develop a graphic representation strategy to communicate their research in a clear, consistent, and graphically compelling way. The students presented their findings to their classmates in a presentation and compiled their research into a "field guide" that remained in the studio for future reference.

Phase 2—Positioning and Testing

During the second phase of the studio, students were asked to define their own unique approach to bring together textiles and landscape to reimagine the future of the Blackstone River. To help transition from the initial material studies and research into the design phase of the studio, each student developed three "warm up proposals" for potential projects that were based on their initial site response. Following the review

Figure 6D.2 *Willow Spiling Workshop*
Source: Emily Vogler

Figure 6D.3
*Furniture student
Madeleine Young's
material experiment
exploring the
relationship of
cotton, textiles,
postindustrial decay
and rust on the
Blackstone River*
Source: Madeleine
Young

and discussion of each student's proposal, students selected one proposal to move forward with. While we encouraged students to collaborate on their final project, only two students chose to work together, the other students chose to work independently.

There were 14 unique projects that emerged from the studio: Some projects focused on the ecological restoration of the river; others focused on interpreting the complex history of the river and its relationship to textiles; and others chose to explore how to create new spatial and experiential opportunities for people to connect to the river. Depending on each student's approach, there was a range of ways that the students could resolve their projects, including speculative design, gallery pieces, site installations, and material development. Some students chose to narrow into specific sites, some stayed more focused on the overall length of the river and developed a design framework for the river and then narrowed into a specific site to test their logic. While we had hoped at the beginning of the semester that more students would be able to do full-scale site installations, the reality of the time and construction made it difficult. Therefore, many projects remained speculative with prototypes, models, and full-scale mock-ups that allowed them to test their ideas 1:1. Below, I will provide a couple of examples of student projects from the class:

While basket weavers use fibers to shape 3-dimensional *objects*, landscape architects have the opportunity to use weaving to shape 3-dimensional *space*.

Figure 6D.4
Weaving 3-dimensional space to entangle people at the water's edge
Source: Yumeng Yan

Yumung Yan, a landscape architecture student, chose to focus on the spatial experience of being near the water's edge. He shifted the scale typically associated with basket weaving to create a structure to "entangle" people near the water's edge. Yumeng was able to prototype a scaled-down version of this design on a site along the river to test his design ideas—although he eventually imagined the structure being made out of ash bark strips, for the sake of time and cost, in the prototype he used multiflex bendable plywood sheets to construct the woven structure.

Traditional geotextiles were first developed in the 1950s to reduce erosion, stabilize slopes, and drain the landscape. Although many contemporary geotextiles are made out of plastic, there are exceptions including the use of coir (coconut fibers), jute, and straw mats. Natural materials decompose over a period

Figure 6D.5
Material studies of how geotextile would interact with plant growth
Source: Yuxiao Liao

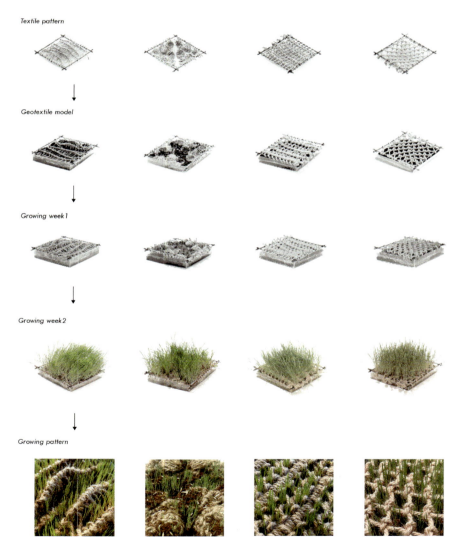

of two to five years and as they biodegrade help to build the soil. Yuxiao Liao, a landscape architecture student, wanted to build on this knowledge to consider how the restoration of a contaminated old mill site along the river could be combined with the design of the human experience of visiting the site to create a network of "Remediation gardens." In the first part of the semester, Yuxiao did a series of experiments to create a layered system of geotextile "pillows" which included a layer of a woven jute fabric, coir fibers as a growing medium, and vegetation. Combined with a gridded framework of poplars, the ecological goal of the geotextile "pillows" was to build soil and introduce plants that could help with the phytoremediation of the site. The jute geotextiles were intended to be woven during workshops to bring the community into the restoration process and build a culture of stewardship and care. To test his ideas, Yuxiao conducted elaborate material studies throughout the semester—growing grass in the geotextile "pillows," weaving different scales of jute and coir materials to determine the appropriate scale, and building a full 1:1 mock of one of the geotextile remediation gardens.

A third landscape architecture student, Leigh Miller, chose to knit a large-scale "soil scarf" to draw attention to flooding conditions along the river and reduce soil erosion. Given the scale of the work and the material properties of working with natural fibers, Leigh began her project by constructing her own knitting needles out of 3 inch diameter dowels. She used the needles to knit paper fiber rush into large panels. The panels were intended to serve two potential functions—(1) acting as an artful flood datum at river access points that immerse the human body into the scale of anticipated flooding, and (2) as a geotextile material to stabilize the river's edge, enhance porosity and infiltration, and prevent and capture sedimentation. To test her ideas, Leigh constructed four 15 inch by 3 inch panels that together were 60 feet long and 180 square feet. She took the woven panels to the site multiple times during the semester to test how the panels could be installed to achieve her two main goals. She photographed the installations and also left some of the panels staked to the ground to see how leaves, sediment, and other materials settled into the open woven mesh.

While many of the landscape architecture students proposed site-based projects that focused on the ecological restoration of the river, Natiana Fonseca, a textiles student, chose to focus on the complex cultural history of the river and the connection between the historic textile mills on the Blackstone River and slavery. The mills of the Blackstone River depended on cotton to make textiles, however, cotton did not grow within the region. The textile mills of Rhode Island were inextricably linked to plantation slavery of the South where the cotton was grown. As the textile industries grew along the Blackstone River and throughout New England, the plantation regime of American slavery grew to keep up with the demand.[7] Natasha made two textile tapestries to represent the Blackstone River and the Alabama River. She used woven and felted cotton and wool fibers to narrate these histories and distort the cartographies to draw the connection between these two distant rivers, landscapes, and histories.

Figure 6D.6 *Leigh Miller's "soil scarf"*
Source: Leigh Miller

Figure 6D.7
Foraged plants and natural dyes developed by textile students Mindy Kang and Clara Boberg for dying their woven textiles
Source: Mindy Kang and Clara Boberg

Mindy Kang and Clara Boberg, both from the textile department, chose to partner for their final project. The two shared an interest in natural dyes as a critique of the use and negative impact of chemical dyes on the Blackstone River and other rivers around the world. Their project began with them traveling the length of the river to forage plants to use as a natural dye. Some of the plants they harvested

Figure 6D.8
Students learning hands-on by being emersed in the river
Source: Emily Vogler

included Pokeberry, Mugwort, Oriental Bittersweet, Japanese Knotweed, American Chestnut, and Sumac. In addition, they collected water from the river to use in the dye bath. For their final project, they made two woven panels and a documentary journal about their journey and the plants they used. One woven panel was made from the yarn dyed with natural dyes from along the river, and a second woven panel explored the history of the mills and dye houses that contributed significantly to the pollution of the river today.

CONCLUSION

While new technologies increasingly allow for digital design to be directly translated into physical form, in this studio we wanted to reorient students to the value of physical, spatial, temporal, and material knowledge that comes from spending time interacting with real materials, landscapes, and people. Students were emersed in the landscape (literally standing and sitting in the river), they were meeting and interacting with people who work and live along the river, and they were in the studio wrestling with willow, coir and rush. By adapting the core principles of critical making into the studio, students learned about the interconnected social and ecological issues along the river, developed skills and material knowledge of working with textiles, took a stance on the issues they wanted to address through their creative practice, and translated those goals into material and site-based responses. By bringing the textiles into the landscape and the landscape into their textiles, students in the studio reconfigured the historic connection between the Blackstone River and weaving to reveal the complexities of this relationship and suggest new visions for the future of the river.

Project Details:

Chapter: GEO | Textiles: Weaving Restoration Ecology and Cultural Narratives Along the Blackstone River

Professor/Project Lead: Emily Vogler (Landscape Architecture) + Mary Anne Friel (Textiles)

University/Organization: Rhode Island School of Design

Students:

Natalie Paik (Textiles)
Natiana Fonesca (Textiles)
Clara Boberg (Textiles)
Mindy Kang (Textiles)
Madeleine Young (Furniture)
Yesuk Seo (Printmaking)
Chloe Zimmerman (Brown University—Literary arts)
Leigh Miller (Landscape Architecture)
Sirui Wang (Landscape Architecture)
Yuting Chen (Landscape Architecture)
Yuxiao Liao (Landscape Architecture)
Yumeng Yan (Landscape Architecture)
Chenfang Gang (Landscape Architecture)
Shreya Kaipa (Architecture)

Project Location: Blackstone River—Massachusetts and Rhode Island
Donations/Financial Support: RISD Academic Enrichment Grant

Project Studio Timeline:

Material Studies and Site Research:	4 weeks
Initial site response:	2 weeks
Design and Fabrication:	8 weeks
Total:	14 Weeks

NOTES

1. Rosanne Somerson. *The Art of Critical Making: Rhode Island School of Design on Creative Practice*. Edited by Rosanne Somerson and Mara Hermano. 1 edition. (Hoboken, NJ: Wiley, 2013).
2. See Emily Vogler. "Critical Making in Landscape Architecture," in *Conceptual Landscapes: Critical Perspectives in the Earliest Stages of Design*, ed. Simon Bussiere (Abingdon, England; New York, NY: Routledge, Forthcoming publication).
3. *Blackstone River Valley Special Resource Study*, 2011. National Park Service: https://sem-spub.epa.gov/work/01/480751.pdf
4. Winthrop Packard. "America's Hardest Working River," *Technical World Magazine*. Vol. 12, Number 2 (October 1909).
5. *Re-Zapping the Blackstone: Keeping the River Recovery Going*! Shasten Sherwell. 2021.
6. www.livingwillowfarm.com
7. Seth Rockman, "Slavery and Abolition along the Blackstone River," In *Landscape of Industry* (Lebanon, NH: University Press of New England, 2009).

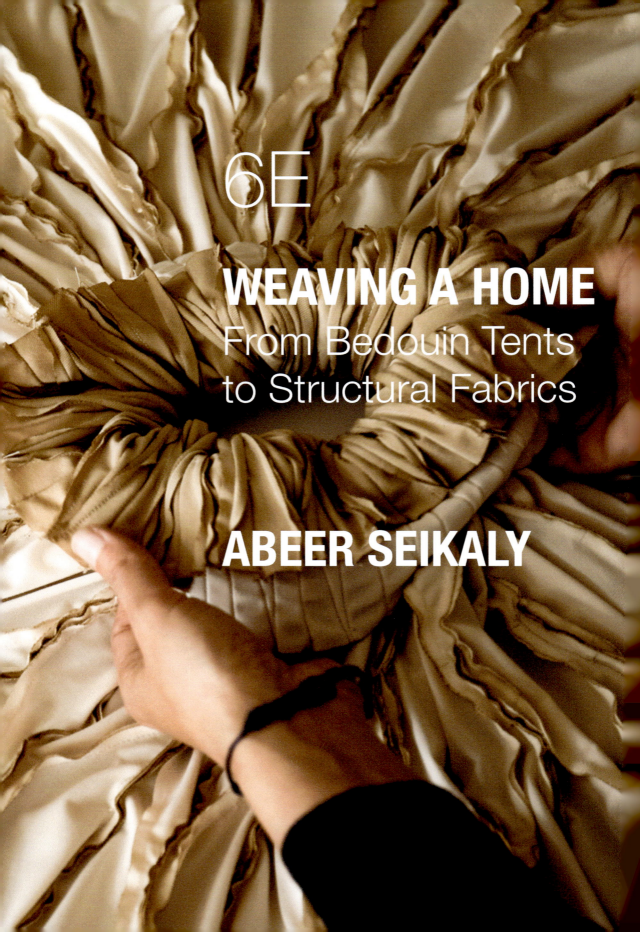

WEAVING A HOME
From Bedouin Tents to Structural Fabrics

ABEER SEIKALY

6E Weaving a Home

Abeer Seikaly

INTRODUCTION: THE BEDOUIN RUG

A decade ago, in 2012, I inherited a traditional Bedouin rug that was hand-woven by my great grandmother. Traditionally passed on through the family, this rug is characteristic—through its colors and pattern—of the holy town of Madaba in Jordan that dates back to the Middle Bronze Age and that is mentioned in the Bible. While each Bedouin tribe marks its weavings with distinct designs, each piece is infused with the individual memory of its own maker, history, and context. In present day Jordan, rugs continue to be woven by Bedouin women on traditional ground looms, constructed of stones, sticks, and other available materials. These women also built the homes of their tribes, known as *Beit-al-sha'ar*, a traditional Bedouin mobile tent made using local resources like goat and sheep wool.

In the same way that Bedouin tribes in Madaba—and my great grandmother— each left their own distinct markings and their memory in the threads they wove, the tents are woven in an intimate and embodied experience that reinforces the relationship between (wo)man and the environment. From the material extracted from animals indigenous to the land, to the tools used—including the woman's body itself—to aid in the building process, the tent becomes infused with elements of both its maker and its environment. Fabric architecture, through communal practices inspired by the way Bedouin women came together to weave their homes, can help revive that intimate relationship with building. This notion of cradle-to-cradle architecture—proposed by architects William McDonough and Michael Braungard in their hallmark book[1]—can help challenge the alienated architectural production that defines contemporary building practices in the post-industrial era. These are often marked by rigid structures, toxic waste, and a detached architecture that is antithetical to the—both physically and socially—dynamic openness of woven structures like the Bedouin tent.

Studying the at once arduous, intuitive, intimate, and communal process of the making of that tent has informed my own practice and the making of my self-structured, livable and foldable tent—the project that has culminated into *Weaving a Home*—that aims to challenge contemporary modes of living. It also pushed me to research a wealth of other material cultures—that similarly challenge contemporary architectural practices—through months of research for a design studio I taught at Yale School of Architecture during the fall 2021 semester, Conscious Skins. As I worked on developing my latest prototype of the dome, a separate yet interlinked

DOI: 10.4324/9781003138471-14

Figure 6E.1 *The traditional Bedouin rug woven by my great grandmother is referred to as the "Fijjeh" and is characteristic—through its colors and pattern—to Madaba, a holy city in Jordan*
Source: © Abeer Seikaly, 2012

Figure 6E.2 *My great-grandmother, Eideh Shuwayhat with her twin daughters, Marta and Elaine, 1940*
Source: © Abeer Seikaly, 2012

platform emerged. *Meeting Points*, a self-structuring tapestry woven by 40 Bedouin and rural women across Jordan, became a model for how architecture and design processes can act as instruments for social change. Marrying contemporary methods of design and building with indigenous and cultural modes of place-making through communal collaboration resulted in a multi-faceted body of work that positions the self as an agent in a sensorial and embodied field of social and material production.

THE BEDOUIN TENT ARCHETYPE

The Bedouin tent or *Beit-al-sha'ar* has been the subject of much reverence for decades, for its beauty and for the poetry of its construction; a process that has evolved through a continuing heritage of women, to whom the construction and erection of these structures has been traditionally tasked. Yet the legacies of its

Figure 6E.3 *"Matters of Time" (2019), video stills. Long and narrow strips of heavy cloth woven from goat hair are sewn together by Bedouin women to form the great rectangle used as the roof of the Bedouin tent*
Source: © Abeer Seikaly and Tanya Marar, 2019

Figure 6E.4 *"Matters of Time" (2019), video stills. A laborer mixes concrete to build tourist lodges in the midst of Wadi Rum in Jordan, a construction process that has taken precedence over traditional tent-making practices*
Source: © Abeer Seikaly and Tanya Marar, 2019

cumulative and communal design ingenuity continue to be disregarded within the contemporary canon of design knowledge in Jordan, and are instead marginalized as architecture without architects. A product of a humanized process and relationship to the environment, the Bedouin tent is a responsive archetype and performative architecture which should be asserted as a composite material structural design, and attributed to the lineage of Bedouin women who have communally and intuitively engineered it.

The embodiment of indigenous tent-making knowledge—passed on through generations—and the consistent dynamic response to changing climate conditions, also position the tent as a permanent and continuous structure in architectural processes and practices. The word "tent" in itself is derived from the Latin *tendere*, meaning "to stretch"; a signifier that the structure of the tent has always had potential beyond its basic structural topology. By approaching architecture with the lens of "weaving" as a conceptual framework and a way of thinking, we can imagine the exterior of a structure as a (conscious) building skin that can be stretched and woven into a performative form that can become a physical catalyst for creating meaningful interactions between space, occupants and their environment.

HANDS, INTUITION, AND COLLECTIVE METHODOLOGY

The weaving of the tent makes use of a number of tools, but one of the most pertinent and often overlooked tools is the woman's hands directly interacting with the material from which the tent is made. Her weaving, building and handcrafting skills reside directly in the fingertips of her intelligent hands and are embedded within her lived reality. Such craft-led, sensorial practices use the hand, body and mind synchronistically as tools to expand thinking through material, therefore informing functional requirements and aesthetic considerations. The care and rigor of working with one's hands also releases the unexpected during the interplay between maker and material.

The role of the hand in architectural practices has long been diminished with the rise of modern technologies, erased along with the traditions that had once embedded it in everyday life. However, technologies of handcraft, merged with the digital processes of today, can lend a fluidity to contemporary architectural and design practices that can produce a complex interrelation of systems and a deeper understanding of the interdependent nature of material, geometry and structural form, and their adaptive response to the environment.

In my exploration of creating skins that are both flexible and structural, I worked with existing materials and navigated through different geometric patterns and traditional handcrafting techniques. This allowed me to redefine a material's property as its ability to stretch through geometry and topology. I focused on alternative weaving and knitting techniques of three-dimensional fabric and studied material flexibility, strength, and stability at various geometrical configurations.

These different methodologies came together and manifested themselves into a broader process of architectural exploration during my studio at the Yale School of Architecture. While designing the syllabus, one important aspect was to blend together intuitive methodologies such as the use of our hands with academic research and digital manipulation. Working with textiles also allowed for active engagement with different materials, knowledge systems, and practices, and a deeper understanding of the spatiality of the task of making. This mélange of different methodologies and materials allowed myself and the students to bring a more communicative configuration to conventional understandings of structures as notionally static load-bearing forms.

Through the studio, the students researched a variety of indigenous material cultures that were then expressed in different ways in their projects, and through each individual lens. The outcome of the studio was always the process of creating the structure, and not the end structure in itself. This helped them develop a more mindful, intuitive relationship with their work that allows them to actively think through the process of making.

Despite the nuances of the projects and the personal and affective engagement each student had with their work, similar concerns and challenges to what I have faced in my own work manifested themselves in different ways. Treating the process of making as the product of the studio was challenging for some who could not visualize an end product for their work. Working through these challenges and understanding the importance of the process as a collective group helped broaden my own understanding of the myriad shapes that an architectural process can take.

Figure 6E.5
Bedouin women push their bodies through fatigue and pain as they process goat hair and sheep wool into yarn. These materials were used to knit the three-dimensional tapestry for "Meeting Points" (2019)
Source: © Abeer Seikaly and Tanya Marar, 2019

Figure 6E.6 Morgan Kerber's project, "Woven Together" (2021), was a result of the "Conscious Skins" studio I taught at Yale School of Architecture. The project sought to work with a group of people to weave a structure which embodies the postures of making within its form. Spanning 28 ft across and utilizing innovative weaving techniques, this textile became a space through which collective processes and communal dialogue are expressed and embodied
Source: © Abeer Seikaly and Dylan Beckman, 2021

The ongoing research I conducted for my projects was not an independent practice, but stemmed from this collective approach to learning that allowed me to build on my practice in various contexts and from different positionalities. On one hand, the ethnographic research I conducted with Bedouin communities for the construction of *Meeting Points* reaffirmed and developed my understanding of the role of hand-making and craft-led methods in architectural design. On the other hand, my studio allowed me to learn from and build on my students' individual investigations, which presented different forms of architectural representation, and different understandings of how architecture is produced and communicated.

WEAVING A HOME: A SOCIAL ARCHITECTURE

Historically, communities in the Arab world were inextricably connected to nature and their surroundings, both inside and outside of their homes. In a modern world governed by consumerism and urbanism, and threatened by a burgeoning climate crisis, the notion of cradle-to-cradle living and design, which embeds nature and sustainability into all processes of life, is needed now more than ever. Shelters need to invite new creative potentials grounded in active engagement with materials, tools, and technologies, and to become a space that supports the thriving of the human spirit and its environment.

Initiated in 2013, *Weaving a Home* is an ongoing project that was initially designed as a lightweight tent structure for displaced communities, which is able to withstand varying climatic conditions, integrates water collection, harnesses renewable energy, and allows for controlled ventilation; providing many of the comforts of a dignified contemporary life. By examining traditional architectural typologies of tent shelters, which inherently marry locally sourced materials with suitable construction technologies, the solution offered is that of a technical, structural fabric that expands and contracts within an innovative structural design.

The geometry of the configuration capitalizes on the performative capacity of pre-stressed radial frames linked together to form a stable and durable double membrane enclosure. Through the technical fabric, which acts as a decentralized integrated energy system, the product is a resilient, collapsible, and potentially "energy independent" form that can also yield different material applications that can be utilized in other building and construction typologies. In the process and timeframe of its technical development, it required an active engagement not only with specialists but with different local communities, and different materials, tools, and technologies.

The project sought to unlock the potential of local knowledge within Bedouin, rural and displaced communities in Jordan, and to contribute towards the livelihood of women by (1) exploring innovation in craft/material technology (material systems and tent-craftsmanship), (2) promoting the development of a sustainable fiber-based processing industry, and (3) developing a program of local resource management, research dissemination, and training and community development to foster equal opportunities for women.

My cooperation with an engineering practice based in the UK—Atelier One—was initiated in 2014 and has resulted in design documents and multiple prototypes for the tent in which the latest prototype was completed in March 2020. With research, field, and lab work spanning seven years, I undertook a critical examination of traditional and contemporary architectural typologies of tent shelters. The journey took me to my Bedouin roots, and to examine the intuitive process of the

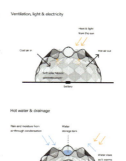

Figure 6E.7 *"Weaving a Home" (2013) is the first iteration of the tent I designed and an ongoing development of performative structural fabric systems, exploring the social implications of creating homes for displaced communities. The tent integrates water collection, harnesses renewable energy and allows for controlled ventilation*
Source: © Abeer Seikaly, 2013

construction of the *Beit-al-sha'ar*, which I found the need to document in a short video piece titled *Matters of Time*.

As I archived the women's building practices, which involved weaving yards of tent material from goat hair and sheep wool, an act that they came together within their communities to do, it became clear that weaving these homes had been about more than simply creating shelters. Weaving these fabric structures was a cultural practice and a performative means of expression that they used and communicated through their bodies in the face of societal submission. For them, responding to the environment through weaving these structures had been a way of life. The *Beit-al-sha'ar*'s contextual link to land, culture, and heritage further highlighted the need to consider the wellbeing of different communities when constructing my tent structure, beyond simply providing functional solutions for a single community. It opened up questions like: How can the design of a shelter truly create added value that can be repurposed for centuries by generations to come?

One of the main challenges I faced in the evolution of the project has been in identifying the parameters of what it has the potential to become. This led me to establish a separate, yet inherently linked, platform called *Meeting Points*; a communal architecture program which shares much of the goals and objectives of *Weaving a Home* with the same sense of urgency, and which evolved through the growing interest of a wide community of users, designers, individuals, and organizations.

MEETING POINTS: BETWEEN MATERIALS, COMMUNITIES, AND DESIGN PRACTICES

My interaction with Bedouin communities and my deep exploration into Bedouin tent-making techniques revealed the potential of evolving these processes into the development of the structural material system that I had envisioned for *Weaving a Home*. The collaborative and cumulative quality of the Bedouin tent archetype became a significant drive for *Meeting Points* to establish an understanding of

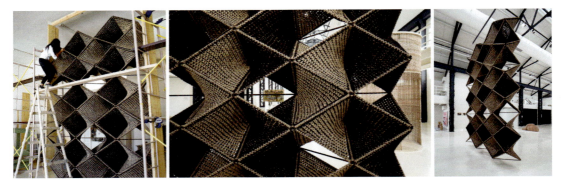

Figure 6E.8 *"Meeting Points" (2019). The three-dimensional material system merges traditional Bedouin tent-making techniques with contemporary design practices. The structural and spatial exploration is an interplay of materials, construction techniques, and delicate and precise design processes*
Source: © Abeer Seikaly and David Walters, 2019

architecture as an embodied process rather than a purely material outcome, thereby aiming to integrate traditional modes of making into contemporary design and fabrication processes.

Through multiple iterations of physical modeling and digital manipulation, the new reconfigurable and adaptable creative-cultural form explores the meeting points between *material and structure*, *nature and designed space*, and *designer and community*. It challenges conventional understandings of structure, from notionally static and load-bearing forms, to a more communicative and socially dynamic configuration. This is manifested through a structural context, which facilitates the cultural empowerment of indigenous communities and marginalized peoples, not through a nostalgic and stagnant continuation of ancient crafts, but through new forms of innovative place-making.

Through the communal efforts of over 60 rural and Bedouin community members from various governorates across Jordan (40 of whom were women), the first prototype has already helped foster new opportunities for individuals to contribute to and benefit from the social, cultural, and economic development within their respective communities. The prototype used local resources and was designed and built in coordination with a community of shearers, spinners, knitters, and craftspeople. The new system synthesizes traditional Bedouin construction, contemporary design, and community participation within a new cultural form; a material experience that draws on the environmental rootedness of indigenous Bedouin knowledge, thereby aiming to integrate traditional modes of making into contemporary design and fabrication processes.

The design of this work begins with an understanding of weaving, craft, and making as complex technologies. The novelty of this self-structuring and communally hand-crafted tapestry is in its coordination of various technological meeting points: digital manipulation and analogue knitting work culminate in a composite structural network of locally sourced plant and animal fiber, wood, and steel connectors. The structural material tapestry was showcased at Amman Design Week's main Hangar Exhibition in October 2019, and at La

Manufacture: A Labour of Love (2020) at Gare Saint Sauveur Cultural Institute in Lilles, France.

The second iteration of *Meeting Points*, which I am currently working on, will continue engaging communities in design processes for the advancement and refinement of the structural material system. This emergent communal architecture program aims to become a flagship for how architecture and design processes can act as instruments for social change. This ongoing project aims to advance innovative material and structural research in shelter design, and build awareness of how architecture, as a social and cultural process, can generate dynamic spaces for collaborative creativity where local communities are empowered to thrive.

FULL CIRCLE: CRADLE-TO-CRADLE ARCHITECTURE

Through this long process of researching, archiving, and communal development, I was able to rethink my approach towards the building of the dome shelter—from its geometrical and material configuration to my relationship to it as its architect. The latest prototype for *Weaving a Home* is a performative structural material system that honors the notion of cradle-to-cradle architecture—where buildings and spaces become part of a natural lifecycle, with infinite potential for repurposing—and challenges contemporary modes of living.

Weaving a Home became more than just a sheltering solution, morphing into a comprehensive creative building process that has the potential to advance new knowledge of pre-existing solutions developed by previous generations, placing itself within a continuum of tradition, and synthesizing structural systems and design processes with traditional knowledge and natural, local building materials and techniques. *Weaving a Home* was a result of my specific engagement with the material and the spatial conditions I constructed with it. However, the process of working through textile making in different contexts—whether in my Yale School of Architecture studio, with Bedouin communities for the construction of *Meeting Points* or when creating the various prototypes of *Weaving a Home*—has elaborated new terrains in how architecture is produced and how these modes of production can facilitate new tectonic landscapes and spatial conditions.

Created through a holistic approach towards material systems that encompasses their geometric behavior, manufacturing constraints and assembly logics, the new iteration of *Weaving a Home* is intrinsically elaborated through the system's own topological capacity. The central vision was to reposition the process itself as a central aspect of building, focusing not on the resulting structure but on the embodied and affective process of hand making and form finding through which we can synthesize material, structure, and function in the process of creating structural fabrics. The outcome of this working process is an architectural space where thinking consciously about material and its properties is mediated through a performative structural skin, thus challenging the narrow view of architecture as a static artifact and as "matter"; treating it instead as a dynamic, living process. The outcome involved creating a structure that is from the earth and adapts to its environment.

Figure 6E.9 *"Weaving a Home" (2020), tent at Al-Namara, overlooking the Dead Sea in Jordan. This ongoing development of the performative structural material system honors the notion of cradle-to-cradle architecture and challenges contemporary modes of living*
Source: © Abeer Seikaly, 2020

Using local resources and the intuitive hands of a community of crafts-men and women, the new material system merges mechanics and design, while drawing inspiration from traditional tent-crafting methods that have community and sustainability at their core. Resilient and collapsible, the dome represents a continuity in the evolution of place-making that is not linear but rather circular—rooted in the present, but watered, fed, and nurtured by its past.

Figure 6E.10
"Weaving a Home" (2020), one-quarter scale tent prototype. The pre-stressed radial frames are linked circumferentially with the patterned geometrical membrane to form a stable and durable double membrane enclosure
Source: © Abeer Seikaly, Tanya Marar and Hussam Da'na, 2020

CONCLUSION

The evolution of these projects highlighted the neglect of a wealth of traditional craftsmanship knowledge, harbored mainly by Bedouin women—the silent architects behind *Beit-al-sha'ar*. This loss of knowledge and intangible heritage for the country and its communities constitutes a waste of valuable economic potential. Realizing the fruits of fabric architecture, especially when merged with digital design practices, can help create sheltering solutions that advance and innovate traditional forms of place-making, while reviving notions of cradle-to-cradle architecture that hold sustainability, connection, and intuition at the core of the process of making of a home.

The projects advocate for participatory community development by empowering women through training, integration, and visibility to explore alternative sheltering solutions and share knowledge on traditional tent-craftsmanship to create an enabling and safe environment for them to thrive. The projects together weave the relationship between nature, tradition, and technology to propel new solutions to how we build, interact, and dwell in the 21st century; redefining shelter as a social, artistic, and cultural process that continues to evolve with our collective values.

Project Information:

Chapter: Weaving a Home
Professor/Project Lead: Abeer Seikaly
University/Organization: Yale University, Yale School of Architecture
Teaching Assistant: Gabrielle Printz
Students: Adare Brown, Elise Barker Limon, Hao Tang, Jun Nam, Morgan Kerber, Serge Saab, Smaranda Rusinaru, Stav Dror, Sydney Maubert, Taiga Taba
Project Location: Jordan and United Kingdom
Donations/Financial Support: Private support/Self support
Awards: 2012 Lexus Design Award

Project Studio Timeline:

Introduction to Fabric Structures:	1 Week
Textile Traditions and the Felt Idea:	1 Week
The Craft of Translation:	1 Week
Transformable Surfaces in the Making:	1 Week
Stretch	1 Week
Travel Week	1 Week
Weave	2 Weeks
Midterms and Desk Crits	1 Week
Deconstruct/Reconstruct	2 Weeks
Program (is the process)	1 Week
Fall Recess	1 Week
Third Space	1 Week
Final Review	1 Week
Total	**15 Weeks**

NOTE

1. Braungart, M., & McDonough, W. (2002). *Cradle to cradle: Remaking the way we make things.* North Point Press.

PROFESSIONAL INQUIRY

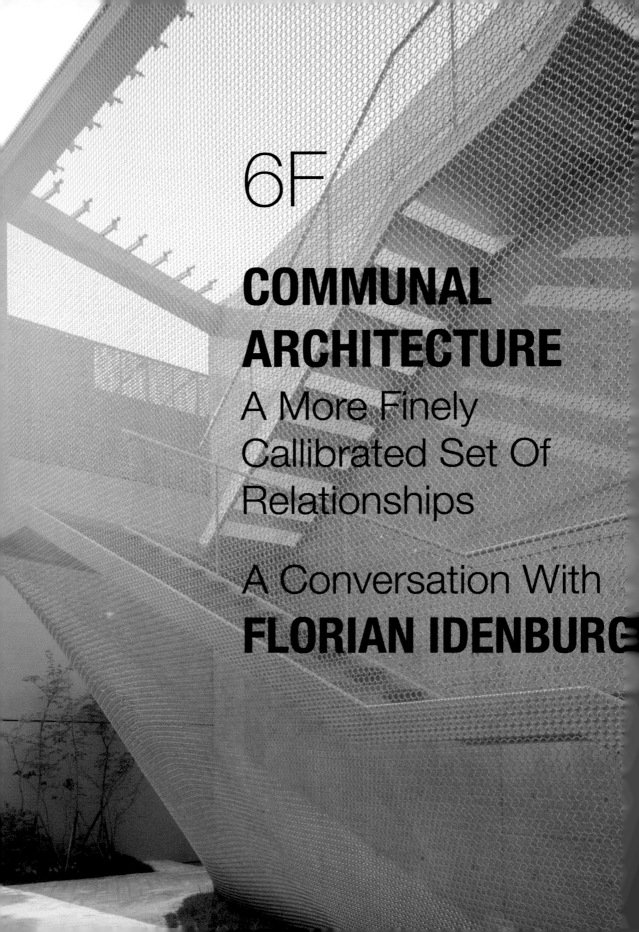

6F

COMMUNAL ARCHITECTURE

A More Finely Callibrated Set Of Relationships

A Conversation With

FLORIAN IDENBURG

6F Communal Architecture

A More Finely Calibrated Set of Relationships,
A Conversation with Florian Idenburg

The following chapter is based on a conversation with Florian Idenburg, cofounder of SO–IL, an internationally renowned architecture firm based in Brooklyn, New York. Idenburg discusses the firm's innovative and multifaceted use of fabric in their projects, from the shrouding mesh of Kukje Gallery to the ephemeral anti-walls in the Logan workspace. Consistent throughout SO–IL's work is a commitment to the exploration of architecture as a tool for innovation and change.

KUKJE GALLERY

Kukje Gallery is one of the more renowned art galleries in Asia, located in the center of a historic district in Seoul, South Korea. The neighborhood where it is located is close to the old palace, where there are many traditional courtyard homes with beautiful detail and refined textures, called hanoks. Kukje is in an historic district and thus three levels of historic approval are required for a building permit, approval from the local neighborhood, from the district, and then from the city. When we were hired to design the project, the client was already in the planning phase of the building, the excavation was under way and there were numerous restrictions on the structure since the site was extremely confined. Still, we essentially started from scratch in designing the gallery within the existing constraints.

The concept for the building's fabric skin builds on the site context itself, within a traditional hanok neighborhood, where the staff of the courts lived. Hanok neighborhoods are comprised of one-story houses, with exquisite detail, craft, and ceramic rooftops. On the left of Figure 6F.1 is a large avenue and on the other side is the ancient palace. Within these two anchors is the neighborhood where the gallery is located. Because this area is such an attractive, walkable part of Seoul, it has been revitalized and is now a popular place for cafes and little galleries, with small stores starting to move in. The three buildings, K1, K2, and K3, all are newly constructed elements of the gallery. K1 is the first building, which grew over time, K2 is the second building, a large box, and K3 is the third building, which SO–IL was asked to design. SO–IL needed to reorient and review the larger master plan and landscape plan to integrate all the buildings into a cohesive whole within the site.

The goal of the client was to create a strong presence within the neighborhood and cement Kukje Gallery's stature within the Korean and Asian art scene.

DOI: 10.4324/9781003138471-16

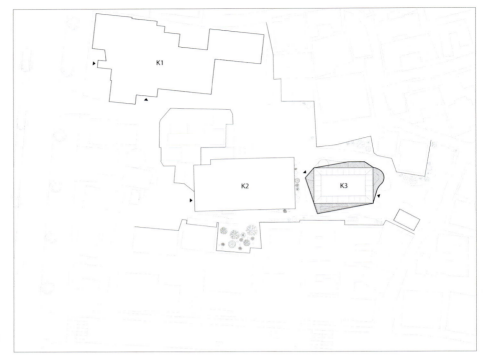

KUKJE GALLERY SITE PLAN
SCALE: 1/400

The gallery organically grew into the neighborhood, and now has evolved into a campus of sorts.

Figure 6F.1 *Kukje Gallery site plan*
Source: SO—IL copyright

The idea of a big white box, a large contemporary art space, was a given from the beginning. We asked the question, how do we situate a very absolute typical white cube into this sensitive, small-scale and refined neighborhood? Intuitively we thought of the idea of wrapping the box with a permanent fog that would literally shroud the box with a skin to soften the hardness of the white cube.

This contextual design objective needed to be juxtaposed onto the client's desire for the largest box possible to house large works of art—think Anish Kapoor—so, our goal was to maintain the size of the building and at the same time lower the reading of the volume within that neighborhood. We were interested in a softer form, which related to the imperfect form of traditional Korean ceramics. Importance was placed on relating to the vernacular surroundings—the challenge was to insert a large modern building into the traditional neighborhood where there is so much detail and craft and attention to texture. We needed to be sensitive to those conditions and mindful of the client's program needs. We explored how to reduce the effect of the height of the building and considered the idea of almost covering the building with a roof, something that falls into its form, that has a certain imperfection to it and appears less massive.

Our ultimate solution was to drape the skin of the building such that it pushes out and falls between forms and results in a feeling that is very similar to the courtyard roofs. To demonstrate this, we literally made a drawing of the

Figure 6F.2 *Kukje
Gallery concept
models*
Source: SO—IL
copyright

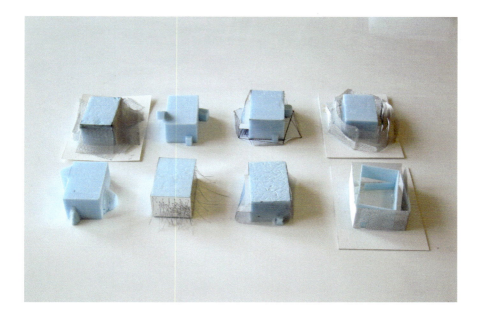

neighborhood that showed all the vernacular roofs and then Kukje's roof that rises up a little bit higher. Based on those diagrams and the narratives, ultimately the project was approved. We brought a conceptual model to our first presentation, and the client said "go ahead and make it." And, of course, we didn't really know what "it" was . . . yet.

A COMMUNAL FAÇADE

Between 2001 and 2006, I worked with SANAA[1] on the Glass Pavilion for The Toledo Museum of Art, where we worked with Petra Blaisse from Inside Outside. On that project, Blaisse shared with me a beautiful chain link sort of fabric, reminiscent of medieval armor, which was both very pliable—it can take on any sort of double curved shape—and also very strong. With Kukje Gallery, we were not interested in constructing a specific shape, we were interested in the drape—the process and how the material falls. I recalled the fabric Blaisse introduced me to years before with the Glass Pavilion and it inspired the design for the Kukje Gallery. The material is a beautiful contradiction between being both very strong and at the same time, being very elastic and soft.

In Figure 6F.4, you can see us experimenting with the way in which this mesh works, with its clear directionality. It is not elastic in two ways, but rather is stiff in one direction and very pliable in the other. This is, in fact, what makes it possible to work with; if it were elastic in two ways, it would not hold its shape, and fall. It is literally the weave itself, the way the rings tie together, that gives the material pliability and at the same time, stiffness. When we knew we wanted to pursue this path, the material studies we undertook became more detailed,

starting with purchased chain link. This allowed us to understand the mechanics of the weave, from which we transitioned to mockups that we fabricated ourselves out of cardboard.

On the left of the image below, you see the chain link at the scale of the body, because it's designed for body attire, rather than building attire. We knew we needed to scale up, to figure out the right scale for this architecture. We didn't want the rings to be too big, because they would become overly graphic, like circles. And yet, we also didn't want the fabric to be too dense, so we had to establish the perfect balance between density and graphics that would set the scale of the ring for this building.

Once we determined the right scale, we knew we needed to engineer the skin. We contacted friend and colleague Mike Ra, from Front, façade engineers. Ra first said we needed to understand the performance expected of the material because at the time there was no knowledge of its use at building the scale. We began testing to determine the structure of the ring, thus gaining understanding

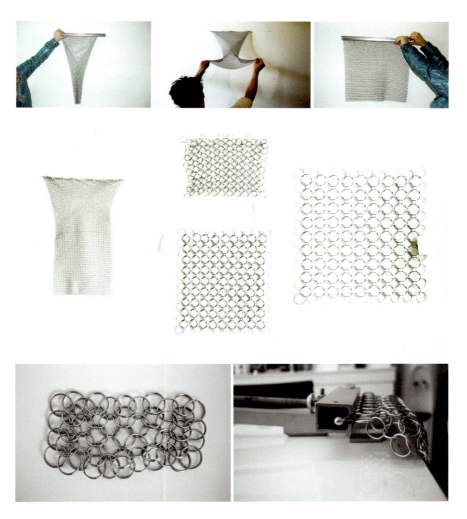

the force within the ring itself. On the larger scale, we started to test the overall fabric, as we had a basic idea of the geometry of how the forces would distribute themselves through the building skin. At the same time, we were doing physical material testing, we simultaneously worked on a digital model of the skin, resulting in an understanding of the geometry of the way the rings come together and how the forces of the fabric fall. Obviously, the rings at the top needed to absorb all the weight of the rings that came below. It was very important that the force was distributed, as the mesh could not hang from the single ring. The material needed to act as a whole, a communal façade, where the skin acted symbiotically together to form a cohesive system.

The engineer dove into the full set of calculations and created a digital model. They asked us to make a physical model to verify their findings and to understand the count of the rings. We bought the largest size of rings on the commercial market, which gave us a certain scale. Based on that scale, we built a model that was three meters by two meters. Once we made this model, we realized we could make the skin seamless by replicating the method used in the model in which the rings were welded together.

At this point, we had the computer model and we had the physical model. Based on that, we thought, okay, we now know enough. But then the big question became, are we going to write this into the specifications for the construction, because there was no product that fit. Realizing the challenges, we decided to try to make it ourselves. We went to AliBaba.com and literally, through many failed attempts, found a manufacturer/welder in the town of Anping, a small town in the middle of China, about six hours from Beijing. After communicating on Skype, the shop sent us samples. We traveled to China and found their workshop, a very small, muddy shop where the brother of the woman we'd been communicating with was welding the rings together by hand, one by one. A small mockup took the shop a month to produce, and we realized that it was going to be impossible to produce what was needed in a single shop. It turned out that the town actually had many metal shops, so we combined multiple shops together and then developed a method of welding where multiple people could work together in a much more systematic way. (We have continued to work with the metal shops in Anping, using this method at a much smaller scale, to make similar ring-based furniture.) The shops each produced large swaths of the welded ring fabric. These were degreased at the local car wash, and then all the welds were checked with quality control. We then tested the swaths in the local yard to confirm they would really work, and they were well received.

When we finally got the mesh to the Kukje Gallery building site in Korea, nobody wanted to install it. We were forced to be creative in our search and ended up working with an installer who worked with fishnets, which share simi- larities in that they cannot be carried from a single point. The installer used his net gear to distribute the loads and fabricated a beam with multiple hooks on the end. This allowed the fabric ring swaths to be quite elastic, with everything acting as a pin connection so the individual components could move freely. The most important thing was that the force needed to find its own path, rather than get stuck somewhere. It was critical that the skin maintain pliability with a lot of flexibility in the way it draped around the corners, as the material was really heavy. We designed a Halfen channel in the concrete structure that the ball connections could slip into. Seams were closed afterwards by welding and the bottom of the fabric was attached to the concrete foundation underneath the ground and backfilled.

An operational challenge was the mundane reality of how to get *between* the fabric and the building shell for cleaning and maintenance. Because the basement is bigger than the building above, we were able to locate a hatch to the basement, which is hidden under the gravel. This allows access into the space between the building and the skin—it's actually very nice to be in between—where you are essentially inhabiting the poche.

The process of creating the pattern for the fabric was quite interesting. If we had needed to calculate exactly how the fabric would fall and make it like a bespoke pattern in fashion, it would have been too much. Instead, we roughly calculated how

the mesh would fall, attached it, and then trimmed off the excess, which was usually 20–30 centimeters. We considered perfectly calculating how the drape would fall and then optimizing it computationally, but in the end, it was easier to do it like this. Being able to respond on site allowed for more tolerance, acknowledging the reality of how things sometimes go differently than expected.

PROCESS AND TRUST

Our office made the model and showed it to the client, who said "How are you going to make it"? In the beginning, we didn't know. We decided to supply the metal fabric skin ourselves, in collaboration with Mike Ra, from Front. We needed to estimate how much the material and fabrication was going to cost. It ended up being about $450,000, which was quite reasonable, and the modest cost was due to the fact that we made it ourselves—with nobody in between—literally going into China to the workshops and paying the fabricators directly. Another interesting development in the process what that because the client was accustomed to moving large artwork, they were able to organize their own shipping, so for them it was very easy to ship and arrange for these big pieces of metal ring fabric. The project was only possible, I think, because we did it like this. It takes a lot of confidence for a client to just say "okay, sure, go ahead—just make it." Our client was perhaps more open to this process because she was used to working with artists who often have an idea but need money to realize it. It takes a client with a certain attitude and belief that something powerful will emerge, and a confidence in the architect to make it happen. I think it was really because of the vision and understanding of the client, who gave us some room and believed in the process, that the project was successful. There was a tremendous amount of trust.

At the time of the Kukje, I was teaching at the Harvard Graduate School of Design on Tuesdays and Thursdays. On Thursday night I would land in La Guardia

Figure 6F.7 *Kukje Gallery completed*
Source: SO—IL copyright

Figure 6F.8 *Heavy and light applications of fabric in LOGAN* Source: SO—IL copyright

and take a car to JFK. I would fly to Korea, be on site Saturday and Sunday, and fly back to Boston on Monday. I did that almost every other week for two years. There's no way to do this other than just being there. Looking back, it was pretty demanding.

THE EVOLUTION OF THE USE OF FABRIC IN SO–IL

Fabric as an idea for building material has evolved in our practice. Because we didn't want to drape every building with chain link, we have thought more about the way in which fabric can be used in different applications, like fabric formed concrete or in place of traditional interior walls. Fabric formwork requires heavy computations and integration of the fabric's material qualities, which you must have certainty about. You need to know the weave and the behavior of the fabric under pressure and the predictability of the elasticity of the weave for instance, so you can anticipate what will occur when you fill it with concrete. We have worked on buildings using this method but have run into insurmountable roadblocks when we tried to find builders in the U.S. because the construction industry is so regulated by insurance companies. In Korea you can experiment more, and builders are generally quite good with fabric formwork.

We have also explored fabrics in interior spaces as well. On an interior project for Logan, a bi-coastal production company, we channeled installation artist, Robert Irwin, with fabric walls, using a combination of translucent lightweight walls and heavy felt walls. This constantly changing work setting required very few personalized work stations and room, but a high level of flexibility. Building on Logan's dynamic working model, we developed a flexible working system that allows fluctuating staff while creating an environment that fosters collaboration and collectivity. The Logan project was primarily not about solid walls, but the idea of realms, which suggests that we are connected at different levels. Logan is a good example of a space where people work together, but are all freelancers, and so are not part of one community, and are not even always working on the same project. The main question with this project was: at what level do you want to show *the other* or allow for *the other* to be legible?

MESH AND CONNECTIVITY

Our first project was the winning design for the MoMA PS1 Young Architects Program[2] installation. In some ways it's really a great metaphor for how our office works. The installation is made from a collapsible fabric mesh, bungee cords, and surf mast bases. The project looks at the cartesian grid, channeling ideas of modernism and modernity and the idea of how a structure can govern. But with PS1, the structure is pliable, it is weak, and it could collapse—everyone is jointly responsible for its stability. The only way the installation could be built was collectively, because one component could not be held up without the other. We have pictures of 20 people holding up a pole while other people are tying it together—and obviously it collapsed a bunch of times. This is the idea that we are trying and testing as an office: that we allow things to collapse and fall apart and embrace that idea rather than the idea of a hierarchical office where nobody is allowed to fail and it is governed by fear.

My work with SANAA, and the way Sejima ran the office, had a big impact on the way I think. She gave everybody a sense of ownership of the work by allowing people to participate in the process. And so, in our office we too tend to give people a lot of freedom in the beginning of the design process. We say we don't know, because we ourselves also need to go down an undefined path. The ability to accept input during the process and the effect this has on the outcome is very important for us. We don't know what the pathway will be. We like to work with people who are quite serious and are interested in figuring

Figure 6F.9 *Pole Dance in use at PS1* Source: SO—IL copyright

Figure 6F.10 *Breathe MINI Living models and steel structural diagram*
Source: SO—IL copyright

things out, people who are not afraid to fail, but also not afraid to tell you that things don't work.

BREATHE MINI LIVING

For this project, we were approached by Mini, the car company, to participate in their competition. Mini realized that they must build their knowledge around not just making cars but also trying to figure out the people who buy their cars currently. Mini has been really trying to win the heart of a younger generation that likes design, redefining itself more as a lifestyle brand rather than a car company. And so, Breathe MINI Living is based on the premise of how well-designed small things for people who like to be in the city could translate into a living concept. Mini began the conversation by reaching out to an audience that thinks about living small and living in a dense urban setting and asked SO–IL to develop a sketch and a concept.

We first needed to address the inherent challenge of working with a car company, so our first move was to design a skin that cleans out the toxins that the car actually produces. The other concept we explored was the question of small, light and nomadic, questioning the idea of mobility itself and asking what if your house can be with you forever, more like a coat. So, Breath Mini Living is a structure and a coat, a collection of frames that fits into a shipping container that can be stacked up, and then you just put on your coat that can adapt depending on where you are in the world. This house was about a connection with the city, an architecture that heightens your awareness of where you are in the world, because we're all on our screens continuously, with no idea where we are anymore. And so we looked at how architecture can be an instrument to help us connect. This first concept was meant to be a provocation to an extent, because it is not really climatized or even watertight. It was taking the idea of porosity and openness to an extreme.

In Figure 6F.10 you can see the steel structure that fits within the shipping containers like puzzle pieces. We also used a Japanese fabric that literally absorbs the toxins in the air so that the dirty toxins stay attached to the skin,

Figure 6F.11 *Breathe MINI Living interior and exterior*
Source: SO—IL copyright

which the rain can wash away. The house contains a living room, dining room, and a shared room with two sleeping areas, along with a larger room with the bathroom, and finally the garden that catches the rainwater which is then used in the building itself.

There are two layers of fabric: an inner layer for privacy which is elastic and double curved and then the outer fabric layer, which is patterned through a computer model, prefabricated, and then stitched and grommeted together. We developed the exterior fabric with a sailmaker. We wanted the users and the onlookers to be aware of others within this space, so at night it lights up and you see the second layer inside of the first layer. There are two types of fabric, one stretches so you can tuck and fit it, and the other is not elastic. This means you need to know the pattern beforehand. Stretchable fabrics don't work as well on the exterior because they are very sensitive to UV light and lose their elasticity and start to become weak over time.

This is why exterior fabrics need to be made out of stiff materials that hold their form, which is what makes them so fascinating. The Kukje Gallery fabric is elastic in one direction, but stiff because it's made of metal. The elasticity doesn't come out of the material itself; it comes out of the geometry of the rings when formed together, and that is what I find really exciting: you can make elastic forms with a solid material.

You can think about fabric in a holistic sense in terms of how fabric contributes to flexibility and adaptability in architecture resilience. Everything is a fabric to an extent. In any material there's something and there's nothing. Even if you look at the structure of atoms, there is solid and there is void. So, in some way, everything is a mesh. The question we deal with is: at what scale do we apply the mesh? If we only decide as architects where there's something and where there's nothing, then our job is to figure out at what scale the "something" is the most productive.

We have used this idea of fabric at the scale of the city and the scale of building. When you think about porosity, the question is how much do you need the surfaces that you introduced to allow things to pass through them? In general, I would say that idea of thinking through fabrics is found in all of our work to an extent. Sometimes it's air that has to move through, and sometimes it's people that have to move through.

On a more philosophical level, glass was one of the products that modernity originally suggested as the material of total transparency and connectivity. This has changed with the advent of our digital total connectedness, which has not created a universally connected humankind a cohesive field, but instead many more realms. Glass suggests that every connection is equal, but we've become much more precise in our levels of connectivity. Now we think of connectivity as a gradient. Digital culture has made us much more skilled in the ways we are connected, which now involves more layers. And that idea of layering, rather than total connectivity, has shifted for us. This is an example of how we have been thinking about fabrics both metaphorically and literally, as a way to work on more finely calibrated sets of relationships.

Project Information:

Chapter: Communal Architecture: A More Finely Calibrated Set of Relationships
Project Lead: Florian Idenburg, SO–IL
Project Location: Seoul, South Korea; Milan, Italy; New York, New York
Client: Various
Awards: Kukje Gallery, Design of The Year, Design Museum London, 2012
Innovation By Design Awards, Fast Company, 2012
AIA New York Design Award, 2011

NOTES

1. SANAA, Architecture office based in Japan, co-founded by Kazuyo Sejima and Ryue Nishizawa.
2. MoMA PS1 Young Architects Program "The Young Architects Program founded by MoMA and MoMA PS1 is committed to offering emerging architectural talent the opportunity to design and present innovative projects, challenging each year's winners to develop original designs for a temporary, outdoor installation at MoMA PS1 that provides respite with shade, seating, and water." Moma.org

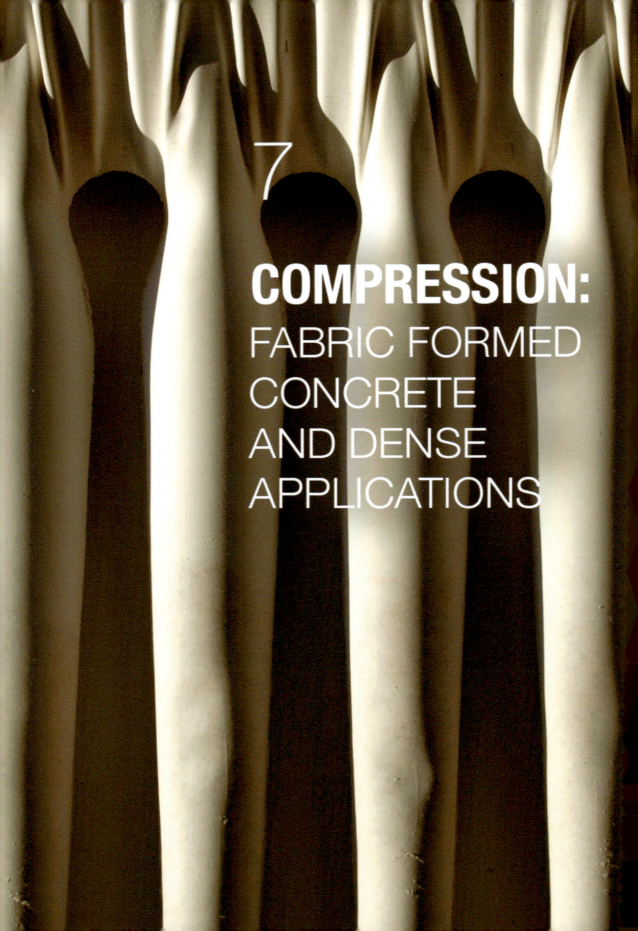

7

COMPRESSION:
FABRIC FORMED CONCRETE AND DENSE APPLICATIONS

ACADEMIC INQUIRY

7A

SPACER FABRIC PAVILION
Advanced 3D Textile
Applications in
Architecture

JOHANNA BEUSCHE
and CLAUDIA LÜLIN

7A Spacer Fabric_Pavilion—Advanced 3D Textile Applications in Architecture

Johanna Beuscher and Claudia Lüling

The future of the building industry will be shaped by resource-saving, lightweight concepts. These textile-based constructions offer new and future-oriented options for lightweight, material-efficient and equally highly functional construction elements. The focus is on 3D textiles and in particular spacer textiles: materials assembly that consist of two cover layers that are joined by pile yarns in an industrial weaving or knitting process. These materials and methods are not altogether new and are previously known in the automotive industry as breathable mattress or seat covers. Thanks to their sandwich-like structure these special textiles can also play a special role in the field of future construction. Research into the development of textile-based components has accordingly been taking place at the faculty of architecture Frankfurt University of Applied Sciences for some time now. The research is accompanied by courses in which students in design- and process-oriented seminars go beyond the use of classical materials and techniques such as wood, steel and concrete construction to explore ideas and designs for the development of new materials and components in lightweight construction.

SPACER FABRIC_PAVILION

In the summer semester of 2015, a group of master's students had the opportunity to realise a lightweight pavilion made of partially foamed spacer textiles as part of a design seminar. Under the generic term "FabricFoam©" the task was to combine two materials that the course participants were previously familiar with from completely different contexts: textiles and foams. The design seminar was tasked with combining 3D spacer textiles with the incorporation of self-curing foams to develop new structural components and construction systems, as well as with the investigation of their load-bearing capacity, usability and design options. With its modular dome construction, the resulting experimental building exemplifies the future possibilities of construction with 3D textiles.[1]

Within one semester, a summer pavilion was designed and built from concept to realisation using foamed spacer textiles. A simple and fast manufacturing process and on-site textile foaming was included in the design process. The design, form-finding and construction process was integrated and developed in parallel to allow a first construction attempt for the student team in the shortest possible time. The design process therefore included numerous analogue simulations of the material

DOI: 10.4324/9781003138471-19

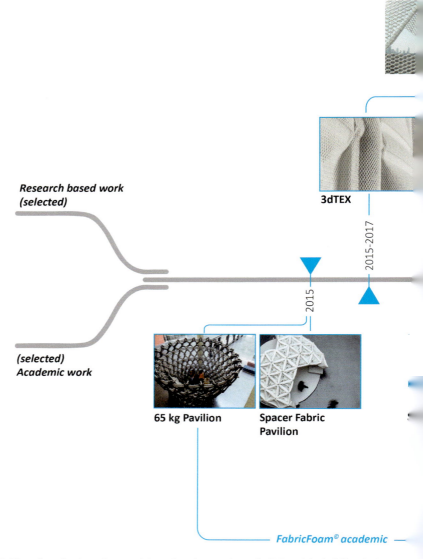

Figure 7A.1 *Map of academic and research-based work towards textile lightweight building design at Frankfurt UAS*
Source: © Johanna Beuscher

ReFaTEX
transparent, translucent
facade elements

am® research

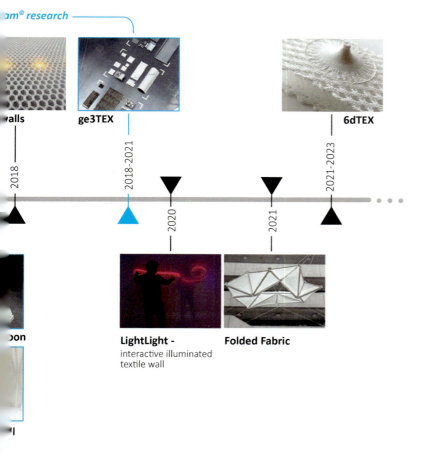

valls   ge3TEX   6dTEX

2018   2018-2021   2021-2023

2020   2021

LightLight -   Folded Fabric
interactive illuminated
textile wall

oon

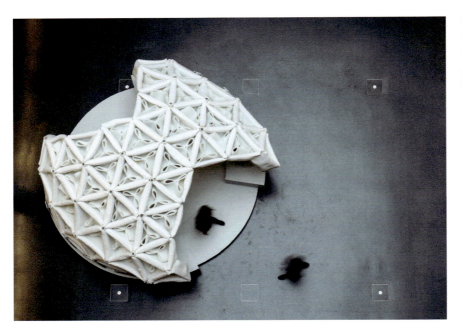

Figure 7A.2 *Spacer Fabric_Pavilion, exterior view from the top*
Source: © Christoph Lison

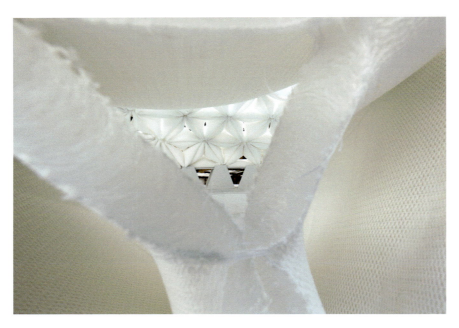

Figure 7A.3 *Spacer Fabric_Pavilion, interior view*
Source: © Christoph Lison

in models, as well as tests in the handling of foam and textiles in order to explore the material properties and workflows in detail. Based on these characteristics, the task was to develop shapes that would be aesthetically pleasing, sustainable and feasible under the given experimental conditions. In addition to the initially entirely unknown 3D spacer textiles, foams were already familiar to great group from their use in the construction industry, but they differed greatly in their properties, such as their final strength, composition and environmental compatibility. Finally, a suitable self-curing polyurethane foam was used, which was readily available, promised sufficient strength in terms of design and, due to a large expansion capacity, seemed suitable for filling cavities in the textile. In contrast to the use of conventional construction materials, the focus initially was on gaining in-depth knowledge of the individual textile and foam systems, their material-dependent behaviour and their design potential when combined. At the same time, this had to be repeatedly checked at the design level and in the spatial context of a pavilion structure. Since the combination of textile and foam is a new composite system, it was not possible to use characteristic values for load-bearing capacity (compressive strength, tensile strength, deflection); instead, different load-bearing systems were tested in experimental trials and scales using mockups.

Methodically, the seminar was structured in such a way that, at the beginning, research was conducted on topics such as experimental construction, different textile fibres and production techniques such as knitting, weaving or warp knitting, in order to bring the basic findings on textile processes and the most interesting innovations in textile construction research and development to the group as input for all the participants via short presentations. Field trips to the Institute for Computational Design and Construction at the University of Stuttgart (ICD), the German Institutes of Textile and Fiber Research and the "Techtextil" international trade fair also served to provide an introduction to the subject. At the same time, each of the students developed their own design concepts for the pavilion during the first half of the semester and presented them regularly. For form-finding purposes, there was a deliberate shift away from thinking about tent-like constructions and Frei Otto's imposing, wide-span membrane roofs from the 1970s, in order to develop textile structures that are both tension- and compression-resistant thanks to the foam-fibre combination. Soon, three typologies emerged from 15 design concepts among the foamed support structures: folding, gridshell and modular structures. These were further investigated in three small teams who then started weeks of intensive hands-on testing with small mockups, picking favourites within the group and then accumulating their design ideas into one proposal per category. At this point most students would see aspects of their work represented and were eager to contribute, while all three teams developed a slight sense of competition against each other. Weekly presentations and discussions with the entire studio group were held to compare aspects of feasibility and structural integrity and see how special attributes of spacerfabrics such as translucency, for example, could be brought to the forefront. Designs were altered, compared and voted on until there was a common sense of understanding within each team. By midterm the seminar group decided after a long and intense debate by majority vote to realise Marie Vogel's module structure as a prototype on a 1:1 scale.

During the following test and optimisation phase, numerous details were developed for joining the individual parts, further experience was gained from the material behaviour and the necessary production steps for the construction of the pavilion were clarified. A 30-mm-thick spacer fabric with polyester cover layers was used. The connecting threads, so-called "pile threads", are polyester monofilaments with recovery behaviour, which also gives the textile stiffness despite some elasticity. Individual teams at different workstations cut open pyramid-shaped modules from them according to templates, folded them, sewed them together in the middle and turned them inside out. Similar to a hat, this gives them additional stability. The modules were joined together by foaming defined cavities between the modules in the spacer textile. The individual parts of the pavilion finally fitted together during erection due to the tapered nature of the discrete elements to form a dome. The foamed material combination is stable, heat-insulating, sound-absorbing and translucent and optimally combines constructive as well as haptic properties. Placed on a wooden base, a space is created that is soft, airy and translucent, and which has seating for meeting, lingering and celebrating.

The pavilion, with a diameter of five metres and a height of three metres, documented not only as an initial test the spatial qualities but also the stability of the new FabricFoam© composite material, and was actively used by students and passers-by on the campus of Frankfurt University for several weeks. The experimental building also gained recognition beyond the borders of the university by professionals in the construction and textile industry, and the team's work was recognised by several press publications[2,3] and awards[4,5].

FABRICFOAM© FURNITURE: SPACER FABRIC_SHELL AND SPACER FABRIC_COCOON

In the 2015/2016 winter semester, a smaller group of students investigated the other alternative load-bearing principles—"shell" and "folding". The work continued to be predominantly analogue without the use of digital models to simulate material and load-bearing behaviour; physical models made of paper and textile as

Figure 7A.4
Assembly of all modules flat on the ground, before pulling it up into final shape.
Source: © Frankfurt UAS

well as small 1:1 mockups were used to form-find and design the structural geometries. Thus, as a supplement to the pavilion structure, two experimental pieces of lounge furniture were created, each of which uses the principle of folding or a shell structure to further explore the potential of the composite material. The folded structure was realised using manually-made channels in the textile, which were placed on a shaping formwork and foamed out. The resulting spacer-textile cocoon is self-supporting and surrounds a stable lying surface, which is held by climbing ropes. The entire element can move freely in space, and provides a place on which to relax and explore the textile surfaces. The second piece of lounge furniture explores the effectiveness of the composite material as a shell structure and covers a lounge seat for 1–2 people. The textile is traversed by diamond-shaped, machine-prepared channels which, when filled with foam, form a lattice-shell supporting structure. Following the catenary principle, the textile was foamed in a hanging position and turned over after curing, or when the load-bearing capacity of the arch form was reached. Placed on an ergonomically shaped, slightly swinging seat, the shell allows the user to retreat into an acoustically-muted atmosphere and is ideal for relaxation. The created structures inspired further reflection: First, to think about 3D, complex textile geometries in which the elastic and rigid areas in the textile are already defined during production, so that the textile is deformed in a controlled manner on interaction and when the foam is introduced. The polyurethane (PU) foams, used in combination with polyester textiles, could be ideally used here for the rapid development of load-bearing, aesthetic shapes and components under workshop conditions, as they were easy to obtain or provided through sponsorship. Second, the open questions regarding the environmental compatibility and recyclability of the polyester/polyurethane material composite initially led to more concrete material research into alternative foams and fibres, both inorganic and organic in origin. The search revealed that both spacer textiles and foams can alternatively be created from more sustainable polymeric or mineral materials to open up a wide

Figure 7A.5
SpacerFabric_Cocoon, partially foamed folded structure from spacerfabric Left: Exterior view, Left: Interior view Frankfurt.
Source: © Christoph Lison

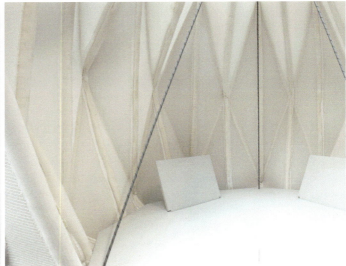

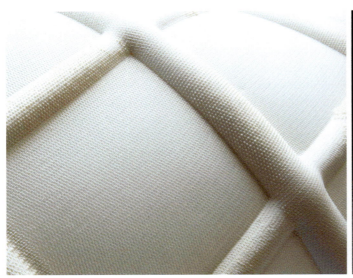 

range of applications when combined. This further development of novel material combinations and manufacturing methods for opaque, self-supporting components made of foam and textile was subsequently advanced by the "Textile Lightweight Construction" research group.

Figure 7A.6
SpacerFabric_Shell, experimental gridshell from spacerfabric with foamed cavities.
Source: © Christoph Lison

APPLIED RESEARCH TOWARDS TEXTILE LIGHTWEIGHT BUILDING DESIGN

Technical textiles, with their great potential for lightweight construction, are increasingly coming into focus as part of the construction industry's search for alternatives to conventional construction materials. As exemplified by the "Knit Candela" project[6] by Block Research Group at Eidgenössische Technische Hochschule (ETH) Zurich, which transported premanufactured custom knitware for a lightweight concrete shell pavilion to the site via two suitcases, technical textiles can be transported as individual semi-finished parts with low volumes and small ecological footprints and used directly on site without extra formwork for very lightweight, free-formed structures. Also in Frankfurt, a team of researchers, led by Prof. Claudia Lüling, has worked intensively for several years on the development of textile, partly free-formed lightweight elements. The aim is to develop textile semi-finished elements from 3D textiles that receive their final finish on site. Together with textile and fibre specialists and numerous partners from industry and research, application-oriented research is carried out, for example in the combination of textiles and foams,[7] to find solutions for opaque as well as translucent, movable wall and roof elements or solar protection elements. The research serves the development of new material concepts and the production of prototypes, which are closely interlinked with the teaching in design and in-depth seminars, as the implementation of the SpacerFabric Pavilion shows. What is interesting about textiles and foams is that both are not materials but technologies. Both technologies, however, allow very different materialisations and both are techniques that can be used to process a wide variety of materials.

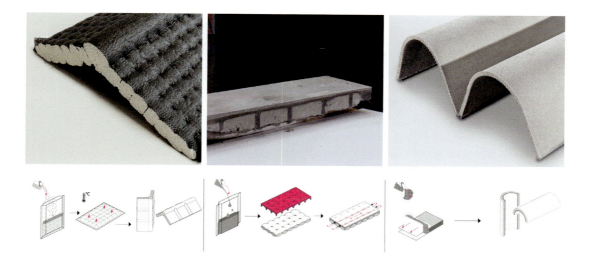

Figure 7A.7 *Top, left to right: ge3TEX — composite building components from recycled PET, basalt fibre with cement foam and grass fire with expanded glass. Bottom, left to right: Filling technologies for particle foam, foamed concrete and expanded glass granulate.* Source: © Christoph Lison

Until now, the two technologies have been considered separately. For the first time, the Textile Lightweight Construction Research Group is showing how a wide variety of composite options are conceivable, depending on functional requirements and sustainability criteria. Thus, complex 3D textiles, or spacer textiles, are in principle based on traditional techniques of weaving or knitting, just like single-layer textiles, and in their behaviour are more or less stretchable. In addition, spacer textiles have great potential for new architectural building applications due to their spatial structure and flexibly adjustable parameters such as the material thickness, density of the pile yarn geometry, nature of the cover layers and elasticity. Foamed materials, on the other hand, can have gradually different densities and porosities as a filling and have very different expansion and filling behaviour depending on the choice of material. Like the fibre material used to make the textile, the used foam can also be of mineral or polymer origin. In the "3dTEX" research project in Frankfurt, by combining both process technologies, spacer textiles were for the first time successfully developed into tension- and pressure-resistant as well as insulating composite components for the building envelope. In addition to the student experimental buildings, the research project showed that it is possible to develop highly functional single- and double-layer wall elements made of foamed spacer textiles with an integrated rear ventilation layer and that 3D textiles can be transformed into high-quality wall elements.

SUSTAINABLE COMPONENTS MADE OF TEXTILES AND FOAM

Globally, the construction industry is one of the main causes of our enormous, climate-damaging consumption of resources and energy. According to the UN Climate Report 2020,[8] approximately 40 per cent of greenhouse gas emissions are caused by the construction and operation of buildings. Resource-saving lightweight construction will therefore be part of an urgently needed building turnaround that counteracts these effects. It will encompass optimised and form-active support structures in order to produce correspondingly lightweight components using a minimum of materials while maintaining high efficiency. If sustainable manufacturing processes and recyclable materials are used, this represents a significant contribution to the energy transition. In the "ge3TEX" research project[9] at Frankfurt UAS, the next step was therefore to improve the material composite of textiles and foams and to investigate three recyclable, single-origin composite materials. The focus was on combinations of basalt fibres and foamed concrete, glass fibres and expanded glass, as well as PET fibres and PET foams.

In addition to the mineral, non-combustible material combinations, the investigation of PET fabric and PET particle foam was of high interest for the following reasons: The plastic used, PET, belongs to the polyester group and is used today in large quantities in the production of bottles, food packaging and films. As a thermoplastic, PET can be moulded under heat, remelted accordingly and returned to the cycle as granules. Thanks to optimised sorting and recycling processes, recycled PET in the form of flakes or granules is also increasingly being used as the starting material for fibres and foams. To produce technical textiles, thin films, and so on, are made from this so-called r-PET, cut into fine tapes and then woven to create a spacer fabric. A new type of PET particle foam was used as the foam filling for the textile which expands like popcorn when exposed to heat and more than doubles its volume. This industry innovation in sustainable particle foams was originally designed to be foamed within complex moulding tools and to supply foam cores that can be used directly and do not require any further processing by cutting or milling. At Frankfurt UAS the material behaviour of the particles within a textile former was investigated for the first time. For this purpose, the textile was filled with loose foam beads, 3–4 mm in size, and closed with a seam. Thermal reaction in the oven was then used to cause strong expansion and densification of the foam beads and to achieve bonding to the textile shell. In cooperation with the manufacturer of the PET beads and tapes, the formulation and production steps were further developed in an iterative process and optimised to such an extent that a hard, stable and load-bearing lightweight panel made of foam and textile could finally be produced from an initially loose filling. It was shown that, in addition to panel components, form-active, material-saving rib structures and folds can be foamed in a single process step. With appropriate prefabrication of the textile, there is high potential for programmable, formwork-free self-deformations. Made from 100 per cent recycled PET, the textile and foam component reduce the use of finite resources such as petroleum. At the end of its useful life, it can be shredded and returned to the cycle in its entirety via proportional recycling or downcycling, for example, as injection moulded parts.

In total, one composite component was developed for each of the three material classes of the ge3TEX research project and these were compared at the end. Accordingly, the associated manufacturing processes have been optimised so that foam and textile ideally complement each other in terms of load transfer, insulation and fire protection. For this purpose, the completely different filling methods of the more liquid foamed concrete, the mortar-like expanded glass mixture and the post-expanding PET particle foam were investigated. In addition, the textile geometries of the 3D textiles were further developed, including for the first time 3D basalt textiles.

The textile as a lost formwork has a decisive form-giving effect. It serves as an outer shell for weather protection as well as for the load transfer of tensile forces and the optimisation of shear force transmission. The project followed a holistic design approach: the overall use of materials is reduced, a maximum of functionality is achieved with a minimum of material, the material comes mostly from recycling cycles and the components are single-origin and are to be recycled again. In a cross-comparison, the PET components have the highest recyclability at the same time as being the lightest, while the mineral components made of glass and concrete are in return non-combustible and generate lower CO_2 equivalents but are recyclable to different degrees. For all components, downstream material consumption, for example, through formwork and construction waste, is also reduced during manufacturing. In addition, production directly on site can reduce transport volumes considerably. The materialisation of the components, in this case their internal structural fabric as well as their external form, results in a textile surface that aesthetically reflects the functionality of the components.[10]

REVERSIBLY FOLDABLE ENERGETIC 3D TEXTILES FOR SOLAR PROTECTION

In addition to opaque, self-supporting components for walls and roofs, spacer textiles also have a wide range of applications on facades. The "ReFaTex" research project[11] therefore investigated light, insulating and stable solar protection facade elements whose movement mechanisms are defined via the textile structure and which are already integrated into the textile. Here, the textile components can contribute to the control of daylight incidence as well as to insulation against overheating. Their material thickness is adjustable and the programmable size of the surface perforation and elasticity offers many possibilities for functional design, so that their appearance can in some areas vary from opaque through translucent to transparent. Through movements within the 3D structure such as bending, compressing, stretching or folding, the elements can be controlled and structured depending on the incidence of daylight. If, for example, the two opposing cover layers of a spacer fabric are moved in opposite directions and parallel to each other, their overlap changes so that more or less light penetrates the fabric and spaces behind receive more or less diffuse daylight incidence. These movement mechanisms of the 3D textiles were investigated on the macro level within the textile and with a view to the entire solar protection element, and in the medium term could function mechanically, electrically, pneumatically or even adaptively. In addition, it is possible to integrate light- and heat-conducting fibres. In this project, robust and low-maintenance product ideas were developed that temporarily reduce the energy loss of the building envelope, but at the same time allow glare-free solar radiation when unfolded or open.

Currently, the "6dTEX" research project is investigating the extent to which 3D textile structures can also be supplemented and stabilised using additive 3D printing processes independent of foaming. The aim is to develop new lightweight composite materials combining two manufacturing processes and to receive single-variety composites. The challenge lies in particular in printing the elastic sandwich structures of spacer textiles and the composite behaviour between the textile and the printed material. Insights into prefabricated semi-finished parts or self-supporting secondary components in the construction industry are expected, including associated joining options. The components can optionally be rigid or flexible, opaque or translucent, manufactured to fit over a large surface area or can also be stretchable and correspondingly tolerant. The interdisciplinary linking of different key industries,

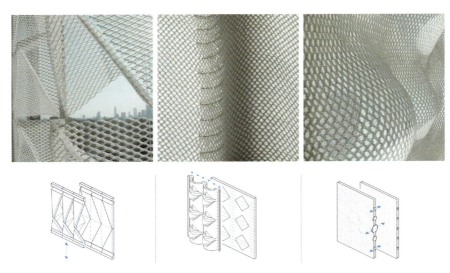

Figure 7A.8 *Top: ReFaTex—solar shading devices from warp-knitted spacerfabrics. Bottom: Folding, bending and stretching strategies to improve daylight control*
Source: © Frankfurt UAS

such as the industrial application of 3D printing technologies and mechanical engineering for highly specialised textile machines, holds enormous potential for the construction industry and can make a decisive contribution to circular construction.

SpacerFabric Pavilion was the initial design-build project and therefore ideal testing-grounds for lightweight structures made from spacerfabric. Since then, a wide range of applications within the scope of architecture and lightweight building elements was researched and demonstrated. Besides putting the capacity of textiles for freeform design to the test, each of the following projects also looked into specific aspects such as optimising material choices towards circularity, finding insulating solutions, solar shading and light-transmission mechanisms or combining 3D-printing with textile technologies in order to find new options for skeleton construction in the future.

Project Information:

Chapter: SpacerFabric Pavilion

Professor/Project Lead: Prof. Claudia Lüling

University/Organization: Frankfurt University of Applied Sciences, Faculty of Architecture • Civil Engineering • Geomatics

Students: Lena Aust, Johanna Beuscher, Sascha Biehl, Marianna Cicala, Jasmin Dittmann, Katarina Gregurevic, Michele Haas, Edda Krücke, Nina Lüer, Natalie Micheev, Ismena Micorek, Maria Simlesa, Chiara Sotgia, Marie Vogel, Alexandra Zgodzinski, Isabella Cursio

Project Location: Frankfurt am Main, Germany

Material Donations: Essedea GmbH & Co. KG

Awards: materialPREIS 2017, Study and Vision category; Competitionline Campus Award 2016, Prize for Innovation

Project Studio Timeline: Design and Fabrication of SpacerFabricPavilion

Introduction and impromptu design task:	1 Week
Precedent research and presentations:	1 Week
Field Trip:	1 Week

Material Exploration and initial designs:	5 Weeks
Field Trip, midterm review with decision about final design:	1 Week
Material Testing, Mock-Ups 1:1:	2 Weeks
Fabrication:	5 Weeks
Total:	16 Weeks

ACKNOWLEDGEMENTS

Research on projects "3dTEX", "ge3TEX" and "6dTEX" in this article is supported by Forschungsinitiative Zukunft Bau, funded by the Federal Ministry of Living, Urban Development and Building (BMWSB), Germany. "ReFaTex" was supported by "IFOFO funding, State Chancellery of Hessen, Germany. The authors would like to express their utmost gratitude towards all partners, colleagues and students for their support, valuable input, enthusiasm and helping hands.

PROJECT RESEARCH PARTNER

Deutsche Institute für Textil und Faserforschung Denkendorf, ITA—Institut für Textiltechnik of RWTH Aachen University, Institute of Structural Mechanics and Design TU Darmstadt

FOR MORE INFO VISIT

Our website: www.fabricfoam.de
Video on ge3TEX: https://bit.ly/FabricFoam

NOTES

1. Sauer, C., Stoll, M., Waldhör, F.E., Schneider, M. *Architectures of Weaving: From Fibers and Yarns to Scaffolds and Skins*, pp. 160–163 (2022), 1. Aufl., JOVIS.
2. Beuscher, J., Biehl, S. "Spacer Fabric", (10/2016), Zeitschrift AIT, pp. 64–68.
3. "Innovationen aus der Uni", (4–6/2016), Competition Ausgabe, p. 7.
4. Award for SpacerFabric Cocoon and SpacerFabric Shell: Famab New Talents Award 2017, Finalist.
5. Awards SpacerFabric Pavilion: Material PREIS 2017, Study and Vision Category; Competitionline Campus Award 2016, Prize for Innovation.
6. Popescu, Mariana, et al.: Structural Design, Digital Fabrication and Construction of the Cable-net and Knitted Formwork of the KnitCandela Concrete Shell, *Structures*, Volume 31, pp. 1287–1299 (2021).
7. Lüling, C., Richter, I.: Architecture Fully Fashioned—Exploration of Foamed Spacer Fabrics for Textile Based Building Skins. *Journal of Facade Design and* Engineering, Volume 5, pp. 77–92 (2017) https://doi.org/10.7480/jfde.2017.1.1526.
8. United Nations Environment Programme. 2020 Global Status Report for Buildings and Construction: Towards a Zero-emission. *Efficient and Resilient Buildings and Construction Sector*, p. 20 (2020).
9. Lüling, C., Rucker-Gramm, P., Weilandt, A., Beuscher, J., Nagel, D., Schneider, J., Maier, A., Bauder, H.-J., Weimer, T.: Ge3TEX-Multifunctional Monomaterials Made from Foamed Glass-, Basalt- or PET-based 3D Textiles. *Powerskin Conference Proceedings*, pp. 37–51 (2021), www.powerskin.org.
10. Lüling, C., Rucker-Gramm, P., Weilandt, A. et al.: Advanced 3D Textile Applications for the Building Envelope. *Applied Composite Materials*, pp. 1–14 (2021). http://doi.org/10.1007/s10443-021-09941-8.
11. Lüling, C., Beuscher, J.: 4dTEX—Exploration of Movement Mechanisms for 3D-Textiles Used as Solar Shading Devices. *Powerskin Conference Proceedings*, pp. 159–172 (2019).

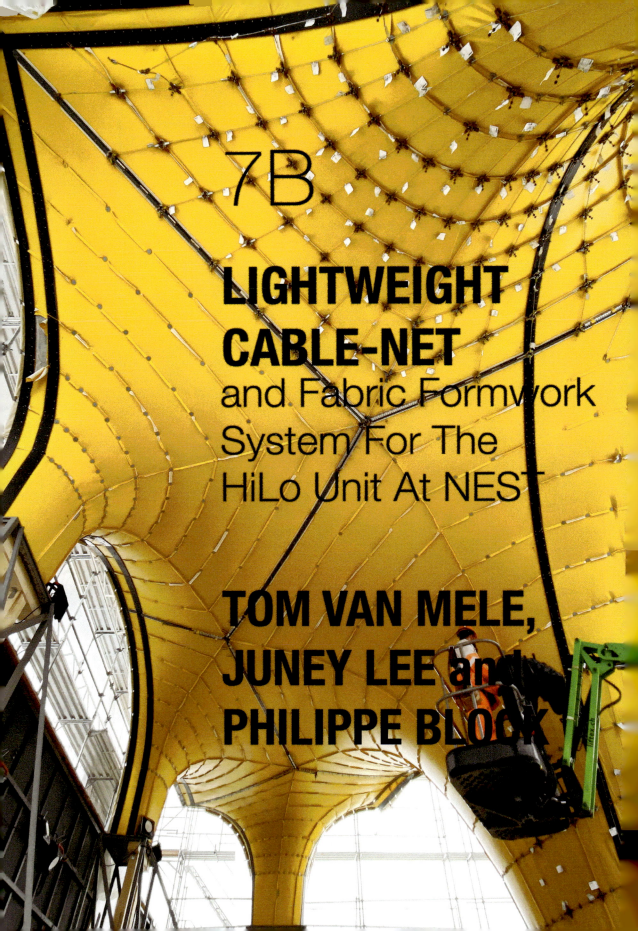

7B

LIGHTWEIGHT CABLE-NET
and Fabric Formwork
System For The
HiLo Unit At NEST

TOM VAN MELE,
JUNEY LEE and
PHILIPPE BLOCK

7B Lightweight Cable-net and Fabric Formwork System for the HiLo Unit at NEST

Tom Van Mele, Juney Lee and Philippe Block

INTRODUCTION

The HiLo research and innovation unit for the Next Evolution in Sustainable Building Technologies (NEST) platform at Empa in Dübendorf, Switzerland, demonstrates how High (Hi) performance can be achieved with Low (Lo) embodied and operational emissions by combining lightweight concrete structures with novel fabrication and construction methods, and integrated and adaptive building systems. The doubly-curved concrete roof of the HiLo unit, spanning an area of 7.85 m by 17.20 m, was realized with a lightweight and reusable cable-net and fabric formwork system. Such innovation in construction allows the reintroduction of efficient, doubly-curved thin shell structures without the typically associated high labor, time, and resource investments. The unit serves as a two-story collaborative and flexible workspace with two closed offices and multiple shared, open office areas.

HiLo's roof is a "sandwich" shell, with two thin layers of reinforced concrete of only 5 cm (inner layer) and 3 cm (outer layer) thick. Spaced 10 cm apart by insulation blocks, the layers are connected by a grid of thin (3 cm) compressive stiffening ribs and vertical tension rods to activate the entire depth of the section. Combining this lightweight, two-layered structure with the strength derived from the roof's highly curved geometry, the roof stands freely on five supports, covering an unobstructed space of 120 m^2.

CABLE-NET AND FABRIC FORMWORK SYSTEM

While concrete shell structures can significantly reduce the amount of material required to cover large spans, their non-standard geometry require custom form-works that typically use massive amounts of cut timber or milled foam as shuttering (temporary mold into which concrete is poured); the production of these single-use molds requires large amounts of material and manual labor, therefore making shell structures expensive and time consuming to build, and wasteful.

As an alternative to conventional rigid formworks, cable-net and fabric form-work systems, built from a largely reusable kit-of-parts, have the potential to drastically reduce this material consumption and construction waste. Furthermore, using fabric as shuttering offers additional benefits: it provides an appealing surface finish to the final concrete with minimal use of material and without the need for a release agent; it is flexible and can be patterned to adapt to the complex geometries

DOI: 10.4324/9781003138471-20

Figure 7B.1 *Exterior view of the HiLo unit at NEST* Source: Roman Keller

of shell structures with minimal labor; it is easy to store and transport to site; and it produces structures with "softer" surfaces, because of the slight pillowing of the fabric under the weight of the wet concrete.

The anticlastic geometry of the HiLo roof balances aesthetic, functional and structural requirements and constraints, such as head clearance along evacuation routes, solar orientation for electricity production and maximum deformation of the cantilevers in relation to the glass facade, and so on. The overall design process consisted of the following main steps:

1. Define the layout of the cable-net that will be used in the formwork.
2. Define a feasible target shell geometry using this cable-net as a form-finding mechanism.
3. Design a balanced cable-net geometry on the target, taking into account (geometric) constraints related to features of the space below.
4. Find a distribution of forces for the designed cable-net that matches the target shell geometry as closely as possible when loaded with wet concrete.

The structural analysis and fabrication design of the cable-net were developed simultaneously and had a symbiotic and parametric relationship. This was necessary because requirements of one process served as constraints for the other and vice versa. For example, the bounds on the force densities for the form-finding procedure were derived from the allowable stress in the elements that were sized based on constraints related to the fabrication and assembly process.

The cable-net and fabric formwork system consists of the following components: reusable steel scaffolding; timber boundary beams; steel cable-net; fabric shuttering; and edge clamps (Figure 7B.2). The primary structure of the formwork is the cable-net tensioned between reusable or recyclable timber boundary beams supported by standard scaffolding props. The cable-net consists of a kit of parts of individual steel cable segments and custom-detailed nodes that facilitate the logistics and application of the many layers of the roof structure. Once the concrete is sprayed onto the formwork and cured, the remaining components can be removed.

Construction sequence of the cable-net and fabric formwork: a) touch down supports; b) boundary beams and temporary scaffolding; c) cable-net; d) fabric shuttering; e) first layer of concrete; f) insulation foam blocks; g) second layer of concrete; h) removal of boundary beams and scaffolding; and i) waterproofing layer

CABLE-NET

The steel cable and rod segments are cut to specific lengths to be stretched into the designed shape in its loaded state. Through the specially designed system of nodes, the cables and rod segments can be easily assembled in patches on the ground then connected to one another in between the boundary beams (Figure 7B.3). These nodes connect the cable and rod segments while providing the degrees of freedom required for the final shape. Each node's central threaded rod holds two small black spheres spaced at defined distances beneath the fabric shuttering. These spheres are used to measure the as-built location of each node via a photogrammetry-based measurement system with sub-millimeter accuracy.

The pattern of the cable-net structure is a quad mesh consisting of five patches and five extraordinary vertices called the "singularities" (Figure 7B.4). Each patch creates a funnel towards its corresponding "touch down" support and thus the lowest anchoring points of the net, while the boundaries between the patches create a set of main structural lines connected to the highest anchoring points. These main lines, called the "spine," control the overall geometry of the cable-net, are largely responsible for generating prestress, and carry the bulk of the forces generated from the weight of the concrete. The spine also serves as the structural cold joint, which has been developed and integrated in the cable-net formwork such that the first concrete layer of the roof can be sprayed section by section resulting in a process that is more manageable from the mobile work platforms.

The density of the pattern is designed to reduce the number of tie segments and nodes, as well as control costs and fabrication time and avoid congestion of the funnels towards the supports, while maintaining acceptably small face sizes in

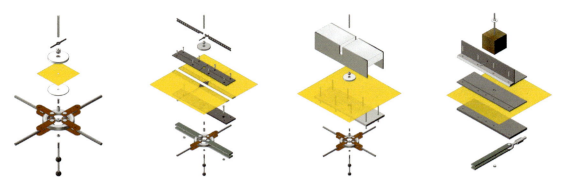

Figure 7B.3 *Four types of cable-net nodes (left to right): typical node; node at the cold joints; node at the facade channels; and node at the boundaries*

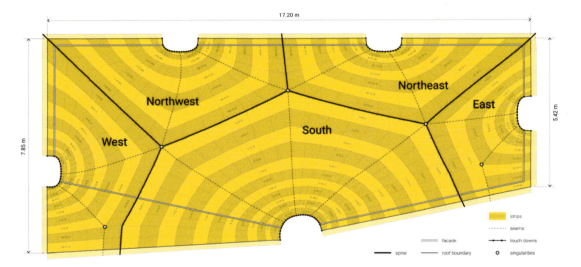

Figure 7B.4 *The five patches of the cable-net and the fabric shuttering*

the central regions of the net. Controlling the size of the faces is important because it influences the magnitude of the pillowing of the fabric shuttering and thus the amount of additional, non-structural dead load carried by the shell.

Having defined the topology, density and connectivity of the cable elements, the target mesh was generated. The mesh geometry was designed manually using an interactive form-finding tool based on the force density method, following as closely as possible the preliminary design. The mesh was subsequently subdivided and smoothened. For this purpose, a smoothing algorithm was applied that works by moving the vertices to the average location of the centroids of the surrounding faces, weighted by the respective face areas. Specific groups of cable elements were constrained to straight lines corresponding to the HiLo unit's glass facade to be installed underneath. This not only significantly simplifies the connections between the glass and the concrete, but also allows for the glass to be cleanly integrated in between the pillows of the surface as opposed to across the surface.

Figure 7B.5 *Strips of the "East" patch*

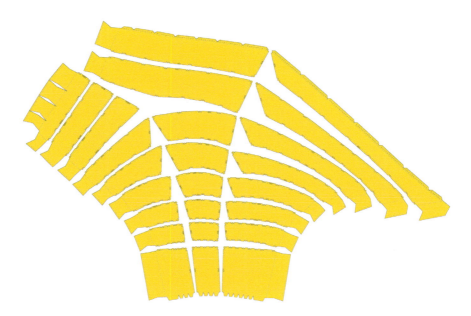

FABRIC SHUTTERING

The shuttering layer is a thin fabric attached to the nodes and tensioned together with the cable-net to form a taut surface. A woven polypropylene fabric is used as shuttering, which has a plastic finish on the bottom to retain the moisture content of the concrete during the curing process, which must be controlled to minimize the formation of cracks. This is particularly important for thin shells that have a high surface area to volume ratio. The exposed weave on the top provides an appealing finish to the final concrete without the need for a release agent. At the boundaries, plastic clamps fix the shuttering layer in a smooth curve to define the edge of the concrete mold.

Due to the doubly-curved geometry of the shell, the shuttering layer cannot be cut from a single continuous roll of fabric. The shuttering layer is first divided into five main patches that match the five sections of the cable-net. Each patch is then further subdivided in horizontal strips around each of the five supports. The discretized strips of each patch are sewn together and attached to the cable-net at the nodes. Once all five patches have been attached to the cable-net, the five patches are sealed together along the spine.

At each node, the fabric is elevated precisely 2 cm above the rings. This elevation of the shuttering layer creates a continuous surface that will sag under the weight of the concrete, creating a gentle "pillowing" effect that is a unique aesthetic feature of the shell. Along the seams of the fabric patches, higher stiffness and rigidity causes the fabric surface to sag less, which results in a hierarchy of pillowing pattern: hard break along the spine; sharper pillowing along the seams; and smoother pillowing within each of the strips.

The amount of sagging needs to be controlled to avoid over-accumulation of concrete. Because the fabric is much more elastic than the cable-net, the fabric shuttering is designed and fabricated to be 1% smaller than the actual cable-net geometry. This geometric discrepancy ensures that under the proper amount of tension in the cable-net, the fabric shuttering layer forms a taut surface that will limit the pillowing and the resulting extra weight. The scale factor for the fabric shuttering was informed by physical tests with 1-to-1 mockups and prototypes.

The shape of the flexible formwork is a function of the applied loads. The change in geometry between various loading conditions or induced by changes in the boundary conditions can be significant. Therefore, the non-uniform prestress in the cable-net is defined such that under the weight of wet concrete, the formwork deforms to the shape of the designed shell without exceeding the capacity of the members at any stage of the construction sequence. To introduce the correct level of prestress before the concrete is applied, the lengths of the cable segments at the boundaries can be controlled individually with a simple threaded anchor connection until the cable-net matches the designed target shape. The ability of the cable-net to achieve sufficient stiffness to support the concrete, with acceptable tensioning forces, is tied to the geometry and curvature of the target shape. For this reason, the design of the cable-net is strictly related to the design of the desired concrete shell, and vice versa.

To allow for compensating for unavoidable deviations from the designed geometry due to fabrication and assembly tolerances, the entire system is detailed such that its actual stress state can be precisely calculated from measurements of the geometry. Custom-developed control algorithms translate the deviations between the measured and the designed state to adjustments of the lengths of the boundary cables. This feedback loop is repeated until the as-built structure matches the designed system up to an acceptable level of precision.

ACTIVE CONTROL

A cable-net is an anticlastic, form-active system with tensile force members and thus no bending capacity. Form-active systems change geometry under the influence of applied loads to reach a new equilibrium state. To limit potentially large displacements, anticlastic systems can be prestressed. Theoretically, prestress could be increased until it fully negates the effects of the applied loads, but practical limitations on element sizes, foundations and anchoring points require an equilibrium state to be found within reasonable bounds.

The allowable forces in the system are limited by the maximum size of the components of the cable-net resulting from constraints related to the fabrication process and the required degrees of freedom at the nodes, and by the magnitude of the reaction forces that can be taken by the supporting scaffolding structure. In addition, the forces are distributed such that they yield a smooth spatial layout of cables. The continuous lines of cables corresponding to the glass facade below should be perfectly straight in plan as described earlier. The process of finding the non-uniform distribution of prestress consisted of the following steps:

1. The cable-net mesh is remapped to the target geometry while allowing its vertices to slide over this mesh and along the constraint curves corresponding to the boundaries and the facade lines, until a balanced distribution of faces is obtained.

2. A fitting procedure is used to find a distribution of forces, within the bounds determined by the maximum element and reaction forces, that minimizes the difference between the corresponding equilibrium state and the current target geometry of the shell.

3. The resulting geometry from the fitting process must be post-processed with the purpose of eliminating residual forces and smoothing the final geometry.

FABRICATION

The success of the cable-net and fabric formwork system relies on the accurate fabrication of precise cable and rod elements, node components, fabric shuttering, and timber boundary beams. For this reason, these elements were digitally fabricated by specialized industrial partners in Switzerland. These partners participated in the planning of most of the components to improve precision, reduce cost, and ensure that everything could be fabricated with their machines. This section describes the digital fabrication processes of the main elements of the cable-net and fabric formwork system.

Each individual cable was cut to its unique length and then swaged and labeled. The cables were connected to the rings using brackets. These were designed to be made from flat steel sheets and pressed into their final configurations, which reduced the price of the brackets considerably without any loss of functionality. The sizes of the brackets were the result of both the force magnitudes and the dimensions of the rings to which they connected. The nodes were materialized as rings. There were four distinct types with diameters of 65 mm, 90 mm, 95 mm and 115 mm determined by strength, fabrication, and assembly constraints. To achieve the highest precision possible, and to ensure the required structural strength, the rings were milled from solid stainless steel discs. This digital machining process also allowed for the profile of the ring to be customized to maximize the cross-sectional area, while still allowing for sufficient rotation of the ties to achieve the required angles. The largest node ring was used for the six-valent singularities of the cable-net.

The fabric shuttering was shaped into the doubly-curved geometry of the shell structure using machine-cut fabric segments, all sewn into one single piece per patch according to a predefined pattern with a specific amount of size compensation to generate a level of prestress that minimizes sagging to the desired extent. The seams of the fabric were aligned with the geometry of the cable-net to avoid leaving an additional imprint in the exposed concrete finish. The pattern was also constrained by the size of the fabric rolls and by the limitations of the computer numerical control (CNC) cutting machine. Finally, flaps were added to the ends of the segments to secure the fabric to the boundary beams and the cold joints.

CONSTRUCTION

The scaffolding consisted of vertical props, vertical ties and diagonal props. The vertical props were installed first to support the timber boundary beams. The beams arrived on the construction site as single straight sections and were assembled on the ground using splicing steel plates and bolts. Once assembled, the beams were

Figure 7B.6
Completed cable-net
Source: Juney Lee

hoisted on top of the vertical props and connected using the precise anchoring positions etched into the wood. The scaffolding system's boundary edge was completed by bracing the beams using the diagonal props and vertical ties. All of these members were installed with the use of small forklifts and a spider crane. The standard scaffolding elements were bolted into the ground with M20 steel bolts. The elevated supports for the touchdowns of the shell at the mezzanine level were made of custom steel landing plates and reusable scaffolding props. These elements had to be positioned with a high degree of precision as some of the cable-net anchors were located on these supports.

The installation of the cable-net and fabric was strongly influenced by the prototype's location within the confines of the Robotic Fabrication Hall, which precluded the use of a crane and demanded the exclusive use of aerial platforms to maneuver workers into the high anchoring positions. The cable-net was assembled into segments on the ground. The size and weight of the sub-assemblies were limited by the maximum amount that could be handled by two workers. The spine elements were assembled first and hoisted to their anchoring locations. The rest of the cable-net was then attached to that spine, segment by segment.

The fabric was delivered as one single element per patch, making it difficult to handle without causing damage. For this reason, the fabric was rolled up, hoisted onto the spine of the cable-net, and then unrolled from the center outwards and

Figure 7B.7 *Installation of the fabric shuttering (from top, left to right): sewn patches; placement of the patches; attaching of the fabric shuttering to the cable-net using steel discs; and joining of the patches at the spine.*
Source: Juney Lee

down towards the touchdown supports. The fabric was then attached to the cable-net at each node using steel discs with threaded holes.

To achieve the required unloaded initial state of the system that allows the cable-net to deflect into the geometry of the final shell under the weight of the wet concrete, the boundary conditions were adjusted by using the on-site control system. First, the boundary cables were set to the designed length in the digital model. The resulting real geometry was measured and compared to the designed version. Then, the deviations between the measured geometry and the digital model were compensated by adjusting the boundary conditions according to predictions made by the control algorithm. Spatial point cloud data was recorded by the positions of the black spherical markers at the nodes and circular stickers on the boundary beams, as measured by the image-based theodolite system. This system uses total stations with modified industrial charged-coupled device (CCD) cameras inserted in place of the eyepiece and is able to provide sub-millimeter accuracy.

Post-processing was required on the raw data, which provided the coordinates of the spherical markers that were successfully recorded during each measurement session. First, data was filtered to ignore nodes that had only one measurement point, that is, one sphere instead of two. When two points were present, the difference vector and the known distance to the center of the rings could be used to determine the exact position of the nodes. By using a two-layered structural

Figure 7B.8
Spraying of the concrete layers
Source: Juney Lee

Figure 7B.9
Removal of the fabric shuttering
Source: Juney Lee

system of steel-reinforced concrete sheets connected by concrete ribs and steel shear rods, sufficient structural depth can be created to resist bending efficiently without adding more material. Given the complex geometry of the structure, the best possible method for the application of the concrete was spraying from aerial platforms. The first layer of concrete is sprayed directly onto the fabric shuttering of the flexible formwork.

A concrete material was designed to be sprayable onto the fabric formwork even at near vertical orientations. The concrete was mixed on-site in small batches and pumped into long plastic hoses at low pressures to avoid damaging the fabric. Workers applied

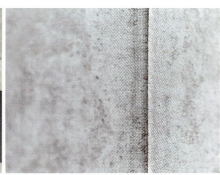

the concrete to cover the entire surface of the shell structure, using the threaded rods at each node as guides to achieve the desired concrete thickness. The ribs are then sprayed in between foam blocks that are placed on top of the first layer, and the second layer of the two-layered system is sprayed on top of the surface formed by the blocks and ribs.

The concrete was left to cure for 28 days before the scaffolding was removed. This process started by releasing the tension on the cables by loosening them from the boundary beams. At this point in time, with the cable-net no longer supporting the concrete, the shell structure was free-stranding with no external forces acting on the boundary beams or scaffolding. These final scaffolding members were disconnected from their anchors on the ground and removed using small forklifts and spider cranes. After the cable-net is detached from the free-standing shell, the fabric shuttering layer is peeled off.

Project Information:

Professor/Project Lead: Tom Van Mele & Philippe Block
University/Organization: Block Research Group, ETH Zurich
Students: Juney Lee, Tomás Méndez Echenagucia, Alessandro Dell'Endice, Cristián Calvo Barentin, Aurèle Gheyselink, Sandie Kate Fenton
Project Location: Dübendorf, Switzerland
Client: Empa
Donations/Financial Support: ETH Foundation, Dr. Max Rössler

Project Timeline:

Research and development	2012–2019
Concept prototypes	2012
Control system prototypes	2015
Full-scale prototype	2017
Architectural mockups	2018
Unit design	2017–2019
Fabrication	2019
Construction	2019–2021
Total	9 years

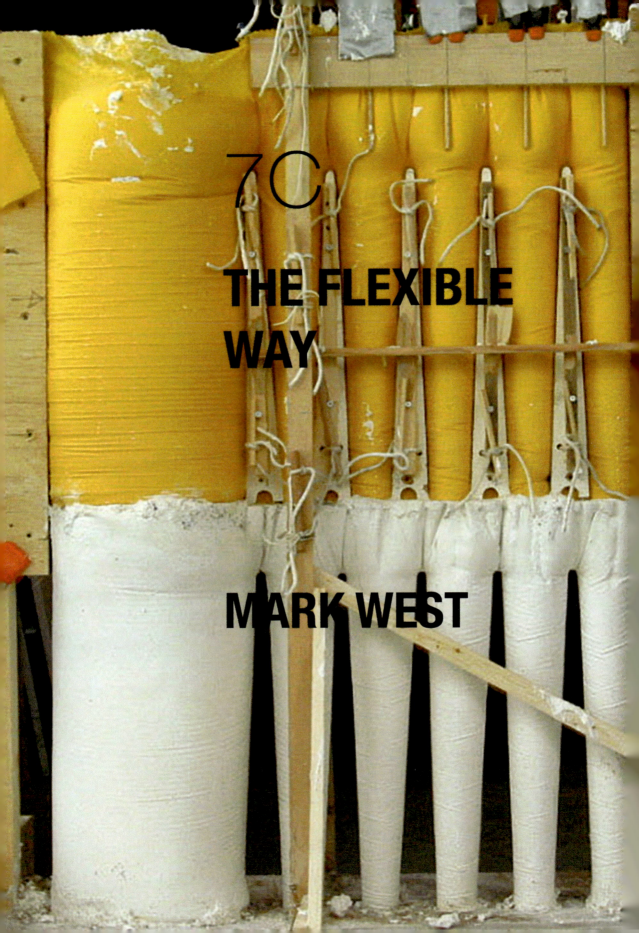

7C

THE FLEXIBLE
WAY

MARK WEST

7C The Flexible Way

Mark West

FABRICS

A piece of fabric in the hand is an unassertive and submissive thing. It offers no resistance—until it is pulled. Only then is this essentially pliant thing transformed into a tenacious structure. Small threads, with very little strength of their own, are cunningly joined in a field of tiny distributed forces, resulting in a cumulative power of remarkable strength. These are communal structures: excessive strains in any particular thread will shed force to neighboring threads, creating a web of shared tension stresses—a self-distributing tension field.

For those of us used to relatively massive, rigid structural members, the thinness of a fabric structure is a marvel. The minuscule thickness of the threads, and the thinness of the fabric sheet they compose, belie the supple structural genius of a textile and confounds the structural intuitions of most builders. Unlike rigid structural members, this strange combination of supple submission and tenacious strength allows a textile to distort itself into the unique shape of its own resistance in tension, allowing us to see, and feel, the struggle it is undergoing.

My own experience with fabric structures is largely limited to their use as moulds for concrete construction. I had the great privilege of building a laboratory building and a research program dedicated to the exploration of flexible fabric formworks—The Centre for Architectural Structures and Technology (CAST) at the University of Manitoba in Winnipeg, Canada. In this lab/studio, specially designed and constructed for this research I, along with my students, associates, and colleagues, played with sheets of fabric for years. What we found through our play were a series of discoveries and inventions that are extraordinarily simple, yet produce some stunningly complex results. Our research adopted several severe constraints in line with a builder's aversion to "complexification." For example, only flat sheets of fabric were used; all these molds are constructed with sheets taken directly off the role—no tailoring of patterning allowed. Only simple, common, construction tools and fasteners are used (even sewing machines are avoided). Primitive methods were always chosen over "high tech" methods with the intention of making our inventions accessible to both low-capital and high-capital building cultures and economies.

RESEARCH

The methods we used in this research combined engineering logic, artistic errantry, construction simplicity, and a hunger for beauty. Our work advanced through a chain

DOI: 10.4324/9781003138471-21

of design+build projects, each one arising, in turn, through the branching discoveries revealed by previous constructions. Because our work was largely funded by fine arts grants[1] rather than engineering grants,[2] we were able to follow the peripatetic and iterative paths of artistic and design practice, avoiding the shackles of engineering research traditions with their requirements for fixed objectives and milestones. We worked closely with our engineering students and colleagues in our lab, but these engineering-based research projects all came to us from the more humid soil of our play-based research/creation. Inventions, after all, are always found rather than formulated. This is why the history of technology is largely a history of mistakes: the broken beaker, the fortuitous misunderstanding. . . . A laboratory is, essentially, an enclosed space set apart from the larger world where, by means of cunning changes in scale, a large number of mistakes can be made in a short period of time.[3]

At CAST, our methods were grounded in the construction of physical analogs. Abstractly, we imagined through drawings, and experimentally, we imagined through small physical models contrived to function as much like their imagined full-scale counterparts as possible: string modeling rope or cables; plaster or sand modeling concrete; light woven fabrics modeling powerful woven geotextiles. . . . We imagine a construction or constructive set-up, then build it in miniature, see where we got it wrong, then build it again. In this process, mistakes provide the richest veins of new ideas and instruction. Failures are embraced and explored. Rather than regret, an attitude of "Hey, look what happened!" is key.

There are, of course, some inevitable differences between the physical behavior of our little models and their full-scale "equivalents" due to scaling factors or differences in materials. But these little models have proven to be extraordinarily accurate predictors of full-scale *events*. In each case these models are not merely scaled objects, but scaled *actions*; they are verb-like as well and noun-like. These are physical parametric models, where the parameters are given by the behavior of the materials themselves, which is why the choice of analog materials is so crucial. Historical precedents for the use of physical parametric models include, for example, Gaudi's hanging model of the Coloina Guell chapel, the soap films of Frei Otto, and the hanging fabric shell models of Heinz Isler.

But unlike these earlier examples, our little constructions are consciously made as "method prototypes" giving us ideas and guidance about methods and procedures for full-scale construction. When one of our little parametric models produces an architectural form, it is, de facto, a *buildable* architectural form. This is an extraordinary bonus, not provided by digital parametric models.[4]

Our research at CAST embraced both sculptural and structural forms. The search for sculptural form does not start with a design, but rather with a choice of materials and methods. Here forms are *found* rather than "designed" as the materials themselves dictate to us their final disposition is space through the urgencies of natural law. Our search for structural form, on the other hand, was more directed as we followed specific, efficient, and calculable, force "paths" through matter. Although certain aspects of these structural forms are decided upon by the materials themselves, the overall structural/geometric schema is established before experimental construction begins.

The search for ways to construct efficiently shaped structures is like attempting to hit the center of a pre-existing target with a rifle. The search for sculptural form, however, is more like shooting a shotgun against a wall and drawing bullseyes around the holes.[5] The "shotgun" approach is "basic research" where we may learn what is possible without imposing artificial limitations. The "rifle" approach is saved for applied research, where discoveries and techniques selected from all those interesting shotgun holes are opportunistically applied to construct some specific instrumental thing (which is not to say that rifles don't sometimes suddenly turn into shotguns).

This way of working is different from most academic research traditions. Scholarly research, based as it is on precedent, fulfills a very different project from invention. Engineering research, based on the scientific requirements of close constraints and tightly controlled parameters, needs to know the "target" one is trying to hit, how one plans to hit it, and the milestones set along the way in that process. Traditional social science research has established similar constraints. The argument is made here for a separate way of doing *architectural* research that employs a variety of heterogeneous and loosely constrained methodologies. For example, if in the middle of our work/play we stumbled upon some unexpected finding or idea, we were free to immediately shift our direction to allow a new line of investigation (drawing a new and unexpected bullseyes around that event/discovery). This is an expansive method of work, built on mistakes and surprises, designed to uncover the new and the unexpected. Artists work this way all the time, and the simple trick here is to strategically adopt this methodological freedom, within specific strategic constraints, for the purpose of architectural, engineering, and construction discoveries.

CASE STUDIES

These projects differ from typical architecture school design-build projects in that they were done within the framework of a research laboratory rather than a design studio class. The participants were a small group of paid Masters of Architecture student research assistants (Aynslee Hurdal, Leif Friggstad, Mike Johnson, and Kyle Martens, Tom Alston, Steven Faust, and Steven Berry) who more closely followed my lead, as the Principle Researcher, and that of CAST Research Associate Ronnie Araya, than would be the case in a design studio class. The *realization* of the fundamental design, however, was accomplished in a very collective manner.

Project 1. Cast Concrete Walls for a Theater Building in Tanzania

In 2009 I was asked by Armstrong and Cohen Architects to assist in the design of a reinforced concrete theater building for the TunaHAKI orphanage in Moshi Tanzania where the orphanage's founder, David Ryatula, taught circus arts to the children. The building would be used for teaching, performances, and also by the City of Moshi for other public performances and events. (The orphanage was restructured in 2010 and the project abandoned.)

The design called for reinforced concrete construction (the local construction standard), but also for a high degree of sustainability. This presented the architects with a problem: Tanzania is a country struggling with a serious deforestation problem, and conventional concrete formworks consume substantial amounts of wood that is eventually rendered as waste or burned. They turned to CAST to see if it was possible to reduce or eliminate the wood consumed in the construction of this concrete building. We were asked to help design fabric formworks for the walls of the theater. These walls were to be highly perforated for ventilation, due to the hot equatorial climate of Moshi.

Crane capacity was limited, so only small lifts of hand-batched concrete were feasible for cast-in-place (CIP) construction. For precast, or tilt-up, construction, only smaller, low volume, lighter weight panels were allowed. We developed proposals for both.

Case 1. Cast-In-Place Wall Proposal

This CIP wall proposal is designed for simple, low-tech construction that can be accomplished without machinery or highly skilled labor. The height of the formwork was limited to allow small batches of concrete to be easily lifted by hand and poured into the molds with buckets.

Figure 7C.1 shows an early sketch of this screen wall and a photo of a 1:10 working model of the formwork. In this case the formwork is used to cast both the screen wall and a larger diameter column for the building's reinforced concrete structural frame. The formwork consists of two flat sheets of woven polyethylene (PE) or polypropylene (PP) fabric comprising the front and back sides of the mould. These extremely inexpensive fabrics are ubiquitous world-wide. The openings in the screen wall are made by selectively clamping the front and back sheets together using rigid, shaped, wooden pieces we call "impactos." These impactos are squeezed together using nothing more than a twisted rope (alternately, bolts could be used for this purpose).

Figure 7C.2 shows a full-scale prototype test of this scheme: on the left, the two flat fabric sheets are shown clamped together by the wooden impactos; the center image shows this mold standing up and filled with concrete, followed by an image of the final casting.

Figure 7C.3 shows the upper portion of the cast in a 1:10 plaster model (Left) and at full scale in concrete (Right). This pleated "entablature" is the most difficult and complex part of the mold. The column-like shafts of the screen are formed, quite simply, by allowing the fabric sheets to bulge outwards in tension between

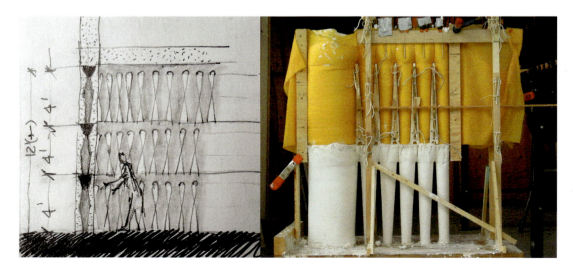

Figure 7C.1 *Sketch (Left) and working model (Right) for cast-in-place wall formwork*
Source: Mark West

Figure 7C.2 *Full-scale prototype formwork and test of cast-in-place wall formwork*
Source: Mark West

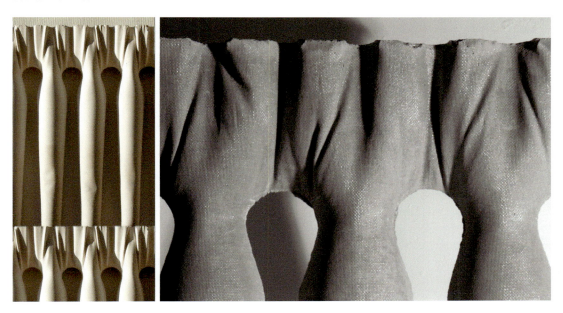

Figure 7C.3 *Detail of the pleated folds along the top, beam portion of the cast*
Source: Mark West

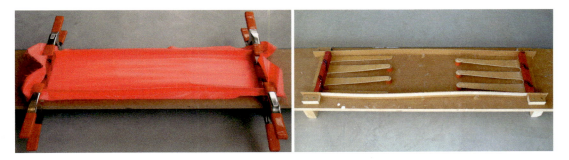

Figure 7C.4 *Working model of a precast, or tilt-up, wall panel formwork, shown with and without its flat fabric sheet*
Source: Mark West

the impactos. The shape of the legs is strictly determined by the profile of the impacto boundaries and their diameter(s) are determined by how much fabric is allowed between the impactos. Filling the legs with concrete, however, causes excess fabric to gather and accordion together along the top "beam" portion of the cast, producing deeply pleated folds. If left entirely to its own devices this loose fabric can fold too deeply into the horizontal beam portion of the cast compromising its structural section, or become captured in the concrete, making it impossible to strip off and re-use the mould. Our solution to handling these wild folds uses a series of cylindrical impactos (dowels or perhaps branches, bottles, etc.) lined up along the horizontal top board of the mould rig. These are visible in Figure 7C.1 (Right), and Figure 7C.2 (Left and Center). Within these mild constraints, the fabric and wet concrete are given free play to negotiate the distribution of this "extra" fabric. This is arguably the most beautiful portion of the casting, occurring as it does "on its own" between the loose guidance of the dowels.

Case 2. Precast Wall Proposal

We also developed a precast option for the theater's walls using a flat fabric sheet laid over impactos placed on the ground. Figure 7C.4 illustrates the general scheme, and Figure 7C.5 illustrates these panels joined together to form a larger facade. Curved edges in the mould frame produce the openings/perforations in the walls. The mould's impactos selectively reduce the thickness (and weight) of the cast panels. Innumerable and varied designs are easily obtained by changing out the pattern of impactos below the fabric sheet, each pattern of impactos producing a differently shaped panel using the same mould rig. Care was taken in the design and placement of the impactos to maintain coherent structural sections throughout each panel for reinforcement.

The flat fabric sheet effortlessly provides a continuous mould surface that negotiates between the impactos and frame edges. As with the free negotiation of the extra fabric in the cast-in-place screen outlined above, the complex geometries naturally produced by the fabric sheet are typically the most beautiful part of the cast. These are geometries given by natural law rather than by human artifice—or perhaps more accurately, it is a cunning combination of human artifice and nature where the simple fabric sheet typically displays more geometric intelligence than the human designer/builder.

Case 3. Fabric-Formed Funicular "Flayed Beam" Vault

The most efficient way to resist an applied load is through linear tension. The second most efficient way is through pure compression.[6] However, arches and compression vaults, efficient as they are, do exert a horizontal thrust on their supports, requiring the provision of tension ties or buttresses.

The least efficient structural mode is bending (i.e. beams, slabs), however bending members have the great advantage of not exerting any horizontal thrust on their supports. The "Flayed Beam" vault is designed as a funicular thin-shell vault that, like a beam, contains its own thrust within itself, thus combining the advantages of structural efficiency

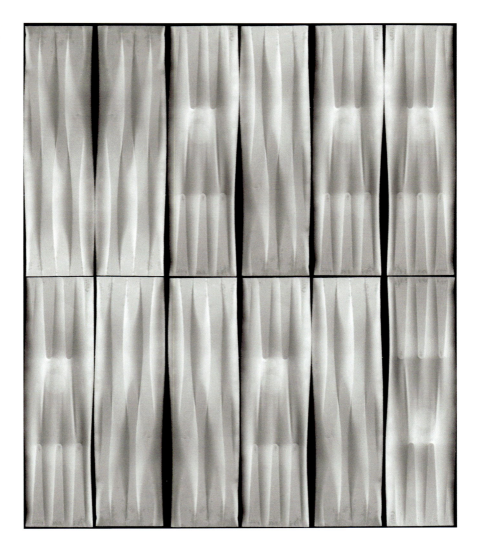

Figure 7C.5 *Photo collage illustrating a perforated wall assembled from precast panels made from the Figure 7C.4 formwork.*

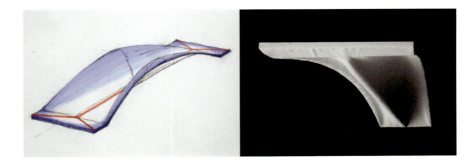

Figure 7C.6 *Drawing (Left) and model (Right) of "flayed beam" design: blue indicates schematic area of its compression field; red indicates schematic location of tension-tie reinforcement*

and construction simplicity. It acts like a beam to its supports, yet its internal forces are all confined to a thin "skin" of concrete—hence the name "flayed beam" (Figure 7C.6).

The mold for this design is made by hanging a flat sheet of fabric between rigid supports and loading its surface with a thin layer of glass fiber reinforced concrete (GFRC), causing the fabric to deflect downwards in pure tension. After the GFRC hardens, the rigidified sheet is flipped over to be used as a mold for the production of the vaults. This production method takes advantage of the deep natural symmetry that exists between tension and compression: a hanging tension "arch," turned upside down, becomes a pure compression arch. Thus, a hanging sheet of fabric forms itself into a pure tension field and, once inverted, provides a pure compression field—in other words a funicular compression vault. The great Swiss engineer Heinz Isler used exactly this method in the design of his complexly curved thin-shell vaults[7] (though not for their construction).

The shell's internal tension restraint is gained by shaping the hanging sheet so that it maintains a straight horizontal line along its centerline where tension-tie reinforcement can be placed. This is accomplished by prestressing the flat sheet with a central "pull-buckle" and providing a rigid horizontal support beneath this central portion of the sheet, as shown in Figure 7C.7. Without this initial pull-buckle, a flat sheet will buckle wildly when it is draped over the central straight-back support; the pre-stressed pull-buckle, in a sense, collects any such buckles into a single gathering. This technique was discovered through innumerable hands-on experiments with flat-sheet model formworks, a form of physical thinking where the materials themselves instruct the designer.

After the sheet has been loaded with its thin layer of GFRC, it is flipped over to present a smooth mold surface for precast production of the flayed beam compression shells (Figure 7C.8). You can also see in Figure 7C.8 the way in which the hanging fabric sheet has formed deep corrugations along its principle lines of tension. Once inverted, these now present deep corrugations along the principle lines of *compression* stress in the shell. This manifestly provides a deep,

Figure 7C.7 *Left: pre-stressed pull-buckle pre-loaded into flat fabric sheet. Right: this sheet hung over its supports being loaded with a uniform layer of GFRC concrete*

Figure 7C.8 *Left: rigidified sheet flipped over to be used as a mold (note deep corrugations formed along principle lines of stress). Right: thin-shell flayed beam vault structure being pulled from this mold* Mark West

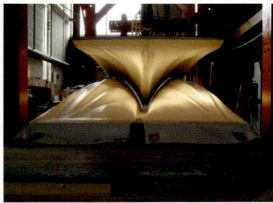

Figure 7C.9 *Photo collage rendering of the underside of a flayed beam roof structure*

buckling-resistant geometry for the shell precisely where it is most needed. A cautionary note is required here: Buckling is a particularly complex phenomena, and not so well understood by structural engineers as one might expect, so blithe claims about the natural buckling of a fabric sheet in a tension field inverting to buckling resistance in a mirrored compression field may be fraught with unexpected complexities. On its face, however, this inverted symmetry seems to be apparent. Figure 7C.9 shows a photocollage of the underside of this vault repeated as a roof.

The projects described here represent a small portion of my work (carried out with the help of many others) using flat fabric sheets as molds for architectural structures. Much of the technical knowledge gained through this work has been collected in *The Fabric Formwork Book*.[8] More difficult to describe, in so many words, are the more subtle lessons made available through this kind of play/work.

The combination of material plasticity and flexibility, applied in an arena demanding prediction and control, challenges longstanding habits-of-mind in the architect and engineer. One important lesson gleaned from this challenge is how to distinguish between those things that need to be controlled, and those that do not. Our professional, if not our cultural training, bends us towards control of everything. But in the act of building, there are moments and events where the material world is best left to its own devices. Indeed, there are more occasions than one might expect where letting go of rigid control and human command allows matter to self-form in extraordinarily beautiful and efficient ways. This lesson, a discovery of freedom within strict and unforgiving constraints, is at once a practical boon and an illuminating metaphor that hints at other, more subtle applications.

NOTES

1. Social Science and Humanities Research Council of Canada (SSHRC) research/creation" grants.
2. We also used National Science and Engineering Research Council of Canada (NSERC) grants to explore the engineering applications of specific formwork methods.
3. This notion is taken directly from Bruno Latour: "Give Me a Laboratory and I Will Raise the World", published originally in Karin Knorr-Cetina and Michael Mulkay, eds., *Science Observed: Perspectives on the Social Study of Science*, London and Beverly Hills: Sage, 1983, pp. 141–170.
4. A quick comparison: physical parametric models are rich in qualitative information but they resist the extraction of quantitative information. Digital parametric models, entirely quantitative in composition, are the opposite: poor in qualitative information and rich in quantitative information.
5. Vogel, Steven, *Cats' Paws and Catapults: Mechanical Worlds of Nature and People*, New York: W. W. Norton & Co. Inc., 1998, p. 3.
6. There is, of course, no "pure" anything—much less pure compression. Every structure, even the most elegantly shaped funicular structure, develops some secondary forces.
7. See, for example: Chilton, John C., *Engineer's Contribution to Architecture: Heinz Isler*, London: Thomas Telford, 2000.
8. West, Mark, *The Fabric Formwork Book*. UK: Routledge, Taylor & Francis, 2017.

PROFESSIONAL INQUIRY

7D

FORM-FINDING

the MARS Pavilion

JOSEPH SARAFIAN
and RON CULVER

7D   Form-Finding the MARS Pavilion

Joseph Sarafian and Ron Culver

In a lecture moderated by Greg Lynn at the Canadian Centre for Architecture, Peter Eisenman asks "whether the saw was invented and so we made tables . . . or we needed a table so we invented the saw"?[1] This question is especially relevant in architecture as we evaluate our fabrication and construction tools, asking, "Were they designed for what we are doing, or have they been reappropriated to realize our intentions?" Gaining proficiency in a tool requires exploring not only its capabilities but defining its limitations.

Parametric design is necessitating a new era of tools. The first generation of these tools was digital and achieved the feat of representing complex design ideas via software accessible to architects. When these complex digital representations outpaced contemporary construction methods, the second generation of computational fabrication emerged, not only realizing design solutions modeled by parametric software, but charting new territories into the previously unbuildable realm. As designers gain proficiency in these tools, they begin to identify entirely new problems that have long been left unsolved and therefore unbuilt. One such problem in the construction industry is the increased cost of design variation. As architects design with increasing complexity and variation, the costs of fabricating such assemblies can increase ten-fold, eliminating them as viable options within a given construction budget.

This dilemma was made abundantly clear in the design of the Broad Museum in Los Angeles. Architects Diller Scofidio + Renfro envisioned their original design for the Broad Museum facade to feature morphing precast concrete apertures with a diversity of geometry. However, excessive cost estimates put this varied design out of reach, resulting in a highly repetitive Glass Fiber Reinforced Concrete (GFRC) version of the original facade. Fewer variations in the apertures meant fewer molds to be fabricated, bringing costs down. If the construction industry could find a way to uncouple the direct relationship between variation and cost premiums, more complex designs could be realized without the need to rationalize the project through value engineering.

This need to realize design variation in the built environment (not only in renderings) became the primary focus of our research at UCLA and permeated into our practice, Form Found Design. We saw mass customization—the means of introducing variation within built elements without additional cost—as an opportunity for creative exploration and invention. If we could devise a way to introduce mass

DOI: 10.4324/9781003138471-23

185

customization into major building components, we could support practical design variation within the construction industry, facilitating a major breakthrough in design opportunity for architects. Not constrained to repetitive patterns or traditional ornamentation, designers could now move past traditional constraints with less financial penalty and greater chance of seeing their concepts actually built.

Our interest in fabric began when we saw the potential for robotic manipulation as an adjustable mold for concrete. We were intrigued by the work of Mark West at the University of Manitoba's Centre for Architectural Structures and Technology (CAST) whose design research on fabric formwork inspired a new generation of ideas on what concrete could become with flexible molds. Andrew Kudless explored fabric formwork on a smaller scale through his San Francisco Museum of Modern Art (SFMOMA) installation, P_Wall. Plaster was poured over stretched nylon and wood dowels, allowing the natural sag of the material and fabric to form both puckering and bulging geometries. Such explorations showed the geometric complexity that resulted from the form-finding inherent in fabric formwork.

Taking a field trip with Greg Lynn's UCLA AUD studio to the San Francisco Bay Area to visit the office of Kreysler & Associates, we were able to witness firsthand the need for both automation and variation in the fabrication of architectural components. At the time, Bill Kreysler's fabrication shop was employing their warehouse-sized computer numerical control (CNC) machine to mill foam molds onto which Fiber Reinforced Polymer (FRP) would be laid to form the facade of the SFMOMA expansion by Snöhetta. Witnessing the custom fabrication of the unique molds, we realized that if automation could be employed to allow variation, this could open the door to much more geometric variation without the cost implications of building unique molds for each variant. We saw an opportunity to couple the precision of robotics with the dimensional freedom of fabric to create a new kind of adjustable mold for concrete. We called this design research "Fabric Forms."

Greg Lynn wisely advised us that if a thesis is strong enough, it can become a life-long pursuit, well beyond academia. Still, this was never our intention when we embarked on an Independent Research Study under Professor Julia Koerner, whose expertise in geometric experimentation and 3d-printing had earned her international acclaim. After our explorations in her "Animated Casting" technology seminar, we realized that concrete as a phase-changing material had untapped potential—if the problems of variation could be solved. (Julia taught this course at the Architecture and Urban Design Department of UCLA in 2015.) Pier Luigi Nervi once said,

> I like reinforced concrete because in it we find all the static, plastic, and structural characteristics of all other materials and, at the same time, it offers almost unlimited and not yet explored possibilities.[2]

Building on the fabric formwork research of Mark West and Andrew Kudless, we explored the multi-dimensional stretch properties of lycra as a mold for concrete. Early tests included both physical tests as well as computational simulations of fabric stretching using Daniel Piker's add-on, Kangaroo for the Rhino 3D plugin, Grasshopper. Comparing the two results allowed us to better understand the material behavior as well as software limitations that prevented us from simulating some of the real-world effects of the lycra when exposed to the fluid dynamics of the flowing concrete.

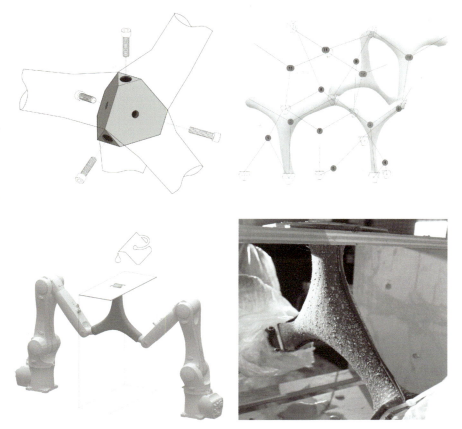

The tools that were being introduced at UCLA's IDEAS campus were the same machines that had been built to assemble automotive windshields, but were given a new purpose in an academic architectural setting. Academic architecture institutions around the world were purchasing and deploying six-axis industrial robot arms in the hope that new fabrication and automation routines could be explored as well as provide new creative opportunities for designers. For us, the six-axis industrial robot was the tool at hand, and we were not only repurposing it, but designing a new fabrication method around its capabilities and limitations. In turn, this new method ultimately allowed us to explore the design of complex geometries that we could actually fabricate with near limitless variation and extreme precision.

Positioning two small Kuka Agilus robots in opposition to each other gave us a working area in the center in which the robots could manipulate a lycra sleeve.

This sleeve would act as a mold for concrete and glass fiber, and when suspended from a fixed armature between the robots, provide a fill point to pour the concrete. Based on this configuration, a three-limbed wishbone geometry was conceived. In order to attach each wishbone, a second "coupler" element was introduced, allowing up to four wishbones of varying geometry to bolt together using the same connection.

By casting a nut into the end of each wishbone and allowing openings in the coupler, we created a four-way bolted connection that could be disassembled easily, all while concealing the fasteners. The shape of the coupler is a truncated tetrahedron, allowing not only the coupling of four wishbones, but creating a three-dimensional connection conducive to a lattice structure or space frame. This predicated a design that was akin to a three-dimensional puzzle of interlocking wishbones.

Digitally, our focus revolved around designing an aggregation of components that could not only be communicated to the robots, but could achieve our structural and material goals. The slenderness ratio of each wishbone was considered in each of its limbs. The final result was a small-scale proof-of-concept, using plastic couplers sufficient to receive the bolt inserted into the nut cast into the end of each limb. Communicating with the robots involved a plugin for Autodesk Maya called BD Move, created by the studio Bot & Dolly. At the time, the novelty of this program was unique in that it allowed robots to be "rigged" like 3D characters in an animation and the motion could be simulated to reveal singularities or other impossible movements that the robots attempted to achieve when positioning the end-effectors. Kangaroo was also used in the Grasshopper environment to simulate the sagging effects of gravity on the lycra. These digital simulations informed our material testing, as we quickly realized the importance of using the robots to precisely stretch the lycra to help the wishbones keep their intended shape.

Concrete was poured into one open end of the lycra sleeve, while custom end-effectors attached to each robot clamped the fabric, and formed the end of each wishbone. The cement chosen was a CTS Rapid Set product called Cement All that would achieve 9,000 psi in compression. A fast cure time meant that we could have a high output rate for casting each wishbone. The glass fiber additive helped increase the tensile strength and reduced cracking and chipping of ends.

When Steven Ehrlich, FAIA, RIBA accepted his gold medal from AIA Los Angeles in 2015, he recited a saying that he had learned while spending time in Africa,

If you want to go fast, go alone. If you want to go far, go with friends.

This quote stuck with us as we began assembling a team to design, engineer, and deliver the pavilion for Amazon. Eventually, we would name it after the conference it was commissioned for, calling it the MARS Pavilion. MARS was an acronym for Machine learning, Automation, Robotics, and Space exploration. Reaching out to the Los Angeles office of Walter P Moore, a team led by Greg Otto, Kais Al-Rawi, AIA MSFE, Trevor Stephen Lewis PhD, PE, FRSA, and Cheryl Luo, P.E., LEED AP BD+C, was a critical first step as their office provided both material and technological support from the early stages of design, to final inspection of fabricated elements.

In order to increase the size of the pavilion without adding significant weight, we designed the overall geometry to behave primarily in compression to exploit the inherent qualities of concrete. Inspired by the way Antoni Gaudí derived the structure of La Sagrada Familia through a hanging chain model, we employed catenary curvature to a digital model by exerting an upward gravitational force using Kangaroo 3D. This optimized the geometry of each wishbone to create a dominant axial compression load path with minimum tensile forces. This ensured that the loads exerted on each member of the pavilion were primarily compressive,

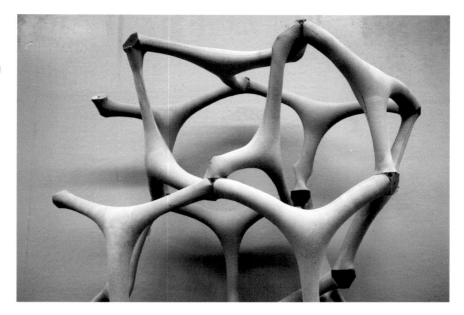

optimizing the geometry to reflect its natural material properties. To encourage interaction with the pavilion, components were strategically removed, allowing for the emergence of three arched portals.

ABB Robotics loaned us two IRB 6700 robots on steel pallets bolted together and we cantilevered the armature's fill point to eliminate tool path collision. Once ABB Multi-Move was installed and calibrated by an ABB technician in our shop, we had both robots working as one 12-axis assembly with accuracy to less than 1 mm tolerance. The robots could not drift relative to each other, and the steel armature was stiff enough that even loaded with the weight of the casting, it would not deflect or be pulled by either robot. Employing the Taco ABB plugin for Grasshopper 3D, we were able to eliminate the manual alignment of the digital model, further reducing the opportunity for error.

The fabric, however, was another story. We quickly learned that lycra wouldn't support the weight of the increased concrete volume, so we embarked on testing materials that would allow enough flexibility to encompass the varied sizes and shapes of each wishbone without distortion, finally settling on a ballistic nylon. While inherently inflexible, once subjected to pre-tensioning by the robots and the pressure of the concrete from within, we were surprised at just how much give there was.

In concert with the testing of the fabric formwork, we conducted experiments with concrete, admixtures, and reinforcing. The Walter P Moore team gave us early design parameters that we used in our digital models that we fed into their Finite Element Analysis (FEA) model, which informed our subsequent design in a continuous feedback loop. Their FEA showed us graphically where the highest stresses would be and set the minimum requirements for our concrete mixes. As "Steve" Lewis liked to point out to us, the pavilion we designed would weigh about 5,000

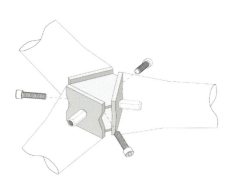

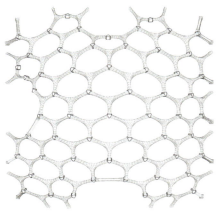

Figure 7D.3
(Clockwise from top left) Steel Coupler diagram showing three-sided bolted connection detail with embedded coupler nut, plan view of MARS Pavilion, Ron Culver, AIA attaching fabric sleeve to robot end-effector, opposing robots positioning a filled, fabric mold
Source: Form Found Design/Tony Castillo

lbs, or the weight of two Honda Civics. 9,000 psi concrete was not going to be strong enough anymore.

After sourcing concrete alternatives from across the country, we came back to Cement All by CTS Rapid Set and experimented with admixtures, fillers, and reinforcing to increase the strength and maintain the fast-working properties. In order to maintain our tight production schedule, it was critical that we could cast each piece and remove it from the robots as quickly as possible. Therefore, the initial cure needed to occur within about 20 minutes so that we could safely handle the freshly-cast pieces without damaging them.

Ultimately, we chose a combination of plasticizer to reduce water in the mix (thereby increasing strength) and Helix Steel Micro Rebar to achieve 12,000 psi compressive and 1,260 psi flexural strength. This combination proved so novel and effective that after our discussions with both CTS and Helix Steel, they did their own testing and started joint marketing efforts to promote the high-strength, fast-curing combination that we discovered.

At the same time as we finished casting the first 20 pieces, we received the first batch of couplers from the foundry. This was a sand-cast aluminum prismatic block that we were to drill out for bolting to the pavilion's wishbones. They were so inconsistent that we could not maintain our tolerances, so we sent the aluminum back to be melted down. It was at that same moment we realized that our digital model driving the robots was one generation old and the 20 pieces of concrete we had just cast were now too short.

Panic quickly turned to the realization that our timing couldn't have been better. By remaking the couplers out of waterjet cut and jig-welded steel, we were able to change their size enough to make up the dimensional difference, eliminate the need to drill holes and solve another problem we knew about but had, until then, deferred: the chemicals in concrete interact with, and eat through aluminum, but steel is not subject to the same reaction.

Our relentless pursuit of accuracy in the casting setup left us down to the wire for the delivery deadline. Even with producing one piece every 75 minutes, we had no time to do a trial assembly prior to setup in Palm Springs for the MARS Conference. With only three assembly days in total, the first day was lost to preparing the platform with anchors for the pavilion base. Once we started erecting the first two pieces, panic struck again. Though our design tolerance was only one-sixteenth of an inch, somehow the two pieces were a full 12 inches away from each other. After moments of anxiety, a quick-thinking intern said "what if these are mis-labeled and one of them is upside-down?" Sure enough, we turned the first piece over and everything worked. That was the only mis-labeled piece in the pavilion.

By the end of day two, all but the final few pieces were installed. Day three saw us fighting all day to get the last pieces to fit into the top of the pavilion, combatting gravity and a seemingly diminishing remaining space. By late afternoon one of our team likened the pavilion to the spokes in a bicycle wheel that need to be adjusted in concert with each other in order to achieve equilibrium. We then realized that in our concern to not have the pavilion collapse during its assembly, we had fully tightened all the coupler bolts as each piece was installed. Within 30 minutes we loosened the bolts enough so that the last pieces simply dropped into place.

The success of the MARS Pavilion brought attention from the media and humanitarian organizations. While initially considering having us build permanent homes based on this technology, we quickly suggested that there might be more appropriate structures devised to meet their needs. Architecture is never a "one-size-fits-all" proposition. Similarly, Maslow's Hammer postulates that "if all you have is a hammer, everything looks like a nail." Because our work is a research-based exploration of design and context, we constantly seek the appropriate technology to meet any given challenge. Integrating structure and ornament, reducing material waste and cost, and speeding project delivery are among our many pursuits.

While we don't consider ourselves to be robotics experts or concrete experts, we have developed a propensity for finding new solutions to new problems. This is why we proposed a radically different building system when The Armenian Relief and Development Association (ARDA) first reached out to us, requesting 3D printed, concrete homes. The 1988 Spitak earthquake in Armenia left devastating damage which is still being felt today as nearly 4,000 families continue to live in crude, temporary shelters, referred to as "Domiks." With access to the computational light-gauge steel FRAMECAD machine at Orange Coast College, we proposed a partially prefabricated panelized structure that could be quickly assembled in

Figure 7D.4 *MARS Pavilion in Palm Springs, CA*
Source: Form Found Design

Figure 7D.5 *MARS Pavilion in Palm Springs, CA with co-founders Ron Culver, AIA (left) and Joseph Sarafian, AIA (right)*
Source: Ben Rose Photography

Armenia. Currently in development, the first such structure is slated to be erected this coming summer, with many more to follow.

Also in development are offshoots of the same concept for low-cost multi-family housing. We are currently designing an entire high-rise multi-family building assembled from factory-complete panels with specialized connections

Figure 7D.6 *MARS Pavilion at the Architecture and Design Museum in Downtown Los Angeles* Source: Tony Castillo

Figure 7D.7 *Robotically prefabricated wall panel system with resulting modular triplex below* Source: Form Found Design

Figure 7D.8
*Robotically
prefabricated
high-rise tower
with undulating
apartment units*
Source: Form Found
Design

and full finishes inside and out, including all mechanical, electrical, and plumbing components.

Our aim is to disrupt the current escalation of construction costs and bring truly affordable construction to facilitate affordable housing projects. Presented with new problems, we continue to find new tools to appropriate into our profession to meet the needs in front of us, making a few necessary upgrades along the way.

What began as a grad school material exploration with fabric and robots launched not only our company, but a new realm of possibilities for realizing complex geometry in architecture. This material exploration showed us that asking the right questions with the right team in place could lead to unexpected results. The multi-directional stretch of fabric coupled with the plasticity of cement, created a material that could be animated through the choreography of highly precise robotics. We had 6-axis robots available to us when the research began, so the forms always had the "signature" of the tool (robots) imprinted on the result. The number of limbs in each wishbone has always been limited to the number of robots available to actuate the fabric. In this case, the tool at hand heavily influenced the product outcome. However, we look forward to new tools being created specifically for the purpose of robotically manipulating fabric formwork. We are optimistic that future research will continue to proliferate, pushing the industry closer to an architecture with fewer geometric limitations in the built realm, allowing architects more design freedom in their work and allowing us all to live in a more uplifting built environment.

Project Information:

Chapter:7D
Form-Finding the MARS Pavilion
Ron Culver and Joseph Sarafian, Form Found Design, USA
Project Lead:
Joseph Sarafian, AIA/Ron Culver, AIA
Project Location: Palm Springs, CA
Client: Amazon
Donations/Financial Support: Walter P. Moore, ABB Robotics
Awards:
2018 AN Best of Design Awards
ArchDaily Best Young Practices, 2020
Project Studio Timeline:
Material Exploration: 3 Months
Industrial Robot Setup and Calibration: 1 Month
Design: 3 Months
Fabrication: 1 Month
On-site Installation: 2 Days
Total: 8 Months, 2 Days

NOTES

1. "The Foundations of Digital Architecture: Peter Eisenman," *YouTube*, uploaded by The Canadian Centre for Architecture, May 21, 2013, https://youtu.be/hKCrepgOix4
2. Peter, John. *The Oral History of Modern Architecture: Interviews with the Greatest Architects of the Twentieth Century*. H.N. Abrams, New York, 1994.

BIBLIOGRAPHY

Culver R., Koerner J., Sarafian J., Fabric Forms: The Robotic Positioning of Fabric Formwork. In: Reinhardt D., Saunders R., Burry J. (eds) *Robotic Fabrication in Architecture, Art and Design* 2016. Springer, Cham. pp. 107–121.

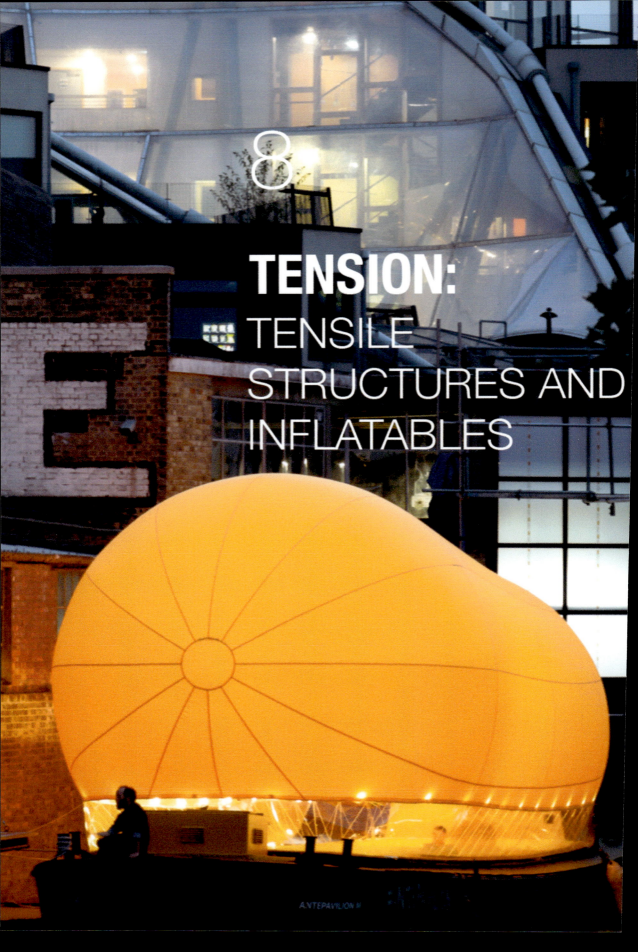

8

TENSION:
TENSILE STRUCTURES AND INFLATABLES

ANTEPAVILION

ACADEMIC INQUIRY

8A

**Fabric[ating]
Act[ivat]ion**

**ANTJE
STEINMULLER**

8A   Fabric[ating] Act[ivat]ion

Antje Steinmuller

INTRODUCTION

The nature and form of urban social spaces has changed considerably over the past two decades, as have the mechanisms for its activation and appropriation. New types of social spaces have emerged through event-based activation that range from guerrilla initiatives to publicly or privately sponsored performances and festivals. In a third form of social space, often referred to as commons, communities come together to create, and steward, collective spaces that cater to specific local need. A critical discourse has emerged in relation to these processes of commoning, investigating how architectural expertise can contribute to the creation of such community-initiated spaces while supporting the longevity of tactical interventions. This chapter puts forward a methodology for a short-term catalytic intervention in such a community project that leverages the familiarity and flexibility of fabric towards a redeployable intervention that enables the activation of an urban space through multiple uses.

The story of Fabric[ating] Act[ivat]ion begins with a summer travel studio at California College of the Arts (CCA), set up to expose students to community-led approaches to urban social space. The destination was Madrid, Spain, whose historic and current evolution of public spaces holds lessons from both ends of the spectrum—from government funded concepts to bottom-up neighborhood interventions in public space. Madrid's recent economic struggle has sparked the evolution of a culture of bottom-up initiatives to impact the public realm, fostering opportunistic and novel urban projects that emerge with and without the involvement of architects. This context of community-initiated projects brings forth questions about the toolkit future architects need in order to productively and innovatively engage with the physical, economic, and cultural aspects of urban space activation today. Recognizing the importance of these questions for architectural education, the participating group was composed of an interdisciplinary team of students in order to spark conversations about the types of expertise needed to support such community projects.

Collaborations between architects and local communities are long-term endeavors in which short studios can only have a limited, yet potentially catalytic role. It was the goal of the studio to expose students to working with a community partner while offering disciplinary expertise within an already ongoing long-term project in which a multivalent intervention was required. Designed by two instructors who

DOI: 10.4324/9781003138471-26

offered combined expertise in tensile structures and bottom-up urbanism, the studio was set up to work with fabric, which, with its ubiquity, familiarity, relatively low cost, weight, and easy deployment was the perfect material for this project. Fabric's traditional association with domestic interiors offered additional opportunities in the conversion of an urban space into what was to be a multi-purpose community gathering space.

FRAMING COMMUNITY CONNECTIONS

The project site, in the San Cristóbal neighborhood of Madrid, is located on the outskirts of the city and home to different immigrant groups. This area generally lacks public spaces, employment opportunities, and social infrastructure. Basurama, a local team of architects and artists concerned with issues of environmental consumption and waste, had been working with the San Cristóbal community through their Autobarrios (Self-Made Neighborhoods) project. Autobarrios reflects a way of city-making that relies on building a network between a range of urban "agents" who contribute their expertise towards a specific goal. In the case of San Cristóbal, the *Autobarrios* project began in 2012 and was centered on the incremental transformation of an abandoned space under an overpass known as Puente de Colores, with the goal to convert it to an evocative urban space by and for neighborhood youth and residents. Local artists Boamistura donated murals, and the French architecture group Collectif Etc contributed multifunctional urban furniture in the form of triangular wooden platforms. Basurama's network of local non-profits, professional partnerships, and industry had supported the project through material and monetary donations and expertise. CCA Summer Programs contributed a modest materials budget to the project. At the time of the CCA studio, the community was managing the programming, use, and maintenance of the space with the guidance of Basurama.

As part of this programming, the community planned to host a TEDx event on the site, hoping that the infrastructure for this event could later serve movie screenings, youth summer classes, and everyday gatherings of local residents. The studio partners Basurama and Teamlabs, a unit of Mondragon University's social entrepreneurship program, integrated CCA students into the ongoing conversations about the TEDx project within the community. During their stay, students were set up to participate in community dialog about entrepreneurial fundraising, collaborative design workshops, and full-scale construction, while contributing their expertise in design, strategizing, and making to a real-world project. The interdisciplinary make-up of the CCA student team (Architecture, Design MBA, and MFA) provided a set-up in which more than one expertise was present, and where productive discussions about the "toolkit" needed for the project could take place.

FRAMING THE PROCESS

The pedagogy for this studio drew on a four-part methodology outlined in Mona El Khafif's book *Inszenierter Urbanismus: Stadtraum für Kunst, Kultur und Konsum im Zeitalter der Erlebnisgesellschaft*[1] (Staged Urbanism: City Space for Art, Culture, and Consumption in the Age of the Event Society). In the context of the multitude of factors necessary for successful public spaces, El Khafif puts forward the terms: *hardware*, *software*, *orgware*, and *brandware* as constituent components of urban space design. The formal-spatial manifestation in dialog with the layer of lived experience and social interactions, have frequently been described as the *hardware* and *software* of a space.[2] The use of the term *software* varies from programming,[3] to ideas and knowledge,[4] to meanings and interpretations[5] through use. Yet, these different uses of the term share the understanding that the physical form is read, understood, and shaped through activities taking place in it. The German term "Bespielung" ("to transfer play onto something") aptly describes *software* as playful interpretation, and the addition of something that adds rules and content.[6] *Orgware* ("organization-ware") has been described by the Dutch research and planning practice Crimson Architectural Historians as the underlying rules and governing structures that enable any project to function.[7] *Orgware* negotiates between software and hardware[8] and connects stakeholders. It can be seen as the organizational intelligence that makes things happen. A fourth parameter is the way a space is conceived and perceived, and, ultimately, represented.[9] This includes the understanding formed through lived experience, as well as the way a space is represented to an audience through various forms of media. Mona El Khafif has described this layer as *brandware*.[10]

The production of a contemporary urban commons differs from the spaces El Khafif applies these four terms to, in that the process of creation is neither led by a government agency nor the purview of a private entity. Instead, it involves close collaboration of and with community members, requiring the design of a process that choreographs the interaction of all stakeholders and ensures the productive use of everyone's knowledge and expertise. This includes structuring workflow, feedback sessions, and team interactions across the involved participants. The process of commoning itself has to be designed. The studio used the term '*formware*' for[11] the design of this process, appropriating the term *form* as it is used in dance choreography, where it describes movement itself, including the occupation of space, timings, and the specific use of the body. Form, in this context, is understood as opposite to content and expression.

Based on the five parameters just described, the scope for the studio was outlined as follows: Students needed to understand the specific qualities of the existing space and produce flexible, deployable structures that could address both short-term and long-term needs for the activation of the space (*hardware*). *Hardware*, here, took on the exploration of a soft material, fabric, and the potential changeability and multiplicity within its deployment. How the malleable applications of fabric might respond to and catalyze use of the space—the *software*—evolved through community meetings, interactive posters, and informal interviews on site. This helped students to link existing social activities, local patterns, and possible future events to the space under the overpass. Local organizations, citizens, and institutions that might benefit from using the space needed to be connected into a mutually beneficial network that could activate the space on a regular basis (*orgware*); and the current perceptions and representations of the space in the local population, as well as the media, needed to be understood in order to contribute to

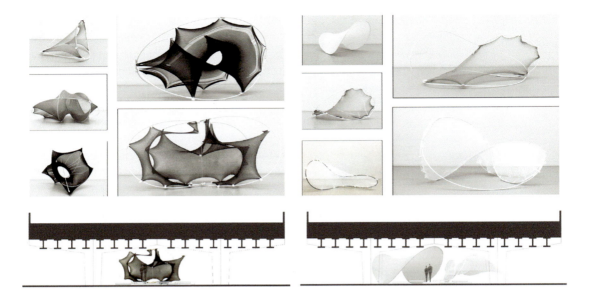

Figure 8A.1 *Fabric studies in small-scale tensile structures*
Source: Photos: studio team

the strengthening of its image and presence (*brandware*). The instructors, Teamlabs and Basurama, shaped the workflow around design and construction, the feedback sessions between student teams internally, and between the students and the community (*formware*).

PRELUDE

To shape an understanding of working with fabric, a three-day pre-travel workshop allowed students to explore the spatial potential of nylon net fabric stretched over flexible styrene plastic rods in small-scale models (Figure 8A.1). This form of "tactile research" used hands-on making as knowledge building, and gave students experiential insight into the forces involved as the interaction of bent rods and stretchable fabric translates two-dimensional soft surface into complex and stable three-dimensional form. The behavior of fabric in tension can be scaled with relative ease. Through the model studies students understood the impact of variations in attachment, bending, and fabric tension within what was termed "form families." Quick drawings and collages tested possible scales and formations for the space under a street overpass (Figure 8A.1). Tensile structures were also introduced through lectures on precedents that ranged from indigenous tent structures and spiderwebs, artwork by Ernesto Neto and Tomas Saraceno, to work developed by co-instructor Mauricio Soto himself at the Institute for Lightweight Structures (ILEK) at the University of Stuttgart.

These early studies of 'form families' were documented and compiled into a booklet that was sent to the partners in Madrid before traveling there, giving the local community a three-week feedback period. Upon arrival in Madrid, a first discussion session with neighborhood representatives and local collaborators served to set a design direction based on feedback on these formal studies (Figure 8A.2). The possible programmatic performance of specific formal approaches was aligned

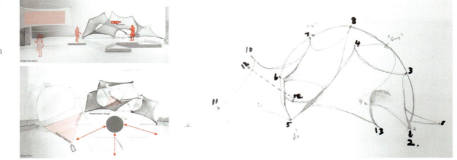

with the desired use of the space for the TEDx event. The selected approach was then refined in further small-scale models and collages (Figure 8A.3) that took into account the attachment points that were available in the form of existing triangular wood platforms on site.

The community prioritized the design of a stage area with specific emphasis on a backdrop that could hide props and interact with lighting. In addition, the definition of smaller zones—as entry points or small activity areas for kids—was a key consideration. Last, a surface for film projection was required for both the TEDx event, and for future outdoor movie nights. Once the general form for the stage was selected and refined through physical models, the attachment of the rods and fabric was mapped and numbered in a rough sketch (Figure 8A.3). All remaining work occurred on site at full scale. Since the construction method was known prior to travel, fiberglass rods had been shipped to Spain from the US as their local availability was unknown. Widely available stretchable fabric was purchased in Madrid together with zip ties, thread, sewing needles, aluminum piping, and other supplies for attachment (Figure 8A.4).

Figure 8A.4
Materials
Source: Antje
Steinmuller

STAGING ACT[IVAT]ION

While the general forces in tensile structures are easily scaleable, the more specific performance of different fabrics and fiberglass rods of different thickness was
not foreseeable without engineering calculations of the complex form. In lieu of
access to adequate computer models, hands-on testing was used by setting up
the rods in their desired formation on site and compensating for excessive bending
by bundling them. Fabric attachment points were clipped temporarily to test ideal
locations. Once these were determined, rings were sewn into the fabric at these
locations, enabling either direct threading of the fabric onto the rods, or alternative
attachment with zip ties (Figure 8A.5). It was here that considerations of disassem-
bly and reassembly became primary drivers for decision-making. One of the main
goals was to take advantage of the lightness and malleability of fabric to allow for
easy storage and reuse, maintaining a maximum flexibility in the use of the space
at Puente de Colores and minimizing waste through reuse. Accordingly, fabric and
rod attachments were minimized and designed for intuitive layperson assembly.
To facilitate redeployment, one of the students used both full-scale installation
and scale models to create a visual instruction manual that detailed the necessary
sequence of assembly (Figure 8A.6). Digital drawings, here, became a retroactive
recording of the construction process of the physical artifact.

The parameters of the studio methodology—specifically *hardware*, *software*,
orgware, and *brandware*—provided the key to structuring group work, and also
allowed the interdisciplinary student team to take advantage of the different
expertise present. To ensure a reciprocal relationship between the parameters
during the process, three teams were formed, each around the intersection of
two categories. Team 1 bridged between *hardware* and *software*. This group was
tasked with developing the physical components for the stage environment, while
integrating the long-term programmatic needs of the community into the design
considerations. Team 2 worked at the intersection between *software* and *orgware*.
Its tasks included engaging the local social context, researching existing activities and desires, and uncovering space needs and potential links between local

Figure 8A.5 *On-site full-scale testing and assembly*
Source: Antje Steinmuller

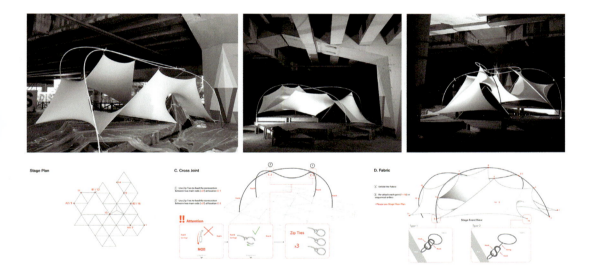

Figure 8A.6 *Final stage assembly and excerpts from the instruction manual*
Source: Jonathan Joong

organizations and institutions. This group structured community visits to the site including community input posters in the neighborhood and a children's workshop on site. Team 3 was concerned with the overlap of *orgware* and *brandware*. Its research assembled all available information disseminated by various stakeholders that had impacted the perception and representation of the space both locally and online in the past three years. The goal was to further shape the site's identity through communication strategies, and to promote it to a larger audience in the process. Two people in each team served as "links" to the respective other teams, keeping them abreast of ongoing work on a daily basis. As part of this "cross-pollination" between groups, design decisions were discussed and critiqued. At the same time, each team member felt a strong association with their team and a sense of responsibility towards the larger group.

The fifth parameter—*formware*—developed the choreography of all stakeholders within the tight timeline of a three-week summer studio. It should be noted that any community relationship that is meaningful necessitates longer timelines. The CCA team was highly aware of its role as invited participants to an ongoing community project and a little-known context. The studio therefore relied heavily on its collaborators in Madrid. Basurama set up initial community meetings and facilitated communication across the language barrier. The studio partners also connected students to Casa San Cristóbal, a local neighborhood organization and cultural center that connected the CCA group to a local children's summer camp, and Fundaçion Montemadrid, a center for culture and social exchange that had played a key role in organizing the TEDx event and visited the site during assembly.

Students took charge of the informal engagement of local residents, conducting interviews on the street, and mounting interactive posters around the neighborhood where anyone could record their aspirations for Puente de Colores in writing or drawing. Engaging local children from the summer cap with the transformation of the site also attracted parents and other community members to stop by and enter into dialog with the student teams. The children, meanwhile, assisted in the production of temporary signage to the space, and were taught new skills as they helped with construction.

OPENING NIGHT FOR FUTURE ACTIVITIES

At the end of the process, the products of the studio touched all parameters for public space activation: a four-part *hardware* fabricated for the site included a stage backdrop with a backstage area (Figure 8A.6 top), a projection screen, and two mobile "shells" that could organize traffic flow for large events, but also define small areas for reading events and sheltered play spaces. While Teams 2 and 3 produced interactions with community members and a larger communications strategy online and in the physical space, the full student group participated in sewing and final installation of the four artifacts. Members of Team 1, who had developed the details and techniques, guided their studio mates in the sewing and assembly techniques. All structures were designed for quick set-up and easy storage when not in use. The studio also compiled comprehensive easy-to-follow visual instructions for all components into a handbook (Figure 8A.6 bottom) that was left with Casa San Cristóbal where the components were to be stored.

In addition to the physical constructs, the studio produced a *software/orgware* document outlining scenarios for the deployment of the structures during specific activities including photography classes, reading spaces, venues for small theater performances, movie nights, and more (Figure 8A.7). This document took into account activity timeframes, the simultaneous presence of different groups on the site, and (where not already existing) proposed collaborations of local organizations and potential sponsors. As part of *orgware/brandware*, a message board was constructed and left permanently on the site to gather further citizen feedback and announce future events, improving their visibility to locals. Bilingual Wikipedia pages about Puente de Colores went live, and the documentation of the CCA

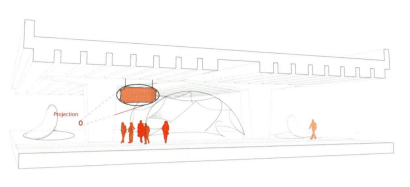

Theater Performances
The structures may serve as set pieces for th
performances for productions both by comn
members and by outside theatre troupe
addition the screen may be used for outdoor cl
projections.

Equipment   Potential Partners   Audience

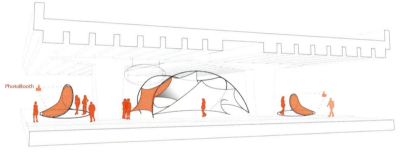

Photography Class and Studio
The structures may be used to create a backdrop for
photography shoots, with the rods accommodating
additional backdrops (colored cloth, props, etc).
Since the community has hosted a photo workshop
previously, the structures could also support
continued learning and skills development. In
addition, since we found that the children were very
enthusiastic about the photo booth activity that
we did, it would be a great way for the community
to capture its members (taking child and family
photos) and even to display some of the photos
publicly by using the structures to create a sort of
gallery space.

Equipment   Potential Partners   Audience

Figure 8A.7 *Excerpt from software/ orgware document for possible space activations*
Source: Jonathan Joong

project was picked up by various blogs and news outlets—a valuable contribution to shaping the evolving image of the space.

On the last day of the travel studio's stay in Madrid, the TEDx event under the overpass took place with six speakers and more than 450 attendees. It served as a proof that the design could live up to its planned ten-minute set-up and take-down period. The student team formally handed over a 30-page document to community representatives with instructions and suggestions for future activation. While the assembly of the fabric structures was designed with great attention towards future layperson users, this manual seemed critical as mediation between disciplinary knowledge and everyday set-up. Similarly, while the manual suggested regular local events to enliven the space at Puente de Colores while making use of the fabric structures, Basurama's role as a mediator and initiator of events was critical. Their work on Autobarrio San Cristóbal would be able to reinforce and guide future use.

While the nature of a summer travel studio prevented further involvement of the students with the site and the any future use of the artifacts constructed, students will carry with them the lessons gained about the reuse and redeployability of fabric structures. Even complex forms like the stage backdrop require few attachment points and can be set up with ease. Considering multiple parameters for the successful production of community commons proved valuable and instilled in the participating students as sense of the expanded toolkit[12] that is required for architects committed to this type of work.

Back in Madrid, the story of Puente de Colores goes on, supported by the possibilities of the fabric structures left behind.

Project Information:

Chapter: Fabric[ating] Act[ivat]ion
Professor/Project Lead: Antje Steinmuller, Mauricio Soto Rubio
University/Organization: California College of the Arts (CCA)
Students: Jessica Ayran, Fernanda Bernardes, Whitney Bush, Lujac Desautel, Joy Fu, Sara Haag, Jonathan Weichung Joong, Pixie Kaminski, Gloria Asaba Kiiza, Ryan Montgomery, Leticia Murray, Brett Petty, Ernesto Preciado-Canez, Emily Robin, Nicole Shiflett, Anne Steeves, Anh Vu, Jessica Zamora
Project Location: Puente de Colores San Cristòbal, Madrid, Spain
Client: San Cristòbal Community, Madrid
Donations/Financial Support: CCA $2,200

Studio Timeline:

— Material Exploration:	3 Days
— Site Visits and Precedent Studies:	1.5 Weeks (overlapping with Design)
— Design:	1 Week
— Fabrication:	1 Week
— Total:	3.5 Weeks

NOTES

1. Mona El Khafif, *Inszenierter Urbanismus: Stadtraum für Kunst, Kultur und Konsum im Zeitalter der Erlebnisgesellschaft* (Saarbruecken: VDM, 2009).
2. see for example Bernhard Butzin, "Was macht die Industrieregionen alt—Das Beispiel Ruhrgebiet", in: *Berichte zur deutschen Landeskunde*, Bd. 67, H.2 (1993), S. 243–254; Rients Dijkstra, Michelle Provoost and Wouter Vanstiphout, "30,000 Houses Near Utrecht", in *Archis*, Nr.8, 1995, pp. 70–80; Mona El Khafif, *Inszenierter Urbanismus: Stadtraum für Kunst, Kultur und Konsum im Zeitalter der Erlebnisgesellschaft* (Saarbruecken: VDM, 2009) among others.
3. Mona El Khafif. *Inszenierter Urbanismus*, p. 20.
4. Dijkstra a.o. "30,000 Houses."
5. Michael Speaks in Rahul Mehrotra, Ed., *Everyday Urbanism, Margaret Crawford vs. Michael Speaks*, Michigan Debates on Urbanism, vol. 1 (New York: Arts Press, 2004), p. 18.
6. Mona El Khafif. *Inszenierter Urbanismus*, p. 65.
7. Dijkstra a.o. "30,000 Houses", p. 71.
8. Michael Speaks. *Everyday Urbanism*, p. 39.
9. see Christian Schmid. "Henri Lefebvre", p. 51.
10. Mona El Khafif. *Inszenierter Urbanismus*, p. 20.
11. Antje Steinmuller. "The Act(ivat)or's Toolbox: Expanded Roles, Actions, and Parameters in the Production of the Urban Commons", in: Corser, Robert, and Sharon Haar (eds.). *Shaping New Knowledges; 104th ACSA Annual Meeting*, Seattle, WA. March 17–19, 2016 (Washington, DC: ACSA, 2016), pp. 52–60.
12. Steinmuller, "The Act(ivat)or's Toolbox", p. 54.

8B

HOLLYGROVE
Shade-Winter Pavilion

JUDITH KINNARD, IRENE KEIL and NICK JENISCH

8B   Hollygrove Shade-Water Pavilion

Judith Kinnard, Irene Keil and Nick Jenisch

PROJECT BACKGROUND

The Shade-Water pavilion was constructed in 2016 on a vacant corner site in an underserved New Orleans neighborhood. The pavilion was part of an incremental urban design and engagement process that began in 2012 and continues today. The project was initiated by community leaders who sought to activate a neglected strip of public land cutting diagonally through the Hollygrove neighborhood. Located in a low-lying district between Carrollton Avenue and the Jefferson Parish line, this residential community was developed in the 1920s along the edges of the raised rail corridor connecting New Orleans north to Chicago. The line was decommissioned in 1955 and replaced with an underground drainage canal below the right-of-way, leaving a 50-foot-wide swath of fenced vacant plots along the mile-long corridor above. The Carrollton/Hollygrove Community Development Corporation (CHCDC) & Hollygrove Market and Farm invited the Tulane City Center to help the neighborhood imagine how the area could be reclaimed as a place of gathering rather than rupture. Students and faculty engaged the project in a design studio and as summer fellows as the project took shape through several phases.

The first challenges faced by the CHCDC were to gain support from the neighbors and access to the site from its owner, the Sewerage and Water Board of New Orleans (SWBNO). Tulane faculty and students did extensive historical research, site analysis, and documentation as they developed materials to facilitate a design charrette with community members. This led to a visioning document for what was christened the "Hollygrove Greenline." In 2012 Judith Kinnard's advanced design studio used this research to ground the exploration of public space strategies along the corridor together with affordable housing on adjacent vacant blocks. Students from the studio continued as summer fellows to develop a master plan using materials from the studio and the community charrette. This document led to a successful proposal submitted to the SWBNO by the neighborhood CDC to convey two key parcels of the Greenline for community use. Though the master plan included a pavilion, play space, shade trees and community gardens, initial grant funding supported only the removal of the fencing and the addition of a concrete path and a line of Nuttall oaks connecting the two parcels. The first iteration of the pavilion was shown in the master plan as a series of shade sails supported by steel posts. The interest in developing the

DOI: 10.4324/9781003138471-27

SITE

structure around the theme of stormwater developed when the SWBNO issued a request for small-scale green infrastructure proposals. The Tulane team developed a schematic proposal for a water-collecting shade structure that would provide educational content on stormwater management. This proposal was funded, and the design was developed by a team led by Irene Keil and Judith Kinnard in 2016.

Figure 8B.1 *SITE: aerial view, site plan* Source: Photo courtesy of James Catalano; Drawing courtesy of Small Center

212

CONCEPT

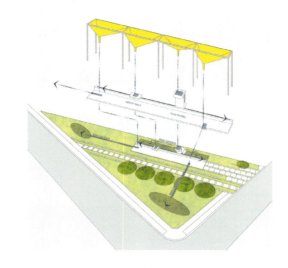

1 - water vessels | drain to rain gardens
2 - linear bench | water trough
3 - table | water cascade
4 - gate | raised water collection
5 - textile funnels | shade; water collection
6 - pavilion structure | 4 x 4 HTS steel
7 - raised water tank | 275 gallons
8 - water gardens

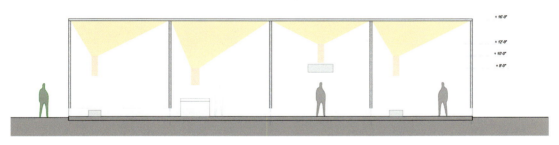

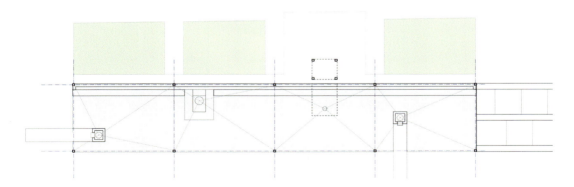

Figure 8B.2 *CONCEPT: project elements, section + plan drawing*
Source: Drawing courtesy of Small Center

WATERWORKS

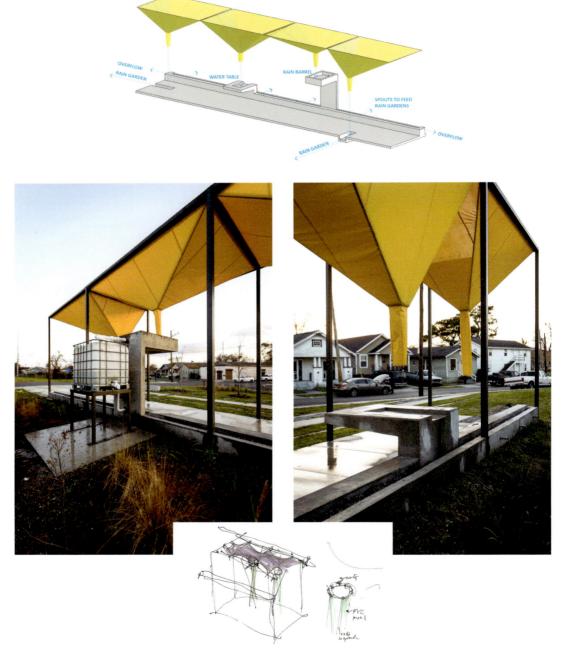

Figure 8B.3 *WATERWORKS: water elements, views of pavilion structure, idea sketch*
Source: Drawings + photos courtesy of Small Center

THE PAVILION DESIGN

As the project developed over several years, the fundamental intent remained the same: to connect the neighborhood by providing an outdoor meeting space. The pavilion is designed to provide shelter while gathering and directing the rainwater into gardens using four elements distinguished by their form, their material, and their purpose: the porous rain gardens, a heavy concrete groundwork, a slender steel frame, and a series of translucent fabric tents. These Semperian elements each play a specific role in establishing shelter. The steel tube framework reiterates the rhythm of the trees and establishes the urban presence of the structure through its scale and proportions. The ground plane and the "roof" membrane work together to address the multiple demands of collecting, shedding, and directing water while promoting airflow. The project accepts and advances the dynamic forces associated with the physical environment, which include hydrology as well as sun and wind. The design team sought to move beyond the notion of a pavilion as a static object and to understand it as continually responsive to the highly dynamic forces of weather and weathering over time.

Figure 8B.4 *SAILS: Fabric and concrete elements*
Source: Photo courtesy of James Catalano

MATERIALITY AND FABRICATION

Though roofs are typically designed to shed water, the need to focus the flow of the water resulted in the inversion of the standard roof form into an upside-down pyramid. These funnel the rain through extended soft "snouts" that engage the concrete elements below. The forms of the "tent" membrane were developed with both physical and digital models. An iterative series of basswood and vellum models of the tents were particularly important to the design process. These were analyzed relative to their visual impact and their impact on the space below. Fabric was chosen for these forms initially for its historic associations with the essence of shelter. Continued research on the specific material characteristics of advanced fabrics showed the potential for varied permeability within the project. The inverted pyramids benefited from a loose weave chosen due to its ability to breathe and to filter light while channeling water. As a semi-tropical city with a hot and humid climate, New Orleans has a long tradition of using canvas awnings to block sun while filtering light and allowing air to circulate. These can be found in both institutional and residential settings and often use color to establish a strong identity. The team engaged local awning fabricators in the design development phase. The final form of the elements of the tent structure and their connections came out of this collaboration. The joining and welding of the aluminum frames, the cutting, stitching, stretching, and lashing of the fabric vessels and snouts were all developed based on their experience with tested methods. Digital design and fabrication had not yet come to the awning industry in Louisiana and visits to the shop floor showed this form of soft construction to be more analogous to dressmaking than to traditional framing. Seams were reinforced to accept movement from wind and the uneven loading from water. The spacing of the grommets and the techniques of tying these to the frames were determined by experience. These skilled craftspeople had sewn custom awnings over decades in a city known for intense rainfall and hurricane force winds.

THE WATERWORKS

The pavilion operates as a machine that facilitates the engagement with water, inspired by the grand waterworks and displays in baroque gardens. Water is intended to be playful, useful, and instructional. It is designed around a series of concrete elements that catch and display rainwater: A long bench coupled with a trough distributes water cascading from a low table receptacle and disperses it through scuppers to the water garden behind. An L-shaped concrete wall acts as a gate but also catches water and channels it to a storage tank behind. Cuts in the slab allow water to drain and be channeled to two rain gardens at the low-lying areas of the site. Fabric sails overhead provide shade and add color and movement to the structure.

TEMPORALITY

The pavilion and the Greenline site are understood to be part of a temporal process both in terms of its materiality and its role in the community. Given the extreme

SAILS

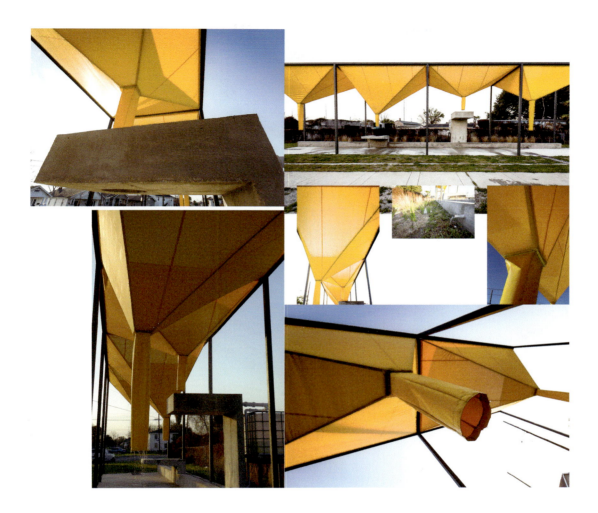

Figure 8B.5
*PAVILION: pavilion
in context of site*
Source: Photos
courtesy of Small
Center

climate in New Orleans, the design team understood that fabric structures in New Orleans will last for 5–10 years before they need replacement. The steel and concrete components will mark the site over a much longer time and the Nuttall Oaks can live for over a century. The fabric canopies can be replaced or transformed to adapt to the needs of the neighborhood, and new gardens can be planted around the structure.

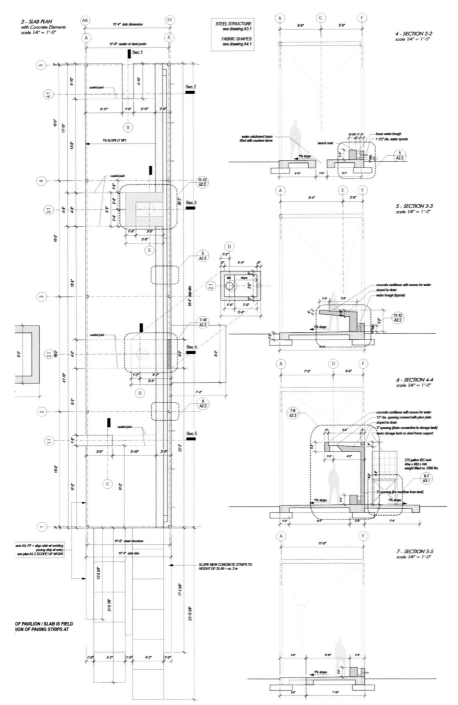

Figure 8B.6
PAVILION
CONCRETE
ELEMENTS:
concrete elements
plan + sections
Source: Drawings
courtesy of Small
Center

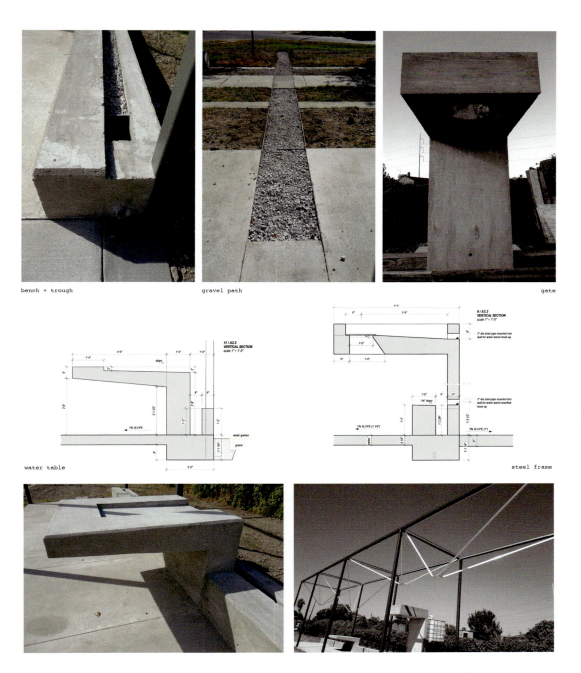

bench + trough   gravel path   gate

water table   steel frame

Figure 8B.7 *PAVILION DETAILS: bench + trough; gravel path; gate; vertical section; water table; steel frame*
Source: Drawings + photos courtesy of Small Center

Figure 8B.8 *COMMUNITY: from top left: planting day with community; brass band at dedication; break during planting day, starting from bottom left: brass band at dedication; cooling down; bottom image: playing*

WEAVING COMMUNITY

The Greenline and the Shade-Water Pavilion are at the center of a community that remains committed to adding value and beauty to their neighborhood. The groups that gathered to celebrate the opening of the structure looked forward to renewing investment in the area after Hurricane Katrina. Economic stability remained elusive, however, and though the Carrollton-Hollygrove CDC helped to maintain the property and facilitated community engagement meetings and input sessions over the project's several years, they recently suspended operations. The SWBNO's maintenance staff has been stretched as well and the fabric surfaces that were once an electric yellow have faded over time and have a patina of age. The SWBNO has recently contracted with a local firm to make needed repairs and the long snouts that children have played with are being replaced. These conditions are understood to be part of the essence of a work made and remade over time. Fabric structures are both strong and fragile. Using materials and methods that are both ancient and advanced, they can be easily renewed by the communities they support and shelter.

University/Organization:

Tulane School of Architecture/Small Center for Collaborative Design

Professor/Project Lead:

Irene Keil, RA, Professor of Practice, Tulane School of Architecture
Judith Kinnard, FAIA, Professor, Tulane School of Architecture
Nick Jenisch, Project Manager, Small Center for Collaborative Design, Tulane University

Project Location:

New Orleans, Louisiana

Client:

Carrollton-Hollygrove CDC and the Sewerage and Water Board of New Orleans (SWBNO)

Donations/Financial Support:

SWBNO, Surdna, Enterprise Holdings Foundation, Emerging Philanthropists of New Orleans

Awards:

AIA Louisiana Honor Award
AIA New Orleans Architecture Merit Award
Louisiana USGBC Sustainable Design Award

Contributors:

Organizations

Project support provided by Sewerage & Water Board of New Orleans, Carrollton-Hollygrove CDC, Emerging Philanthropists of New Orleans, Surdna Foundation, and Enterprise Holdings Foundation.
Tulane City Center, now The Albert and Tina Small Center for Collaborative Design
The Tulane School of Architecture's community design center provides design services to non-profits and neighborhoods across New Orleans.

Judith Kinnard, FAIA (architect), Irene Keil (architect)
Staff: Nick Jenisch, Dan Etheridge, Maurice Cox, John Coyle, Shoshana Gordon,
    Maggie Hansen, Sue Mobley, Donn Peabody, Emilie Taylor Welty
Students: Michael Battipaglia, Michael Cohen, Alisha Croft, Zachary Gong, Chesley
    McCarty, Scott Mikawa, Ian O'Cain, Dorothy Shepard
Carrollton-Hollygrove CDC
    Jarvain Bingmon
Dana Brown & Associates (Landscape Architect)
    Dana Brown, Gaylan Williams
Walter Zehner & Associates, Inc. (Engineer)
    Walter Zehner
Appropriate Technology (Builder)
    William Slattery
C Bel Awnings, now JB Awnings (Fabric fabrication)
    Jay Bonck

PROFESSIONAL INQUIRY

8C

AIRDRAFT

THOMAS
RANDALL-PAGE

8C AirDraft

Thomas Randall-Page

With a boat for a father, and an airship for a mother

In 2017 Russell Gray of Shiva Ltd. a development and property management company based in London, launched "Antepavilion", an arts and architecture charity that aims to "promote independent thought and symbiosis in the fields of art, craft and architecture." At this point they started a relationship with the Architecture Foundation and launched the first of what would become an annual architecture competition to design a temporary and experimental pavilion for one of their sites on the bank of the Regents Canal in Haggerston, East London.

COMPETITION BRIEF

> Architects, artists and designers are invited to propose a floating structure to be sited on the Regent's canal at Columbia and Brunswick Wharf in Hackney. The platform for entries is the 62 foot motor barge, 'Ouse', built in 1934 for canal operators, Canal Transport Ltd for maintenance on the Leeds-Liverpool canal. Ouse is now moored alongside Columbia and Brunswick Wharf as a base for the new structure.
>
> As with its predecessor, the concept of the floating Antepavilion is not pre-scribed. Entries may be purely sculptural, structural or political, or have a real or notional function such as social, habitable or performance space. Proposals for public events to take place in the Antepavilion will need to be self-financing or resourced from the overall budget.
>
> Antepavilion Statement

With the scarcity of opportunities for young architects to build in this city, I was immediately excited by the prospect of entering this competition. Canals are, by definition, not natural, but experiencing them from a vessel that was specifically built for such journeys brought them into focus and made them make more sense. Ouse was just such a vessel, part of a historic industrial infrastructure that was the lifeblood of the industrial revolution in the UK.

BENI AND THE BOAT

I decided to approach my talented university friend Benedetta Rogers to collaborate with. We visited Ouse and were struck by her voluminous open hold, eye-deep and

DOI: 10.4324/9781003138471-29

Figure 8C.1 *Initial competition concept collage, showing the curious grub-like inflatable as viewed from the canal-side walk.* Source: Thomas Randall-Page and Benedetta Rogers

ribbed, like the inside of a whale. Even when empty, her robust iron construction displaced a fair amount of water, leaving the water hitting at waist level. With half of your body below this datum, the interior viewpoint allowed you to peer out at the eye level of other boat/canoe users.

A DESIGN RESPONSE

In response to the hardness of the surrounding warehouse art-space, our site, our first big decision was to offer something wholly soft and comforting, a place where you could kick off your shoes and lounge around like a toddler.

The other early decision was that Ouse should remain mobile, what's the point of being a boat if you can't travel over the water? As barges, when loaded, typically sit very low in the water, the bridges all over the canal network tend to have very minimal headroom between them and the water. In nautical terminology this above water clearance is called "Air Draft" as opposed to "Draft" which is the similar clearance below the water. This constraint leads most barges to be fairly low inside. In contrast, we were clear that we wanted to create a grandiose and lofty space.

Inflatable technology offered the potential solution to both these design ambitions and started us exploring air-supported precedents.

A FASCINATION WITH INFLATABLES

I have always loved inflatables, and whilst an undergraduate in Glasgow School of Art, the extraordinarily holistic "IL" series of books produced by the Frei Otto's Institute of Lightweight Structures in Frankfurt were never far from my desk. Lloyd

Kahn's 1970s masterpiece "Shelter", a bible of counterculture DIY and vernacular world architectures, was bought for me by my dad and there I was introduced to the work of Ant Farm and Buckminster Fuller. These influences sparked a longstanding interest in doing more with less, in lightness and efficiency of structures and spaces.

There is also a sculptural attraction to inflatable technologies, not in a wilful organicism of form making, but in a form which results from physics, from the interaction of fluids, membranes, and pressure differentials. This is a subject I went on to develop a short course around, a course called *Fluids/Fabrics/Forms/Forces*, which I still teach at the Architectural Association.

HAPTIC UNDERSTANDING

Inspired by the can-do DIY approach of Ant Farm and their extraordinary "Inflatocookbook" which I found as a scanned PDF online, I had already run a series of workshops with school-aged kids through the National Art and Design Saturday Club program. With the aim of teaching, in a hands-on way, the relationship between flat nets and 3D architectural spaces, I bought large rolls of cheap clear polythene and dozens of rolls of packaging tape. In single-day workshops we built a series of taped envelopes and blew them up with simple office fans.

They quickly filled with air (and children) and demonstrated in a very immediate way various important lessons about inflatable design. Inflatables want to be spherical, even if you make a cube, once you inflate it the pressure pushes the flat square sides out of plane, forming creases along the lines of added stress. Spheres, cones and cylindrical tubes all work well with little creasing as there are sections in these forms which can be truly circular. Where creases form, one can even cut a slice into the envelope in line with the crease and as it is in line with the tension force, the slit won't open and the inflatable won't lose too much air. These lessons were vital for us in the development of the concept design for AirDraft.

Figure 8C.2 *Inflated 1:20 scale physical model, built to present the project at phase 2 of the design competition* Source: Thomas Randall-Page and Benedetta Rogers

OUR DESIGN PROCESS

Early in the design process, whilst researching inflatables, Beni and I came across the work of artist Jeffrey Shaw who in the late 1960s and early 1970s produced wild and joyful inflatable installations ranging in scale from single person envelopes allowing the user to walk on water, to very large-scale inflatable landscapes. We were totally inspired by the playfulness and softness of these works and of particular interest was the "Auditorium" from 1971, commissioned for an outdoor art exhibition "Sonsbeek buiten de perken", at Park Sonsbeek, Arnheim, Netherlands.

We loved this concept as it delivered a really otherworldly experience by removing all solid elements of traditional architectural spaces and replacing them with soft forgiving surfaces. It also was bright yellow and monochromatic further removing the presumed distinction of floor, wall, and ceiling. It was at this point that we decided that an experimental performance space could serve as a flexible program for the project.

Our initial design used the hull of the boat and a tightly fitting cover to form a high-pressure zone, which supported the weight of the audience, then a lower pressure enclosure wrapped over the top to produce a grub-like amorphous performance space. A small solid stage would be provided between the deck-level entrance and the audience mattress. During the design process we studied historic images of heavily laden hay barges covered in tarps and lashed with ropes. We also took inspiration from early Airship and zeppelin design, where inflated forms and the need for streamlining collide.

We knew we wanted to create a space for performance. When we through to the second round we were able to develop the program further and decided to propose a ten-day festival where AirDraft would travel down the Regents Canal from Hackney Wick in the east, and west to Camden Town, partnering with existing waterside venues along the way.

FABRIC AND FABRICATORS

We searched for fabric engineers and balloon makers and made contact with Cameron Balloons, one of the world's oldest hot air balloon makers based in Bristol. They make balloons of all sorts, shapes and sizes at their factory, but they have also developed a line in other fabric engineering, producing inflatables, installations, and pieces for film and theatre shows. They immediately filled us with confidence and when we asked them if anything in the design worried them, they replied that as it didn't have to fly they considered it at the low-risk end of their spectrum of work!

A WORKING MODEL

Having our competition entry shortlisted, we decided we needed a model to demonstrate the idea to the judging panel. Settling on a scale of 1:20, we produced a model using pillow stuffing and mustard yellow tights to model the

Thomas Randall-Page + Benedetta Rogers

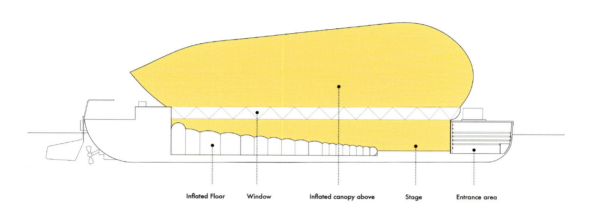

Inflated Floor   Window   Inflated canopy above   Stage   Entrance area

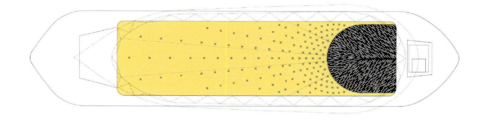

AIRDRAFT
Plan and Section
Scale 1:100

Figure 8C.3 *As built general arrangement plan and section of AirDraft, showing the interaction of the inflated elements with the pre-existing barge*
Source: Thomas Randall-Page and Benedetta Rogers

high-pressure mattress. Points on this surface were sewn down to the hidden base, creating an undulating form similar to a Chesterfield sofa. As we wanted to physically see this interior landscape we decided the top needed to genuinely inflate the model, which was a tricky thing to achieve at this scale. We sourced a pair of centrifugal computer fans that could be powered from a USB battery

Thomas Randall-Page + Benedetta Rogers

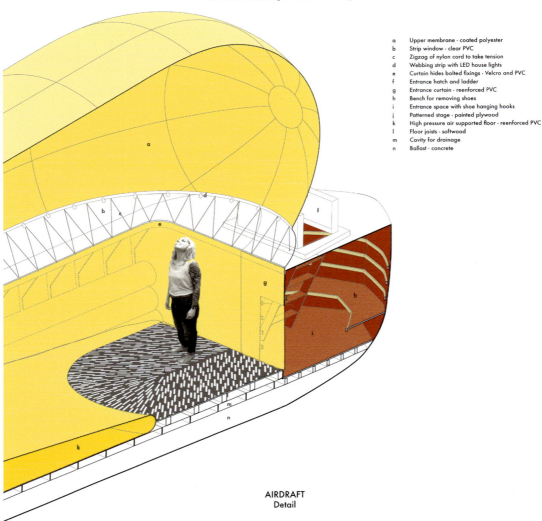

a   Upper membrane - coated polyester
b   Strip window - clear PVC
c   Zigzag of nylon cord to take tension
d   Webbing strip with LED house lights
e   Curtain hides bolted fixings - Velcro and PVC
f   Entrance hatch and ladder
g   Entrance curtain - reinforced PVC
h   Bench for removing shoes
i   Entrance space with shoe hanging hooks
j   Patterned stage - painted plywood
k   High pressure air supported floor - reenforced PVC
l   Floor joists - softwood
m   Cavity for drainage
n   Ballast - concrete

AIRDRAFT
Detail

pack and rigged them beneath the deck of the model boat. Late on the last night before the presentation I set about learning to weld very thin bin-liner with a steel ruler and a tool designed to brand wood similar to a soldering iron but. It was challenging, but finally we had something close enough to the form we were after.

At the presentation we revealed a rather strange and sad looking, deflated model, but whilst he judges curiously looked on, I connected the battery to the fans and with a quiet "whirr" the model began to inflate. Thankfully the delicate welds held and as the creases pulled out, the model found its stable turgid form. The drama of this moment was quite compelling and conveyed well the truly "Pop-Up" nature of this proposal.

Figure 8C.4
Sectional axonometric cutaway drawing, showing the relation of the inflatable performance space, and the entrance sequence down through the barge's converted front hold
Source: Thomas Randall-Page and Benedetta Rogers

DESIGN TAILORING

After we had recovered from the shock of the call telling us we had won, the terror of having to deliver the project set in. Each year, engineers AKT II support the Ante Pavilion competition to safely realise the winning designs. We were relieved to finally be able to ask an engineer all the questions that had been worrying us. We knew we were going to spend the vast majority of the £15,000 budget on the fabric and the labour of having the inflatable envelope cut and sewn. We began to realise it would be hard to provide restraint for the crowd loads which could act sideways on the upper inflatable, especially due to our lack of an airlock compartment at the entrance. Having looked at various options we considered lowering the mattress into the hull, allowing the sides of the existing boat to contain the crowd's push.

This move meant the stage now sat at the bottom of the boat, which simplified the overall construction. Even more significantly, it allowed us to use the hold in the bow of the barge as an entrance space for sitting and removing shoes before entering the pressurised interior. This move also freed up the ends of the inflatable, allowing the form to be much more sculptural. After many explorations and iterations of the silhouette, we settled on having the front end bulbous and domed over the stage and letting the back end taper to a more streamlined form, finishing with a crisp conical point. This form gave a sense of motion, streamlined like a fish or insect abdomen, much closer to the airships we had looked at before. It also was pleasingly vegetable-like, half aubergine half butternut squash.

As the form became tighter and the entrance was now hidden, we realised we needed a way to interface the pure geometry of the upper envelope with the square profile of the top of the barge's hold. We decided to "lift" the yellow enclosure and insert a strip window of clear PVC all the way round. This was about at eye level when you stood on the stage and also at eye level when you sat at the back of the raked inflatable floor. As well as allowing a tantalising glimpse in from outside, it also clarified the zeppelin above, allowing it to "fly" above the barge, like a balloon and basket.

THE HOT AIR BALLOON FACTORY

Once Cameron Balloons were committed to the project, we began working with them directly to develop the form and, from this, determine sensible cutting patterns that minimised waste. Drawing on their experience of making strange novelty shaped hot air balloons we designed a lower mattress filled with internal ties in a pattern radiating from the centre of the stage. Sides made from intersecting tubes with internal tensile gussets were added in such a way that when inflated they would push out under the gunnels, locking the inflatable down into the hold.

The ribbon of window also began to have a form of its own, bulging out like a clear cushion. To achieve this we used a zigzag of parachute cord to take the tension created by the air pressure inside the upper canopy directly to the hull; this

Figure 8C.5 *As the fans begin to fill the lightweight upper envelope with air, the operators hold the slack fabric to prevent out-of-control billowing* Source: Photo credit Jim Stephenson

triangulated zigzag element allowed both boat and balloon their own form and let the window segue from one to the other.

I will never forget my visit to the Cameron Balloons factory in Bristol. The upper two floors of their vast Victorian warehouse house the location where balloon panels are sewn to one another. Dozens of people sat at small sewing machines, surrounded by comically huge mountains of brightly coloured fabric, sewing seemingly endless seams. I was told, whilst being given a tour of the factory, that each balloon is sewn by one person. Each person sews with a slightly different tension in the lines they sew, which results in small changes in length of seams. If they were to change persons mid balloon, unexpected asymmetric strains could be created in the fabric.

Figure 8C.6 *The first audiences make themselves comfortable on a comfortable yellow bed under an equally yellow sky* Source: Photo credit Jim Stephenson

Once the geometries of the two envelopes were defined with a 3D computer model, Cameron Balloons set about developing this into a series of flat panels for cutting. The upper was to be made from lightweight polyester with an airtight coating and the lower was to be made from a heavyweight reinforced PVC similar to lorry siding. There was a limited choice of primary colours in this heavy fabric and we chose a bright buttercup yellow. This yellow was matched in the choice of fabric for the upper, giving a homogenous and sunny interior palette.

MANY HANDS

Having spent almost all our budget on these bespoke fabric elements, we were pushed to keep the rest of the design as simple and low-tech as possible. We sent out an open call to students to volunteers to help Beni and myself realise the remainder of the design.

The inside of the hull had iron ribs and the floor had a rough concrete ballast. To prevent damage or wear occurring, this was covered with a layer of recycled, ridged, corrugated sheet and the ribs were each covered with foam pipe insulation. The rear hold, where the engine was located, served as a plant room and housed the three fans which were to keep the envelopes inflated and at pressure. A pair of centrifugal fans, like those used in commercial kitchens, were used to provide high volume but quiet air flow for the upper envelope and a single bouncy castle fan was specified to keep the high pressure needed for the lower mattress. Each of these sat behind their own hole, cut through the thick iron rear bulkhead of the barge.

To connect the canopy to the upper edge of the hold we designed a plywood plate which ran all the way around and had to be clamped in place with several hundred bolts, each of which needed to be drilled through the iron rim using a mag-drill. To keep the pressure within certain limits, a barometer was installed alongside speed controllers for the various fans that could be operated from the entrance space.

APPLYING PRESSURE

Finally, Ouse was ready to receive the inflatables. First came the mattress, heavy and bulky. It was lowered down into the belly of the barge and unrolled on the protective floor. Prior to fitting the lightweight upper, we did a test inflation. With a little encouragement the tubular sides lifted up, locking the base down to the floor of the boat and wrapping the circular stage. Immediately, the temptation to bounce up and down like a child was irrepressible.

Once we were satisfied that the floor fitted and functioned, we set about attaching the upper canopy to the hull's rim. Starting in the centre of one end we worked our way around, tightening bolts as we went. Next came the zigzag of parachute cord to take the tension, and finally we were ready to switch on the main fans. The world of yellow drapery we had been wrestling slowly began to lift and take shape, rising out of the barge like dough from a tin.

We quickly found that this half-inflated state was when the structure was at its most volatile, being both large enough to really catch some wind but lacking the stability of a taught and anchored balloon. In this state the fabric could whip about and even find itself in the canal. Inside we had installed loops to carry lights or a cinema screen. We soon discovered the trick was to have a couple of people inside holding the loops whilst the thing filled up to keep the fabric in tension and under control.

"PLEASE, NO BOUNCING"

The Architecture Foundation is a social organisation and a mainstay of their work involves putting on events; they throw a hell of a party. As Beni and I approached on the opening night the queue stretched around the block. AirDraft was moored alongside the warehouses and lit up with festoon lights from the inside. Security had a very tough job that night trying to prevent half the young architects in London from drunkenly trying to use the interior landscape as a trampoline. Through the course of the next weeks "No Bouncing" became a phrase that would become second nature.

Over the next ten days we welcomed aboard audiences to see: live bands, stand-up comics, electronic music acts and even a night of contemporary opera. The soft landscape inside encouraged a relaxed atmosphere with people lounging in all positions like piles of puppies. It was very interesting to bring musicians to the space, as there was an extraordinary acoustic quality that none of us had predicted. Low notes were either absorbed or let out through the fabric but high-pitched sounds bounced and reverberated in the space creating a glistening acoustic landscape.

Figure 8C.8
*Audiences sit in
rapture at one of the
many experimental
live performances
hosted in AirDraft's
voluminous belly*
Source: Photo credit
Jim Stephenson

AirDraft arrived in places as an unassuming barge, but the drama of the huge yellow balloon slowly rising up quickly drew a crowd of onlookers, stopped in their tracks by the unexpected spectacle. Between performances we welcomed the public inside to experience the space and as you can imagine it was a magnet for children. Controlling the "bounce factor" became harder than ever.

CONCLUSION

This project could not have happened if we hadn't found the right team of people to help with its realisation. From Cameron Balloons, generations of experience in fabric and air, to the specialist risk analysts who helped us manage the unusual risk factors we found in the design. AirDraft was an exercise in sticking to your guns when it came to design intent, whilst listening to advice from every expert going.

The project was exceptionally well documented both in stills and in a short film both by Jim Stephenson; this led to some really wide media coverage which brought a good degree of exposure for us at an important time. This was also a lesson learnt and something I have continued to do on later projects.

Figure 8C.9 *Reflecting in the dark canal waters and lit from within like an urban-scale Chinese lantern, AirDraft's friendly vegetal form has become an ephemeral London landmark*
Source: Photo credit Jim Stephenson

The experience of making inflatables by hand and explaining their underlying physical principles to students was totally essential for this project. This practical understanding gave me the design confidence in the principle of what we were proposing. I also learned that when you're totally out of budget, just roll up your sleeves and get stuck in building.

Project Information:

Chapter: 10 C—Case Study—AirDraft
Project Leads: Thomas Randall-Page and Benedetta Rogers
Organization: Thomas Randall-Page Studio with Benedetta Rogers
Students: The project was constructed in part with student volunteers from various institutions.
Project Location: Regents Canal, London, UK
Client: Antepavillion
Donations/Financial Support: Budget £15,000
Awards: The project is the winning entry for the Antepavillion Competition

Project Studio Timeline:

Competition Phase 1:	3 Weeks
Competition Phase:	2–3 Weeks
Detail Design:	6 Weeks
Fabrication and Installation:	6 Weeks
Total:	18 Weeks

Credits

Designers and Architects—Benedetta Rogers and Thomas Randall-Page
Structural Engineers—Ed Moseley from AKT II
Fabric Engineering and Fabrication—Cameron Fabric Engineering
Risk Managers—Jackson Coles
Volunteers—Georgia Battye, Quentin Martin, Hannah Sheerin, Seb Birch, Ruby Sleigh, Massine Yallaoui, Felix Scobie, Joshua Richards, Simona De Angelis, Ana Dabija

8D

PATCHWORKS

A Report from Three
Fabricated Futures

JUAN FRANO VIOLICH

8D   PATCHWORKS

A Report from Three Fabricated Futures

Juan Frano Violich

"A fabric presents in principle a certain number of characteristics that permit us to define it as a striated space. First, it is constituted by two kinds of parallel elements; in the simplest case, there are vertical and horizontal elements, and the two intertwine, intersect perpendicularly. Second, the two kinds of elements have different functions; one is fixed, the other mobile, passing above and beneath the fixed. Third, a striated space of this kind is necessarily delimited, closed on at least one side: the fabric can be infinite in length but not in width, which is determined by the frame of the warp; the necessity of a back-and-forth motion implies a closed space. Finally, a space of this kind seems necessarily to have a top and a bottom;

Felt is a supple solid product that proceeds altogether differently, as an anti-fabric. It implies no separation of threads, no intertwining, only an entanglement of fibers obtained by fulling (for example, by rolling the block of fibers back-and-forth). What becomes entangled are the microscales of the fibers. An aggregation of this kind is in no way homogeneous: it is nevertheless smooth, and contrasts point by point with the space of fabric."[1]

PREAMBLE

Our understanding of fabric as a material is inseparable from everyday life. In its more rarefied state as a hand craft we appreciate its cultural value, its simplicity of construction, and its connection to nature. As an industrialized product it is valued for its performance, its ability to adapt to industry, and to create entire new economies. Yet when it comes to an architectural material, our understanding of fabric is more elusive. Where does it stand in the long list of building materials? It tends to resist categorization and in this way is left in a state of "the yet to be imagined", a sort of fabricated *patchwork* condition that is neither here nor there but nonetheless filled with imaginary potential.

The demands for fabric to perform at the scale of a building, to withstand the elements, and to compete against conventional materials is both a challenge and an opportunity that is unfolding before our eyes. Can what has been thought of as a temporary, nomadic, and somewhat limited form of shelter now be explored as having the potential to address the wide number of programmatic, economic, and environmental crisis of our time? The Anthropocene, our current moment where human activity has become the dominant influence on climate and the environment, has demonstrated that natural resources are not in unlimited supply

Figure 8D.1 (Cover)
Oculus under construction, 34th Street Ferry Terminal, New York City, NY, USA
Source:
Photography by KVA

DOI: 10.4324/9781003138471-30

and architecture continues to reveal its insatiable appetite to use materials with excessive carbon emissions at any cost, including economic, human, and environmental. This chapter argues that *fabric-thinking* in architecture can play a critical role in disentangling the dependence it has on hard infrastructure, and open, instead, future territories where patchworks of soft infrastructure can be produced through lighter weight, more flexible and adaptable alternatives. Fabric's inherent characteristics of lightness, flexibility, light transmittance, and tensile strength offers a soft and resilient alternative to its conventional architectural material counterparts like steel, concrete, and glass which, beyond being limited by virtue of their physical characteristics, are major sources of carbon emissions impacting the earth's climate crisis.

As architectural fabrics continue to develop, as Deleuze and Guattari note, from woven *striated* materials that originally used organics, but now use polymer strands, to *smooth* anti-fabric membranes like ethyltetraflourideethylene (ETFE) that use nano-based compounds, they are testing the boundaries of what is considered material: roofs and facades that are stitched and not glued-down, that are referred to as pillows, and that are Heliotropic and produce energy. Fabric has become more and more responsive and adaptable to the urgent need to address resource scarcity, affordability, and energy consumption and in this way provides architects a new material and *way of thinking* within the discipline that can be used as a productive agent for global change.

INTRODUCTION

This is a report about three built projects led by Kennedy & Violich Architecture (KVA) and its research unit MATx where textiles play an integral part of innovative programs in public transportation, missing middle housing, and new forms of teaching and learning. The first report is from Soft House, a row house prototype designed for the International Bauaustellung (IBA), historically significant for pioneering contemporary housing typologies since its inception in 1901. The project is located in Wilhemsburg on one of a series of islands along the Northern and Southern branches of the Elbe River. Wilhelmsburg, a quarter of Hamburg, Germany, is a new city planned by IBA to house Hamburg's growing population and has become the seat of the City's government. The project is a Passiv House that incorporates a textile shading and flexible photovoltaic array that is designed and programmed to follow the sun to optimize solar exposure and radiation. The next report is from the 34th Street Ferry Terminal, a multimodal transportation hub on New York City's East River that uses a double polytetraflourideethylene (PTFE)-coated glass fiber fabric to form a roof over an open-air landing. The roof creates a pillow-like form that glows, providing both ambient and interactive light as it tracks the movement of commuters and the East River's changing tides. The final report is from the Global Flora Conservatory, a research laboratory, teaching facility, and public conservatory for plants in Wellesley, Massachusetts, that uses an air-insulated ETFE fabric membrane as roof and walls instead of conventional glass.

PROVOCATION

Now imagine, however, for a moment that these projects are merely fabrications, imaginary explorations into the possibilities of using textiles in architecture. Each project is written in the form of a *reportage*, a "field report," placing a central focus on how conventional hard building materials used for roofs and walls can not only be replaced by softer, lighter, more flexible and low-carbon ones but exceed their performance by being reconfigurable and providing renewable energy, digital information, and thermal capacity. The three projects work together to create a patchwork of correlations that establishes an alternative way of thinking, a worldview, that resists modernist assumptions of "command and control" from the top down and rather embraces a new ontopological understanding of the need to imagine on grounds of non-linearity, complexity, and entanglement.[2] Design that is sensible and smart, that is hackable and mappable, can liberate the way we think about architecture and its ability to respond to and confront our entangled condition of resource scarcity, energy dependence, and reliance on hard infrastructure.

REPORT FROM WILHELMSBURG ISLAND, HAMBURG, DE

Across the Elbe River from Hamburg, Germany, IBA Hamburg creates a model for new sustainable development and for the future urbanization of this 35 square kilometer historically multi-cultural district. The Soft House site is located on the southern edge, adjacent to a new canal system and public open space. The site plan is based on a traditional linear polder garden typically found

Figure 8D.3 *Flexible fabric solar panels along south façade, IBA Soft House, International Bauaustellung, Wilhelmsburg (Hamburg), DE* Source: Photography by Michael Moser

Figure 8D.4 *Cross-section, IBA Soft House, International Bauaustellung, Wilhelmsburg (Hamburg), DE*
Source: Drawing courtesy KVA

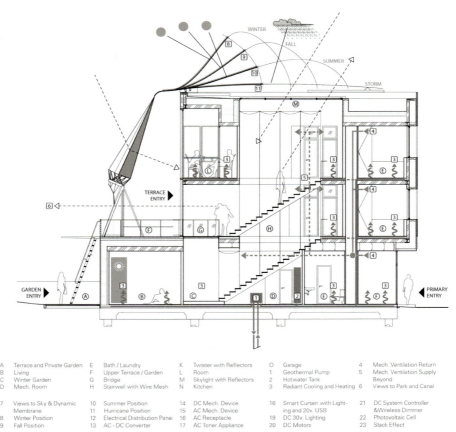

A	Terrace and Private Garden	E	Bath / Laundry	K	Twister with Reflectors	O	Garage	4	Mech. Ventilation Return
B	Living	F	Upper Terrace / Garden	L	Room	1	Geothermal Pump	5	Mech. Ventilation Supply
C	Winter Garden	G	Bridge	M	Skylight with Reflectors	2	Hotwater Tank		Beyond
D	Mech. Room	H	Stairwell with Wire Mesh	N	Kitchen	3	Radiant Cooling and Heating	6	Views to Park and Canal

7	Views to Sky & Dynamic	10	Summer Position	14	DC Mech. Device	18	Smart Curtain with Light-	21	DC System Controller
	Membrane	11	Hurricane Position	15	AC Mech. Device		ing and 20v. USB		&Wireless Dimmer
8	Winter Position	12	Electrical Distribution Panel	16	AC Receptacle	19	DC 30v. Lighting	22	Photovoltaic Cell
9	Fall Position	13	AC - DC Converter	17	AC Toner Appliance	20	DC Motors	23	Stack Effect

in this region where river water and dikes help control flooding. Soft House draws inspiration from the windswept luminous lowland atmosphere and dynamic cloud formations of the Wilhelmsburg islands, known for its maritime traditions, with a material palette that plays with and augments the available natural light.

The Soft House structure uses a traditional *brettstapfe*[β] solid wood panel and deck construction technique based on joining wood planks with dowels. This wood construction is temporally *soft*, as the thickened envelope sequesters carbon and is fully demountable for recycling at end of life. A three-story air *convection atrium* brings daylight deep into the ground floor, creates dramatic vertical views and modulates the rise and fall of warm and cool air with a system of vertically moving interior curtains and operable window vents.

The project provides four row house units or *Reihenhäuser* with the middle and upper floor volume shifted over the ground floor to create a terrace over-looking private gardens, a parkway, and canal. The housing is designed with a *soft* unit organization that accommodates the living needs of families over time. Entry options from the shared driveway, private garden, and terrace connect

◀ Figure 8D.5
Servomotor controlled energy harvesting fabric solar panels, IBA Soft House, International Bauaustellung, Wilhelmsburg (Hamburg), DE
Source: Photography Michael Moser

with vertical circulation, enabling each row house to be configured as a single residence or as a two-level living unit with an independent work unit or garden apartment at the ground level. Plumbing stacks are strategically paired with the wood brettstapfel sheer structure providing owner options for a ground or middle floor kitchen location. Soft House living units are organized around the confluence of soft infrastructure and architecture components. A *thick* party wall zone, which contains bathrooms, stairway, lightwell, and wireless controllers, crosses over the three-story Soft House ventilation atrium, creating balconies, bridges, and overlooks.

Soft House uses a flexible lightweight, smart energy harvesting textile cladding as its façade, which bends to respond to the seasonal changes of the sun and twists to open views or create privacy. This is one of the first responsive facades to demonstrate a two-axis solar architecture capable of rotating a pliable, spring-like structure that integrates textiles and fiber reinforced composite boards to optimize the solar angle of thin film flexible photovoltaics. Daily east–west sun-tracking and daylight harvesting is achieved with simple winch rotation, drawing upon the region's local maritime industries. Adjustments to the responsive façade are made seasonally and daily via a building management system (BMS).

The energy harvesting textile façade is complimented in the interior dwellings with movable LED curtains and a low voltage DC network for household electronics and LED lighting. This new domestic landscape of curtains may be configured to enclose space, prevent drafts, and augment the local thermal

Figure 8D.6
Interactive smart curtain, IBA Soft House, International Bauaustellung, Wilhelmsburg (Hamburg), DE
Source: Photography by Michael Moser

conditions of radiant floor heating. This *smart curtain* allows for real-time monitoring and visualization of outside wind and climate conditions with a play of solid-state lighting that moves along the curtain surface in relation to exterior wind levels—creating a *visual breeze*—an ambient interior luminous expression of the external environment. With multiple, movable soft layers, the Soft House unpacks the thick perimeter of the Passivehaus typology, creating a set of reconfigurable domestic spaces and personal thermal zones that are conceptually allied with the decentralization of domestic energy and information, thus offering homeowners the freedom and flexibility to adapt their homes to fit their personal lifestyle and comfort preferences.

REPORT FROM MANHATTAN ISLAND, NEW YORK, NY

The design of the 34th Street Ferry Terminal takes a non-nostalgic attitude toward the NYC Riverfront. It creates a public architecture which integrates the spatial and environmental experiences of the river front with the expanded virtual experiences of the working commute: the rituals inscribed by the comings and goings of ferries, passengers, and shifting tides. It is situated not along,

Figure 8D.7
Translucent PTFE fabric roof, 34th Street Ferry Terminal, New York City, NY, USA
Source: Photography by John Horner

but above New York City's East River, on Manhattan Island. The importance of the East River to New York and its five boroughs has never been more relevant than it is today. The 16-mile-long regional watershed of the East River Estuary provides ecological services on which the fresh water supply of New York City depends. Yet few urban dwellers are aware that the East River is not a river but in fact, is part of a complex saltwater estuary that stretches from Upper New York Bay to the south, through Hell Gate, to Long Island Bay to the north. As a tidal straight, it has swift moving currents that change the direction of the river flowing into and out of the estuary with daily cycles of low and high tides. It was a pivotal site during the American Revolution and the early industrialization of New York. Reimagined by artists and writers,[4] it continues to be a critical part of the City's maritime activity, and has recently, especially after Hurricane Sandy in 2012, become the focus of our climate crisis and the need for coastal cities to address sea level rise.

The 34th Street Terminal uses design principles of resilient and soft infrastructure, including the integration of a triangulated column structure, open bow trusses, and a fully tensile, structural lenticular roof canopy system with integrated daylighting, LED lighting, and an environmental sensing system, all of which hovers over a 10,000 square foot folded concrete and wood public platform. The structure consists of a double-layer membrane roof stretched on top of steel arches, supported by slender steel pipes. The upper layer membrane, a PTFE coated glass fiber fabric, provides protection from the elements, while the lower layer creates an architectural element that visually conceals the steel structure.

Passenger waiting areas use reflectivity and translucency to enhance the atmospheric effects of water and weather, offering an expanded public experience of the contemporary urban waterfront. An undulating double wall of perforated aluminum panels house the building's infrastructure and provides waiting space

Figure 8D.8 *Oculus detailed construction drawings, 34th Street Ferry Terminal, New York City, NY, USA*
Source: Drawing courtesy KVA

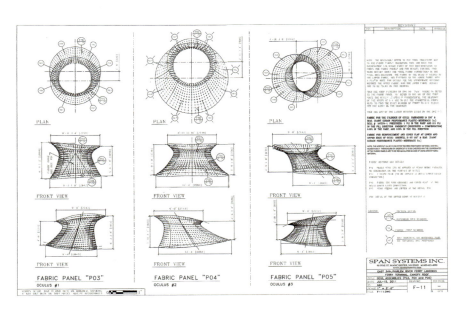

Figure 8D.9 *View across East River toward Queens, NY, 34th Street Ferry Terminal, New York City, NY, USA*
Source: Photography by John Horner

Figure 8D.10 *Global Flora under construction, Global Flora Conservatory, Wellesley, MA, USA*
Source: Photography by KVA

with semi-private and semi-public bench groupings. The digitally fabricated perforated panels are designed to produce moiré effects as passengers move through the Terminal, opening and closing dynamic views across to the water. The curved glass wall and retractable rain screens enable commuters to view the river while being protecting from rain and wind.

The building's cross-section is detailed to emphasize the Terminal's connection to the riverfront through large fabric oculi stitched into the translucent fabric roof, providing generous natural daylight below. Inversely, light is reflected along the underside of the tensile canopy caused by the caustic play of refracted sun light off the surface of the water. At night, the roof's lightwells illuminate through integrated solid-state lighting and motion sensors embedded along the boardwalk, registering the flows of people moving east and west across the pier. This same addressable LED lighting network integrated in the fabric roof tracks the alternating north and south tidal flows of the East River using water sensors. Working together, the design demonstrates how soft infrastructure creates a sensory architecture that brings together in real time the physical elements of architecture, natural data, and digital information, bringing to the surface the ordinary, yet life sustaining changes that exist on-site that at times go unnoticed.

REPORT FROM THE WELLESLEY BOTANIC GARDENS, WELLESLEY, MA

The Global Flora Conservatory reimagines how the design of a sustainable greenhouse can enhance global interdisciplinary science education and deepen a public understanding of nature. Nested in the midst of the Wellesley College's Botanic Gardens, the centerpiece of the American landscape architect and conservationist Frederick Law Olmsted, the Global Flora expands the 1920 vison of Dr. Margaret Ferguson who argued for plant biology as a central part of science education and encouraged students to "listen to" plants and learn through hands-on interdisciplinary experiences. Even a century before our current climate crisis, Ferguson foregrounded the critical role of nature and science education in underrepresented populations and stressed that no lasting economic prosperity is possible without social equity and shared environmental action.

Global Flora is a synergistic set of wet and dry biomes that are heated and cooled using only renewable resources. The light, low-carbon footprint of the greenhouse offers a transferable new model for contemporary sustainable construction. If net zero human comfort can be achieved for tropical and desert environments in the cold and humid New England climate, it can be done anywhere. The building integrates innovative passive and active sustainable systems to meet the net zero water and energy criteria of the Living Building Challenge.[5]

Global Flora meets this performance criteria through the radical integration of natural landscape topography, plant biomes, building form, innovative materials, and sustainable passive systems that minimize energy use.

Figure 8D.11 *Cross-section, Global Flora Conservatory, Wellesley, MA, USA* Source: Photography by KVA

The Global Flora Conservatory confronts two challenges in the use of glass in northern environments. The first is the latitude of Massachusetts is far enough north that natural daylight strategies are limited, requiring more open sky exposure than in southern latitudes. This increases the need for high levels of thermal insulation in the region. The other is that the iron content in glass reduces light transparency, resulting in low levels of UV and light spectrums that, in the case of greenhouses, are required to sustain wet and dry biome life. Ethylene tetrafluroeth-ylene, or ETFE, a plastic polymer resin related to Teflon and originally developed by Dupont in the 1970s for the aerospace industry, was considered as a viable option. The decision to move away from a rigid envelope to ETFE's soft double-layer pillow assembly addresses several problems, including a 95 percent reduction in weight, the reduction of steel structure, and the reduction of carbon required to produce glass and steel. Additionally, the complex geometry of the conservatory produces warped surfaces that conventional insulated glass units (IGUs) cannot accommodate and which ETFE, as a flexible smooth membrane, can.

Global Flora is conceived primarily as a cross sectional exploration of space rather than a sequence of spaces in plan. The need to accommodate different tree heights produces a multivalent space that varies with the site's natural topography.

Figure 8D.12 *Upper* ▶ *walkway and bridge approaching the Wet Biome, Global Flora Conservatory, Wellesley, MA, USA* Source: Photography by KVA

Design in section offers people diverse spatial experiences with different plant forms whether looking down from above or up from below. The Global Flora Conservatory is entirely cooled by natural ventilation. No cooling is added to manage the heat and humidity of Summer. This is done through an automated roof and wall vents system that is integrated into the lightweight ETFE roof membrane. Based on this passive approach, the number of hours per year that the greenhouse goes over 85 degrees, which is the limit of tolerance for plants in arid and humid environments, is limited. When temperatures reach this limit, natural ventilation and shading is deployed through the automated wall and roof vents—all managed by a cloud-based building management system that monitors, controls, and assesses the Global Flora's indoor and outdoor conditions in real time.

Global Flora is a free and public botany lab and "museum" that emphasizes the importance of environmental stewardship to current and future generations on-site and online. Its interactive platform of sensors and data-loggers are integrated into the design as an open-ended system to support global experimentation on interdisciplinary plant-based sciences and sustainability initiatives, accessible to the public, libraries, schools, and international research universities.

POSTSCRIPT

As we return from the field, this reportage on three fabricated futures raises a fundamental question: how do textiles and fabric fit into a practice of architecture that is inextricably dependent on increasing scales of resource extraction and carbon emissions? Fabrics as a building material are to architecture as islands are to continents. For decades, islands have historically provided a critical voice in challenging the mainland's dominant solutionist role in modern world-making.[6] Today, islands are increasingly becoming a topic of anthropocene-thinking for their ability to represent the inevitability when, once faith in modern reasoning collapses, we are faced with the stark realization that "there is no world, there are only islands".[7] As we continue to adapt to this post-Holocene condition of our own making, exploring alternative materials through fabric-thinking present patchworks of correlational approaches with different sets of capacities, affordances, and potentialities to what constitute the making of architecture as we know it.

Project Information:

Project: 34th Street Ferry Terminal
Architect: KVA MATx

Consultant:

Structural Engineer: Schlaich Bergermann & Partner LP
Marine Structural & Civil Engineer: McLaren Engineering Group
MEP/FP Engineers: Lakhani & Jordan Engineers, PC
Security Consultants: Cosentini Associates
Landscape Architect: Ken Smith Landscape Architects
KVA MATx Design Team: Juan Frano Violich FAIA: Principal

Sheila Kennedy FAIA: Principal

Veit Kugel, Dipl Ing: Project Architect

Project Designers: Michael O'Young, Tonya Ohnstad, Ted Steinemann, Sloan Kulper IDSA, Jason O'Mara, Heather Micka-Smith

Project Location: New York City, NY USA

Client: New York Economic Development Corporation

Awards: Progressive Architecture Award, 2002

Design Excellence Award from NYC Art Commission & Mayor Bloomberg, 2006

NYAIA Design Excellence Award, 2014

Architizer Award, 2014

Project: IBA Soft House

Architect: KVA MATx

Consultant:

Executive Architect: 360grad+ architekten (Hamburg)

Structural Engineer: Knippers Helbig Advanced Engineering (Stuttgart)

Climate Consultant: Solites (Stuttgart)

MEP/FP Engineers: Buro Happold (London)

Landscape Architect: G2 Landschaft

Fabric Manufacturing Consortium: Global Solar Energy, Inc; Svensson Global, AG; Philips Color Kinetics Headquarters; Philips Eindhoven Lighting; Automatic Devices Company, Inc.; L-tronics, Inc.; Textilbau Gmbh.

KVA MATx Design Team: Juan Frano Violich FAIA: Principal

Sheila Kennedy FAIA: Principal

Veit Kugel, Dipl Ing: Project Architect

Project Designers: Kyle Altman, Jeremy Burke, Stephen Clipp, Iman Fayyad, Patricia Gruits, Katherine Heinrich, Heather Micka-Smith, Chris Popa, Shevy Rockcastle, Phillip Seaton, Alex Shelly, Nyima Smith, Sean Tang, Diana Tomova, Sasa Zivkovic

Project Location: Hamburg (Wilhemsburg), Germany

Client: Internationale Bauausstellung IBA Hamburg GmbH

Developer: PATRIZIA Projektentwicklung GmbH

Awards: Architect R+D Award, 2007

AIA New England Design Award, 2013

BSA Design Excellence Award, 2014

Architizer A+ Awards, 2014

Architect Master Prize, 2015

Project: Global Flora Conservatory

Architect: KVA MATx

Consultant:

Structural Engineer: Buro Happold (Boston)

Climate Consultant: Transsolar Klima Engineering (Stuttgart/New York)

MEP/FP Engineers: Buro Happold (London)

Landscape Architect: Andropogon Associates (Philadelphia)

Fabric Engineering/Manufacturing: Vector Foiltec GmbH (Bremen)

KVA MATx Design Team: Juan Frano Violich FAIA: Principal

Sheila Kennedy FAIA: Principal

Ben Widger, AIA; Project Architect

Project Designers: Shawna Meyer, AIA LEED AP, Kyle Altman, Bob White, Nick Johnson, Daniel Sebaldt, Michael Bennet, Diana Tomova, Peteris Lazovskis, Mark Bavoso, Lynced Torres;

Project Location: Wellesley, MA USA

Client: Wellesley College

Awards: North American LaFarge Holcim Bronze Award, 2017

AIA/BSA Design Award, 2021

Architizer A+ Awards, 2021

Architecture MasterPrize, 2021

NOTES

1. Chapter 14: The Smooth and the Striated, Deleuze, Gilles, and Guattari, Felix (2013). *A Thousand Plateaus*. Bloomsbury Revelations. London: Bloomsbury Academic.
2. *Ontopolitics in the Anthropocene*, by David Chandler. London: Routledge, 2018.
3. Ramage, Michael H., Burridge, Henry, Busse-Wicher, Marta, Fereday, George, Reynolds, Thomas, Shah, Darshil U., Wu, Guanglu, Yu, Li, Fleming, Patrick, Densley-Tingley, Danielle, Allwood, Julian, Dupree, Paul, Linden, P.F., and Scherman, Oren (February 2017). "The Wood from the Trees: The Use of Timber in Construction". *Renewable and Sustainable Energy Reviews* 68: 333–359. http://doi.org/10.1016/j.rser.2016.09.107.
4. As part of the 1856 publication Leaves of Grass, the American writer Walt Whitman's poem Crossing Brooklyn Ferries describes the experience of taking a ferry across the East River. The poem is written to future readers providing an experiential glimpse into the past.
5. The Living Building Challenge is an international sustainable building certification program created in 2006 by the non-profit International Living Future Institute [1]. It is described by the Institute as a philosophy, advocacy tool and certification program that promotes the measurement of sustainability in the built environment.
6. *Anthropocene Islands: Entangled Worlds*, by Jonathan Pugh and David Chandler. London: University of Westminster Press, 2021.
7. *The Beast & The Sovereign, Vol. 2*, by Jacques Derrida. Edited by Michel Lisse, Marie-Louise Mallet, and Ginette Michaud, Translated by Geoffrey Bennington. Chicago: University of Chicago Press, 2011.

9 Outcomes + Conclusion

Tolya Stonorov

Responsive, flexible, impermanent, fluid and adaptive—fabric interacts with, and influences architecture, offering innovative solutions and increased material responsibility. Documented in FABRIC[ated] are provocative examples of how fabric historically has and continues to inspire and contribute to architectural projects. Foundation and theory chapters establish clear precedent and futures for fabric's position in architectural discourse. Through innovation, sustainability, future forward experimentation and a deep look into the materiality of formwork, fabric emerges as an invaluable contributor to responsible architecture. The case studies examined demonstrate new and fresh methods for addressing sustainability and social justice through the use of fabric in architecture. In each we see novel techniques for dealing with space, culture and need. This transference of the way we think about the materials we use, both conceptually and physically, offers an increased focus on socially driven projects.

In the first case study section, *Veiling*, fabric as a conceptual and literal material is explored as a modifier, a filter, a political act. The inverting of the veil experience turns the user experience into one of introspection and discovery. By inhabiting the veil, the typical power dynamic of the garment is reversed, highlighting complex gender relationships. Further, we look at an examination of the traditional female garment in relation to vernacular architecture and gain a deeper understanding of how women have influenced and continue to influence the built environment. Political and subversive acts are undertaken in the Pipeline Project, yet these are delivered through a deeply beautiful experience of occupying an intertwined enclosure, which will eventually return to the earth from which the woven material was derived. Cultural narratives continue through the lens of river ecology and sustainable acts. Home as a fabric enclosure is explored through the historical and modern reinterpretation of the Bedouin tent. Finally, projects ranging from the veiling of an entire building in mesh to an examination of malleable smart skin uncover the dramatic ways that fabric can define and provide inspiration in architecture. *Veiling* explores gender and fabric as a material of translation and threshold.

The *Compression* case studies investigate fabric as a responsive material, one that both conforms to and determines form, strength and sustainability. Fabric in these examples offers an alternative to the wholly wasteful traditional methods of concrete formwork. *Compression* examines efficiency as a tool and as an impetus for space making. With the dire state of sustainability in the building industry, the

DOI: 10.4324/9781003138471-31

incorporation of fabric formwork can help to transform concrete from a carbon heavy material into a more sustainable one. Fabric formwork addresses waste both in material form and formwork, honing in on where material is most needed and where it can be eliminated. Further, *Compression* offers an utterly innovative look at fabric as a complete building envelope through a thickening of skin. Similar to our own skin's multilayered composition, we see how the building envelope can analogously be thick and thin depending on necessity. In this section we see fabric's ability to be parametrically adaptive.

Finally, the *Tension* case studies draw from historical inspiration of Frei Otto, Antfarm and more. In Otto's dynamic and groundbreaking work, ideas of heavy structure are replaced by light and malleable forms that use dramatically less material, while also creating delight. In this section, fabric provides a more responsive and interactive solar collection system, while heightening the interior possibilities of the user experience. Like the traditional Japanese house, users can adjust their interior space through the use of fabric walls, similar to vernacular Japanese sliding screens. Through the qualities of these translucent materials, daily experience finds richness in the previously mundane. Tensile structures are highlighted as both temporary public manifestations and permanent community solutions. Water is captured, redirected and employed, using fabric as its vessel and director. A discarded barge becomes a playful and interactive cultural space emphasizing real social shifts in the London canal system—the ethereal and temporal nature drawing attention to the shifting landscape of cultural space on this everchanging waterway.

Figure 9.1 *Meeting Points—View from the inside of one of the structuring columns.*
Source: Photography: © Abeer Seikaly and David Walters, 2019

Figure 9.2 *Veiling:*
Transparency
Conceptual Model,
Student Work
Source: Translation
Studio, Tolya
Stonorov, Norwich
University

Each project is political as it responds to public need, whether through increased sustainability or a reinvigoration of an existing blighted space or object.

FABRIC[ated] seeks to offer new possibilities and inspiration for architecture of the future. Through innovation, sustainability and social justice, the uses of fabric outlined in this book chronicle radically different explorations that share a common goal of "architecture for everyone."[1] Through the work of the many authors this book, we see fabric as drape, skin, veil, mold, concept and inspiration. Fabric, in its broadest definition, is an important and innovative material in the development of socially conscious architecture.

NOTE

1. Danny Sagan

Figures

Index

Page numbers in *italics* indicate a figure and page numbers with an "n" indicate a note on the corresponding page